ADOBE
ILLUSTRATOR 88:
THE OFFICIAL
HANDBOOK FOR
DESIGNERS

ADOBE ILLUSTRATOR 88: THE OFFICIAL HANDBOOK FOR DESIGNERS

Tony Bove, Frederic E. Davis and Cheryl Rhodes

BANTAM BOOKS
TORONTO · NEW YORK · LONDON · SYDNEY · AUCKLAND

Trademarks

Apple, Apple LaserWriter, Apple LaserWriter Plus
and AppleTalk PC are trademarks of Apple Computer, Inc.
Linotronic is a trademark of Allied Linotype Company
MacDraw, MacPaint, and MacWrite are trademarks of Apple Computer, Inc.
Macintosh is a trademark of MacIntosh Laboratories, Inc.
and is licensed to Apple Computer, Inc.
Microsoft is a registered trademark of Microsoft Corp.
MS-DOS is registered trademark of Microsoft Corp.
PageMAker is a registered trademark of Aldus Corp.
Pantone Matching System is registered trademark of Pantone
Illustrator 88 and PostScript are registered trademarks of Adobe Systems, Inc.

ADOBE ILLUSTRATOR 88: THE OFFICIAL HANDBOOK FOR DESIGNERS
A Bantam Book/September 1988

Copyright © 1988 Tony Bove, Frederic E. Davis, and Cheryl Rhodes
Cover illustration Copyright © Stanislaw Fernandes;
translated to Illustrator 88 file by Ron Chan; processed and
color separated by Electronic Publishing Center, Inc., New York, NY
Page makeup by the authors; typesetting by Krishna Copy, San Francisco, CA

ISBN 0-553-34629-6

Published simultaneously in the United States and Canada

Bantam Books are published by Bantam Books, a division of Bantam Doubleday Dell
Publishing Group, Inc. Its trademark, consisting of the word "Bantam Books" and the
portrayal of a rooster, is Registered in U.S. Patent and Trademark Office and in other
countries. Marca Registrada, Bantam Books, Inc., 666 Fifth Avenue, New York, NY
10103

PRINTED IN THE UNITED STATES OF AMERICA

BH 0 9 8 7 6 5 4 3 2

Foreword

When we started the development of Adobe Illustrator, our goal was to make a tool that would be easy to use and valuable to both the amateur and professional artist. What we didn't anticipate was how creative users would be. They are creative in the artwork they produce, and in the ways they use the program to solve illustration problems. The users of the program continue to amaze us. They have created astounding pieces of art. They have used the program in ways that we have never contemplated, and they find applications that are new, novel and innovative with each week that passes.

We have always thought that it would be great if someone would bottle the experience the early users have gained so that new users could benefit. Adobe Illustrator: The Official Handbook For Designers fills such a need.

In this book, Tony, Fred, and Cheryl explore the uses of Adobe Illustrator from the perspective of several of the more advanced users. This perspective gives the reader valuable insight into how various illustration problems are approached and solved. They also expose in detail the use of each tool. They discuss the organization and semantics of each menu item, and they discuss the structure of Illustrator files as they relate to the PostScript language. All of these portions provide a valuable reference guide to the program.

If you do not own a copy of Adobe Illustrator, then this book will give you a good idea of how powerful the program is, and what it can do for you.

If you have purchased the program, then this book will be a valuable reference to how the program works and how it is used. In any event, welcome to the creative world of Adobe Illustrator.

John E. Warnock
President, Adobe Systems Incorporated

Preface

Welcome to the world of computer graphics. Adobe Illustrator 88 is a program for designers and professional illustrators that runs on Apple Macintosh Plus, Macintosh SE, and Macintosh II computers. With it you can produce high-quality illustrations and all kinds of line art. It is unique in offering a very accurate display of PostScript graphics, and a collection of sophisticated line and curve drawing and editing tools, for a desktop computer.

This is the second edition of this book; the first described the original version of Adobe Illustrator. Adobe has added major capabilities to Illustrator and renamed the program to Adobe Illustrator 88. The new capabilities include automatic tracing of scanned images, automatic color separations with Adobe Separator, the PANTONE Matching System colors, the ability to show color on any type of color Macintosh II display, the blend tool for graduated fills and special effects, and the freehand tool for freestyle drawing. In addition, the DrawOver program can convert MacDraw PICT graphics into PostScript.

This book starts with a basic introduction to Adobe Illustrator 88 and leads you on a tour through artwork created by professional illustrators. In the artists' own words are their rare insights into getting special effects and high-quality designs.

Chapter One is a basic introduction to the program's features and to the Macintosh system. This chapter explains each icon you may encounter, and provides a brief tutorial on how to draw and create artwork with Adobe Illustrator 88.

Chapter Two shows how maps, charts, and clip art can be prepared with the program. The artists who drew these images describe how they used Adobe Illustrator 88 to do special effects, from building reusable graphics and drawing objects with shared borders to adding paint and the illusion of three dimensions. The artists also explain some of the techniques for placing text in graphics, and how to clone, scale, shear, reflect, rotate, and trace images. The chapter also covers page setup and printing.

Chapter 3 uses commercial art examples to show how an artist would start a large, complex illustration. Artists use multiple transformations and overlays, airbrush effects, strokes and fills for enclosed objects, gray shades, and blends. Artists also show the most effective use of the New Window and Preview Illustration windows, how to rotate text, and how to use gray shades and colors.

Chapter 4 show how Adobe Illustrator 88 can scale images with or without preserving line weights. The artists explain how they used multiple rotations, reflections, and constraints for drawing complex graphics, as well as editing techniques, such as changing straight lines into curves. The chapter covers line styles, stroke widths for setting trap between color images, overprinting, and color separations.

Chapter 5 is a complete reference guide to Adobe Illustrator 88 menus and tools. The menus and tools are presented in the order they appear in the program's display, followed by Adobe Separator and DrawOver.

Chapter 6 is a brief overview of PostScript, the page description language used to describe the graphics created by Adobe Illustrator 88. PostScript files can be used with other applications that support PostScript, and can be printed or typeset on any PostScript output device. This chapter shows what an art file looks like from the programmer's perspective. It is provided for users who are curious about PostScript, but it is not meant to be a complete tutorial.

We are confident that you will find Adobe Illustrator 88 useful. By creating PostScript art you are preserving the artwork in digital form that can be used again and again without any degrading of the image. You are also preparing artwork that can be used in future graphics systems, since PostScript is the standard page description language for publishing systems.

"Only through art can we get outside of ourselves and know another's view of the universe..." (Marcel Proust). May you find inspiration with mouse in hand.

Colophon

This book was written and desktop published by the authors. We used the following software to produce this book: Microsoft Word 3 (Microsoft) for writing and editing; PageMaker 3 (Aldus) for page makeup; and MacPaint (Apple), SuperPaint (Silicon Beach Software), and GraphicWorks (MacroMind) for preparing MacPaint templates. We also used SmartScrap (Solutions Inc.) to keep track of icons and other graphic symbols, and Art Grabber+ (MacroMind) and Camera (Keith A. Esau) to help prepare examples.

We ran this software with the following hardware: Apple Macintosh Plus, Macintosh SE, and Macintosh II computers; Apple HDSC 40 and SuperMac DataFrame XP60 hard disks; the SuperMac SuperView monitor (with the Macintosh II computer); Apple LaserWriter IINT and AST TurboLaser/PS printers; Linotype Linotronic 100 and 300 imagesetters; and Datacopy Model 730, ThunderScan, DEST PC Scan Plus, and MacVision scanners.

We wish to thank the following companies for support and services in the preparation of this book: Adobe Systems, Aldus Corp., Apple Computer, Inc., AST Research, Datacopy, DEST Corp., Electronic Directions (New York City), ImageSet (San Francisco), Krishna Copy Center (San Francisco), MacroMind, Microsoft Corp., PTI Industries, Thunderware, Silicon Beach Software, and SuperMac Technology.

Acknowledgments

The authors wish to acknowledge the people who helped create this book, especially Steve Rosenthal and Mike Schuster, who contributed to Chapter 6.

The authors thank the following artists for their artwork and assistance with this book: Gail Blumberg, Russell Brown, Luanne Seymour Cohen, Pat Coleman, Gary Cosimini, Dean Dapkus, Laura Lamar, Keith Ohlfs, Sumner Stone, and John Warnock.

We also thank Robin Davis, Adelle Aldridge, Paul Brainerd, Liz Bond, Suzanne Doyle, Charles Geschke, Bill Gladstone, Brenda Hansen, Jono Hardjowirogo, Barbara Hawkins, Ric Jones, Lud Kimbrough III, Laurie McLean, Glenn Reid, Tom Reilly, Lenny Schafer, Robert Simon, Laura Singer, Martha Steffen, Kenzi Sugihara, Keri Walker, Diane Wilde, and Paul Winternitz.

Contents

1

Introduction to Adobe Illustrator 88

The touchstone of an art is its precision.

— Ezra Pound

Adobe Illustrator 88, from Adobe Systems, is a drawing program for professional illustrators, artists, and designers that brings a new level of precision to personal computer graphics.

The program can produce an image that is not confined to the fixed resolution (measured in dots-per-inch) of laser printers. The image can be printed on almost any printer, but printers and typesetters with higher resolutions (more dots-per-inch) can do a better job of producing a smooth, yet crisp image. Illustrator has sophisticated curve-drawing techniques to make curves of any shape and size, as well as techniques for drawing any geometric or custom shape and using any pattern.

With Adobe Illustrator 88 you can trace lines, curves, and shapes using a rough image as a template, or draw freehand with or without a template for guidance. Your display becomes the equivalent of an illuminated light table, and your tracing tools are the precise functions of the program which you use by pressing keys and moving a mouse. Lines can be drawn perfectly straight, and curves can be precisely contoured by dragging a mouse with little artistic skill. However, the program is designed for professional illustrators who understand how to use these tools to produce high-quality art and graphics.

To make use of a template for tracing, you can first sketch the rough image on paper and use an inexpensive desktop scanner to scan the image into the computer for use as a template. You can also use other painting and drawing programs on your Macintosh (notably MacPaint, MacDraw, or other programs that can create MacPaint documents) to create or modify a template for use with Adobe Illustrator 88.

Once you have the template image in a MacPaint file (either scanned or painted with a program), you can use it with Adobe Illustrator 88 — the program displays the template as a gray-filled background image while you draw lines, curves, and shapes over it. The program offers automatic tracing over images as well. You can at any time display what you've drawn, only the template, or both drawing and template. You can even see a preview of exactly how the artwork will look when printed.

This combination — precise drawing tools, a template for tracing on the screen, and resolution-independent images — makes Adobe Illustrator 88 one of the best personal computer graphics tools for professional artwork and illustration in publishing and commercial graphics applications.

An excellent example of how the program can make artists more productive is at *The New York Times* art department, which uses Illustrator 88 to prepare the daily weather map and four-day forecast. Illustrator graphics can be combined and edited to form new graphics, so that the art department can produce an image faster and still get high-quality results. The Adobe Illustrator 88 graphics files are transferred to the various daily newspapers owned by *The New York Times* — much like a wire service distributing its news. Art

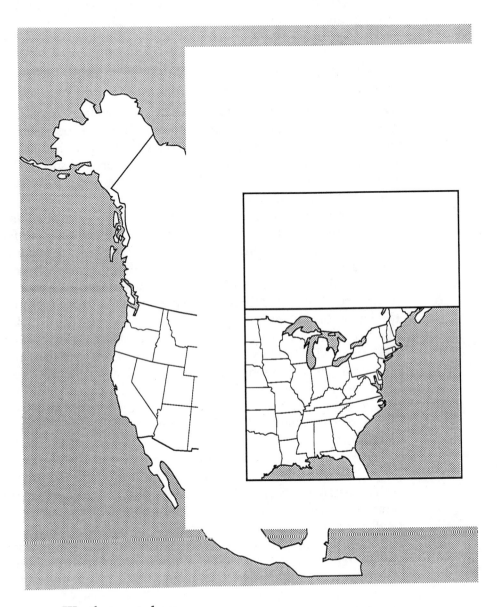

Weather map base:
Courtesy The New York Times, *used with permission.*

director Gary Cosimini explains that his goal is "to automate some mechanical processes so that the artist can be creative without thinking about the processes."

The Role of PostScript

The reason why Adobe Illustrator 88 can produce resolution-independent images that can be printed on laser printers or higher resolution typesetters is that it describes the graphic image in a computer language rather than in a series of spots and spaces. The language, developed by Adobe Systems co-founders John Warnock and Charles Geschke, is called PostScript.

PostScript is generally referred to as a *page description language*. It provides a standard method of describing and transferring images, and even entire pages, which contain text (in fonts) and graphics. The language is used by an application program (such as Adobe Illustrator 88, or Aldus' PageMaker, or Letraset's ReadySetGo!) to send pages of text and graphics to a printer, typesetter, display screen, or other output device (plate maker, film recorder, etc.). This device has a PostScript raster image processor (RIP) unit, which translates the PostScript language into a raster image (a series of dots) that is ideal for the resolution of the printer, typesetter, display, or output device. Programs can use PostScript to take full advantage of the resolution of the printer or typesetter, and produce images without restrictions on resolution.

A PostScript RIP is built into the Apple LaserWriter series laser printers. You can purchase a Linotype Linotronic laser imagesetter with a separate PostScript RIP unit (Linotronic imagesetters can use other RIPs, such as another one Linotype manufactures, called CORA, but the PostScript RIP is the one to use to be compatible with personal computers and Adobe Illustrator 88). The industry uses the term "imagesetter" because, unlike typesetters, these PostScript devices can prepare halftones and color separations as well as produce typesetting and line art.

Resolution, defined by the number of dots per inch (dpi), is extremely important for high-quality graphics. The higher the resolution, the better an image will appear in print. PostScript transcends resolution by describing graphics in an algorithmic language rather than in a series of dots at a specific resolution.

As a result, PostScript makes it possible to "print" the same page on the 2540 dpi Linotronic 300 or 500 imagesetter (with vastly higher quality), that you print on an Apple LaserWriter or other PostScript laser printer at 300 dpi resolution — using the same computer, system, and software (such as Adobe Illustrator 88 and PageMaker). PostScript is compatible with Macintosh system software and applications, and it is also supported on PCs by most of the page makeup and word processing programs.

Why is PostScript so important to publishing, and why does Adobe Illustrator 88 use it to store image information? Typeset-quality output (printing with a resolution of 1000 dpi or higher) is required for most graphic design and illustration and publishing applications. With PostScript, it is possible to automate production from creation all the way to printing, without limiting your output to the resolution of laser printers. Pages can be sent directly to a PostScript-driven plate maker for the highest possible resolution. PostScript files can be transferred over telephone lines and networks, and PostScript can also be used to send information to color printers, film recorders, slide makers, and color electronic prepress systems.

Figure 1-1.
Adobe Illustrator 88 can automatically trace the outlines of scanned images to produce shapes that can be readily adjusted, added to, and redrawn as needed.

Overview of Features

Adobe Illustrator 88 is a comfortable tool for professional artists and illustrators because it uses the paradigm of drawing with mechanical tools. It is also an excellent tool for CAD/CAM and technical line art because you can draw a complex image and scale it to any size, yet preserve the line weights if you want (the lines will not get thicker when you resize the image to be larger).

Artists who have traditionally started with rough sketches may still work that way — the only difference is that "inking" the sketch is done electronically, with more sophisticated tools. The program lets you put inexpensive scanners to good use: converting a scanned bit map into an object-oriented, resolution-independent drawing. The least expensive scanner on the market may be used to scan an image at any resolution — no matter how rough — and bring it into the program.

You can turn the scanned image instantly into line art using the automatic tracing feature (Figure 1-1). The program can automatically outline a scanned image brought in as a template, so that you can start with shapes already drawn.

You can also draw the outlines yourself, tracing the rough scanned image with precise PostScript lines, curves, and filled areas. The resulting file of PostScript code can then be sent to any PostScript device, such as the 2540-dpi Linotronic 300 imagesetter for color separations on film, or the 300-dpi QMS ColorScript color page printer.

The program also provides the ability to assign areas of an image to have a percentage of black (gray) along with a percentage of each of the primary process colors (cyan, yellow, magenta), or a specific PANTONE MATCHING SYSTEM color or custom color. You can then produce a four-color separation (one piece of film for each process color) with or without custom separations (individual film layers for each custom and PANTONE color) for the image using the Adobe Separator program. Adobe Illustrator 88 can display colors on a wide variety of color monitors using all of the Macintosh II color capabilities.

The drawing area can be nine 8.0-by-10.9-inch pages on the Apple LaserWriter, but page size is not restricted to this measurement. You can make drawings bigger than a page, up to a maximum drawing area of 1008-by-1008-points (14-by-14 inches). You can

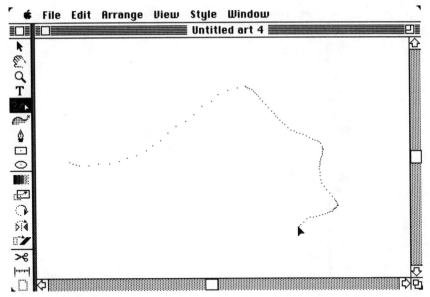

Figure 1-2a.
With the freehand tool you can drag the mouse to draw shapes.

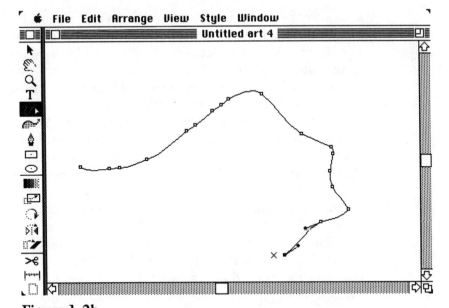

Figure 1-2b.
After sketching with the freehand tool, the program creates line and curve segments resembling your sketch. You can control the precision for freehand drawing.

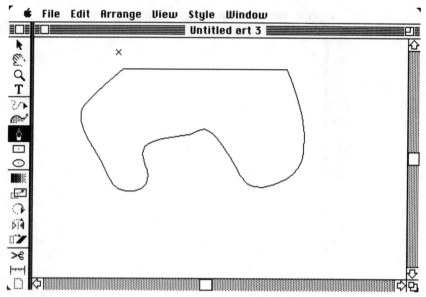

Figure 1-3.
A path of lines and curves connected to form a shape.

then scale the drawing larger or smaller, using a normal Page Setup menu (the PostScript code can be edited to make an image the size of a billboard). Minute detail can be displayed by zooming into an image with the zoom tool, which offers nine zoom levels.

Adobe Illustrator 88 offers a freehand tool for drawing curves freehand, without constraints of any kind (Figure 1-2).

Keyboard controls make the program easy to use. You can switch from one drawing tool to another quickly, or bring up a dialog box for typing specifications for an operation, using combinations of the mouse button, the Option key, the Command key, the Shift key, and space bar. The keyboard controls are close to one hand, while the mouse is at the other hand. You use both simultaneously — and once you learn the tricks, you can draw complex images quickly. You hardly ever go back to the pull-down menus, the palette usually displayed on the left side, or the toolbox — you can keep your eyes and hands on the artwork. For example, to scroll around with the hand, press the space bar for the hand tool; to zoom in and zoom out, use the Command key, the Option key and the space bar; to automatically zoom and scroll at the same time, hold down the mouse when you are using the zoom tool.

As you draw a curve, you can go back and edit it by pressing the

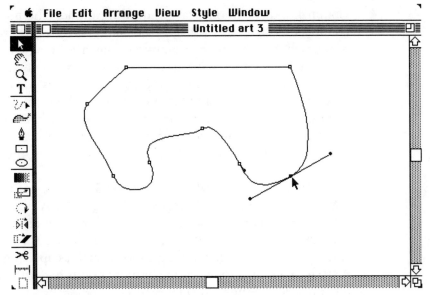

Figure 1-4a.
Selecting a point (direction points connected to the point control the slope and direction of the curve).

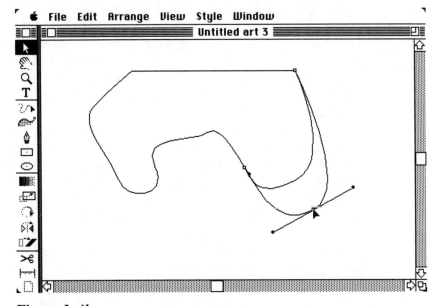

Figure 1-4b.
Reshaping the path by moving one or more points. You can reshape a curve by moving the direction points.

Command key, without leaving drawing mode. The program remembers its state, lets you go back and change things, and then resumes without losing continuity — your hand never has to leave the mouse (which is important for an artist who is trying to concentrate on the work). To build certain types of curves you stretch the curve, press the Command key, pull back one line with the mouse, and then go on. This technique can be mastered to the point that it can become second nature; people who are proficient at it can build curves much faster in this manner than by drawing them with a pencil.

A graphic object in Adobe Illustrator 88 consists of points and segments (lines or curves) connected in a *path*. A path can be a single line or curve or shape, such as a circle or rectangle, or a combination of lines, curves and shapes (Figure 1-3). You select an entire path to perform many operations, such as applying paint or rotating. You can also select one or more points in a path and move them to reshape the path (Figure 1-4).

There are several useful ways to select entire objects and pieces of objects, or just points within them. The standard marquee (selection rectangle) will select every point that's within the marquee (Figure 1-5). When you select just one point, it deselects the other points unless you hold down the Shift key to extend the selection to include both the points already selected plus the new point. The Shift key lets you extend your selection to include a new point, or if the point was already selected, it will be deselected. With the marquee, you can extend the selection, even to another group of points.

Rather than trying to surround an entire path or large image with the marquee (especially if the path is larger than your screen's display area), you can point to the path, hold down the Option key, and click the mouse to select the entire path (Figure 1-6). You can then use Shift-Option-click to extend the selection to another path. This is especially useful when you have a large number of objects — you can select them in a hurry.

Using the Option key with the marquee will grab all the paths that intersect the selection rectangle (Figure 1-7). This is useful for very complex drawings — you can select everything within a certain area, and then deselect certain parts using the Shift key and clicking on them.

The Shift key can constrain movement when you are moving a

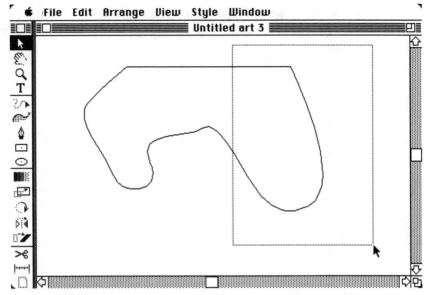

Figure 1-5a.
Draw a marquee around part of the shape to select more than one point in a path.

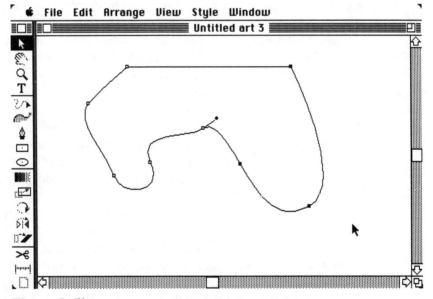

Figure 1-5b.
Only those points that lie inside the marquee are selected.

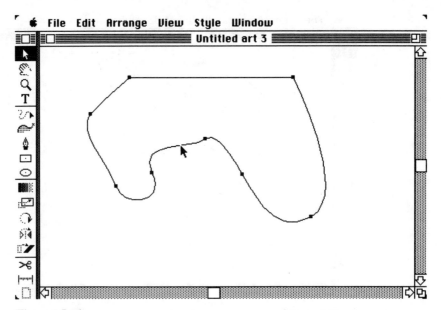

Figure 1-6.
You can select a complete path by holding down the Option key while clicking the mouse.

group or a path. It can also constrain while drawing so that you draw perfect squares or circles. Hold down the Shift key while using the ellipse tool to draw a perfect circle rather than an ellipse (Figure 1-8). You can build a circle or ellipse from center-to-edge rather than from edge-to-edge by using the Option key to constrain. Ellipses are created to align to the x and y axes settings; they align to whatever degree of rotation has been set.

To paste one object between others, you can select the object, cut it, select the next object, and choose Paste In Back to paste the first object behind the selected object but in front of a third object. Any object or group of objects can be interleaved between any other objects (Figure 1-9).

No matter how you select a group of objects, it moves as a group until you ungroup it. This feature can be useful for moving large and complex shapes. Rectangles, ellipses and circles are grouped when you draw them, but you can ungroup them and turn them into other shapes. For example, you can select a circle and ungroup it, then select a point on the circle and Cut it; the circle becomes four Bézier curves that can then be edited. You can also use the Scissors tool to cut the circle into segments for precise arcs.

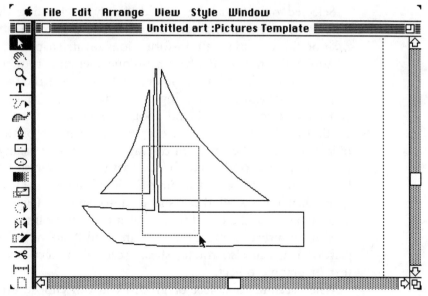

Figure 1-7a.
Hold down the Option key while dragging the marquee to select paths.

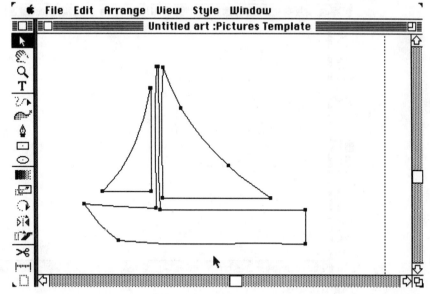

Figure 1-7b.
With the Option key down, the program selects all paths that intersect the marquee.

Selected objects can be cloned simply by holding down the Option key while dragging. You can clone a selected object and then perform a series of transformations on its shape and color.

Adobe Illustrator 88 offers a unique blending tool that helps you blend one shape into another. First you select the two objects or paths that define the starting and ending shapes (Figure 1-10), and after selecting the blend tool, you click one point of the starting object or path and a corresponding point of the ending object or path. The program displays a dialog box asking for the number of steps, or discrete shapes, that the program should create between the starting and ending shapes (Figure 1-11). The program then creates all these shapes automatically (Figure 1-12). You can also use the blend tool to blend one color into another to achieve an airbrush effect (see "Swan" and "Violin" in the color plates). You can also rotate, shear, scale, or reflect any piece of text or graphic object.

When scaling an object or group, you can choose uniform or constrained scaling, preserving line weights or scaling the lines.

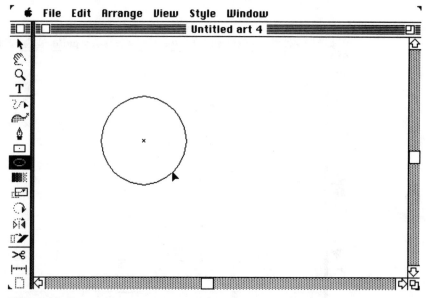

Figure 1-8.
The Shift key with the ellipse drawing tool constrains an ellipse to be a perfect circle.

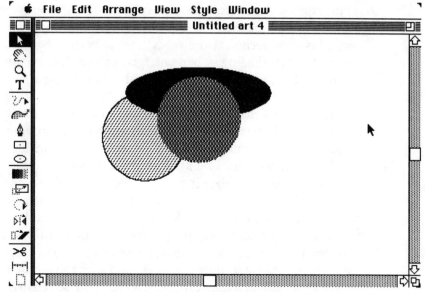

Figure 1-9.
Interleaved objects as they appear in the Preview window.

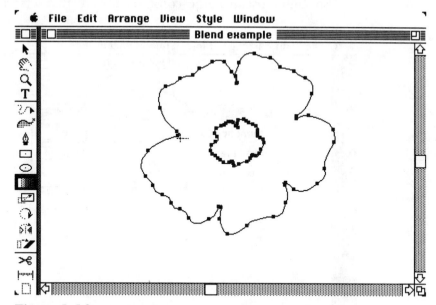

Figure 1-10.
To use the blend tool, first select the two shapes at either end.

For example, you can select everything on the page and scale it down by 33 percent of the original size with preserved line weights. For technical drawings, this is better than using a stat camera. Gray shading, when enlarged or reduced, retains its exact density, because it is repainted with the specified shading percentage.

You can control the text font (PostScript fonts, which are outlines of characters), style, size, leading (vertical spacing between lines of text), kerning (spacing between letters within a word), and alignment (Figure 1-13). With the Text tool, you can select the text and change its size; it changes the size of the outline font in fractional points and allows you to condense character width and even change the outline. Color or shades of gray can be applied to filled characters and you can specify the color and thickness of the stroke. You can use the Rotation tool to rotate text by a percentage you specify, or you can rotate it freehand with the mouse (Figure 1-14). Text and graphics can be selected and scaled together because they are treated in the same manner. At any point you can edit the text by double-clicking on its starting point with the text tool.

Also highly useful is the constrain feature that lets you set a

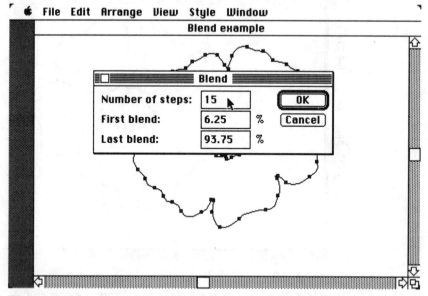

Figure 1-11.
The blend tool displays a dialog box requesting the number of steps, or discrete shapes, that the program should create between the starting and ending shapes.

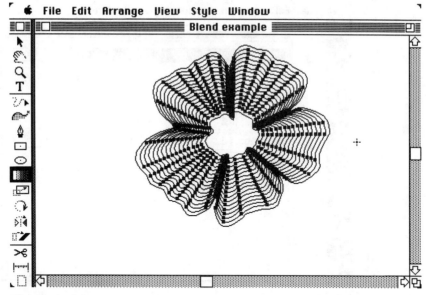

Figure 1-12a.
The blend tool automatically creates a series of objects that are a blend between the starting and ending objects. These objects are grouped so that you can move them or transform them together.

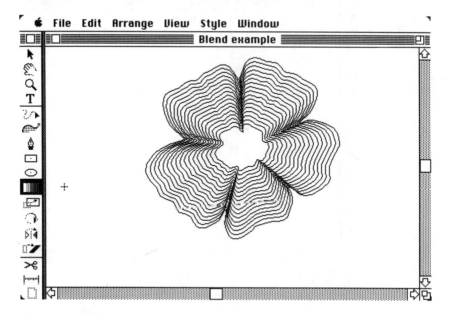

Figure 1-12b.
The result of using the blend tool. Each step of the blend is a regular path you can adjust and paint.

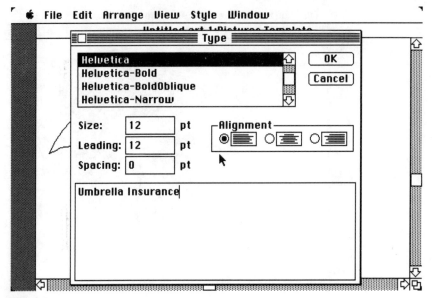

Figure 1-13.
The dialog box for specifying text formatting.

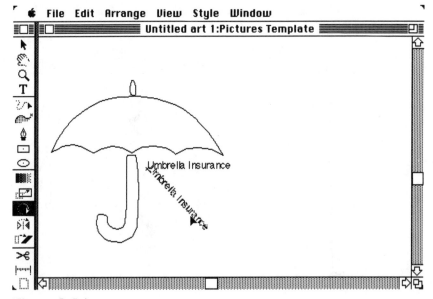

Figure 1-14.
Selecting and rotating text freely with the mouse.

constraining factor according to the axis you draw. If you are doing a road map, for example, and you need to indicate buildings on the map, you can draw a direction, then place graphics to be constrained to go along in that direction. The measure tool displays the exact measurement between two points (Figure 1-15), which can help make drawings accurate.

Adobe Illustrator 88 can create a complete PostScript page, or just the PostScript code necessary to rebuild the image when included with other page makeup, graphics, and word processing programs. You can, for example, save an illustration as a PostScript file using the Encapsulated PostScript (EPS) format and then place the illustration onto a PageMaker page for use in a publication. Adobe Illustrator 88 can save in both Macintosh and PC versions of the EPS format so that an image can be displayed on either type of system.

Those who can program in PostScript will also find Adobe Illustrator 88 useful. You can select any point and insert a comment, and the program inserts the comment in the PostScript file, so you can later find that area and edit the PostScript code. We

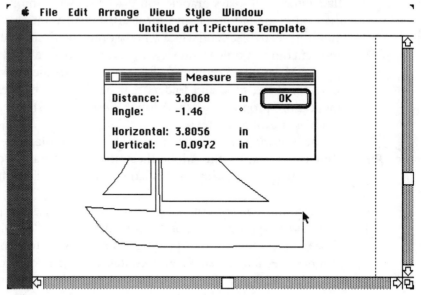

Figure 1-15.
Measuring the distance between two points with the measure tool.

recommend that you consult the *PostScript Language Tutorial and Cookbook* and other books from Adobe Systems for learning about programming in PostScript.

Overview of the Macintosh

Adobe Illustrator 88 runs on any Macintosh computer with at least one megabyte of RAM and equipped with either a hard disk drive or an 800K external floppy disk drive (this configuration includes a standard Macintosh Plus with one external floppy disk drive). It can run with all of the high-resolution color monitors available for the Macintosh II including monitors from Apple, Radius, Super-Mac Technologies and other vendors.

You don't need a color monitor, however, to assign colors to images that print in color on PostScript color printers and can be separated on PostScript imagesetters. A color monitor is useful in previewing color graphics, but it is not necessary — colors appear as different shades of gray on black and white monitors. Adobe Illustrator 88 displays graphics on black and white monitors faster than on color monitors, and most artists will want to work with monitors set to black and white when working with complex images, and set color on only to preview the artwork before printing.

The Macintosh computer displays an electronic desktop with icons for disks, files, and folders that hold files. The files may be application programs (like Adobe Illustrator 88) or data files (such as drawings or text).

The following are icons you might see on the Macintosh screen: Here is the icon for the Adobe Illustrator 88 program. To start up the program, you point to this icon and double-click the mouse button.

The folder icon represents a group of files that are either programs (also called "applications") or "documents" (also called "data files," "image documents," or "graphics files") associated with those programs. A folder usually also contains other folders to further subdivide the files. Folders are useful for organizing the icons for files on the Macintosh desktop.

Folders are the equivalent of *subdirectories* on other computer systems. When you create a new folder, it is automatically named "Empty Folder." Folders usually contain a group of related items, so you should rename your folder to describe the folder's contents. (See your Macintosh manuals for a description of how to create, rename, and move files into and out of folders.)

This icon represents an Adobe Illustrator 88 artwork document (or "artwork file"), which should be named to describe its contents. The Tutorial folder supplied with the Adobe Illustrator 88 files includes artwork documents named "Dragonfly art," and "Flower art" (as well as template files created in the MacPaint format, described later).

An Adobe Illustrator 88 document is a text file which contains the PostScript description of the artwork. An Illustrator document can be opened by either the Adobe Illustrator 88 program, or it can be opened by a word processing program if you want to edit the PostScript code. If you point to an Illustrator document icon and double-click the mouse, the Adobe Illustrator 88 program is automatically started and it opens the Adobe Illustrator 88 artwork document and any template document associated with that artwork document.

This icon represents a Macintosh Encapsulated PostScript document. This file format is used when you want to use Illustrator-created artwork with another Macintosh program such as a page layout program. For more information about creating a Macintosh Encapsulated PostScript file (or PC Encapsulated PostScript file for use with PC applications) see the File menu's Save As command description in Chapter 5. See Chapter 6 for a detailed discussion of Adobe Illustrator 88 and Encapsulated PostScript.

This icon represents a MacPaint file containing a graphic image. MacPaint and PICT files are the only type of documents that can be used as templates for tracing over with Adobe Illustrator 88. MacPaint files have similar icons to files of other painting programs that also save images in the MacPaint format, such as FullPaint and SuperPaint. If you plan to use a paint program other than MacPaint with Adobe Illustrator 88, it must be able save its files as either MacPaint files or PICT files; virtually all painting programs allow you to do this. MacPaint files have a fixed resolution of 72 dpi (dots per inch), which matches the Macintosh display resolution.

This icon represents a MacDraw graphics file saved in the PICT format. MacDraw files in the PICT format and MacPaint files are the only files that can be used as templates for tracing over with Adobe Illustrator 88. If you plan to use another drawing program, it must save its files as either MacPaint files or PICT files; virtually all of the drawing programs allow you to do this. MacDraw

PICT documents have a resolution of 72 dots per inch when used as templates with Adobe Illustrator 88.

Guided Tour of the Adobe Illustrator 88 Display

You start the Adobe Illustrator 88 program by double-clicking the icon. The familiar Apple icon and other Menu titles appear at the top of your screen, but no tools or windows (other than the opening screen) are visible, because no documents have been selected.

Most Adobe Illustrator 88 commands are not available unless a document is open. Unavailable commands appear as gray text in the menus; available commands appear as black text. The only commands you can use from the Adobe Illustrator 88 desktop are New, Open, and Quit from the File menu and Show Clipboard from the Edit menu. No commands can be selected from the Arrange, View, or Style menus.

Choose Open from the File menu (the three dots after Open indicate that a dialog box will appear to request further information). Use the Open option from the File menu to either resume work on an existing Illustrator document or to create a new Illustrator document by tracing over an existing MacPaint file or PICT file that you want to use as a template. Use the New option to create a new Illustrator document with or without a template image to trace.

After choosing Open from the File menu, a dialog box appears (see Figure 1-16). Drag the scroll box if necessary to select an Adobe Illustrator 88 document, MacPaint document, or PICT document. If you select an Illustrator document that already has a template associated with it, the template is automatically opened. If you select a template document (MacPaint or PICT file) a new, untitled Illustrator document is opened on top of the template, and the template becomes associated with that document.

Select the document you want to open, then point to the Open button in the dialog box and click the mouse button. In Figure 1-16, the Illustrator document named "Butterfly.art", located in the folder named "Animals" (on a Gallery images disk available from Adobe Systems) is opened. The template document named "butterfly" is a MacPaint file created by using a scanner to digitize sketches or photographs (or pressed butterflies).

When the Illustrator document and its associated template are first

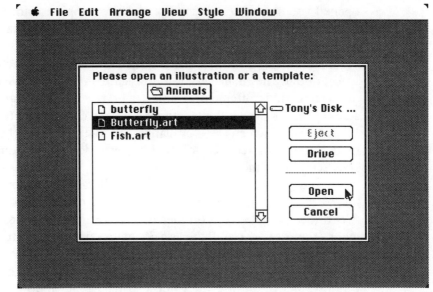

Figure 1-16.
After selecting the Open option from the File menu, a dialog box appears with an Open option for selecting a document.

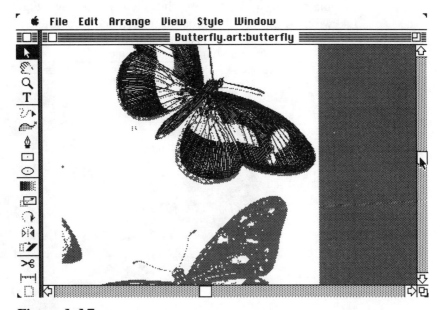

Figure 1-17.
The program displays the artwork in black and its background template in gray so that it is easier to trace.

opened you see both the artwork and the template. Since Adobe Illustrator 88 is often used for tracing over scanned images, the background template is displayed in gray rather than black (see Figure 1-17). The Illustrator document is a 14-by-14-inch work-space; due to the small size of the Macintosh Plus and Macintosh SE screens, it is often impossible to fit the entire image in the active window when the document is viewed at its actual size. Larger video screens — available for the various Macintosh models — let you see more of the Illustrator document at once and save scrolling time.

To find out what view is displayed in the active window, check the View menu. In Figure 1-18, the check mark in front of the Artwork & Template option means that both the Illustrator document (the artwork) and the MacPaint document (the template) underneath it are displayed in the active window. (If your screen shows more than one window, only one window is the active window; click the mouse in a window to make that window the active window.)

Other views of the active window can also be selected from the View menu. To see the template without the artwork, select the Template Only option from the View menu (see Figure 1-19). Likewise, to display the Illustrator artwork without the template,

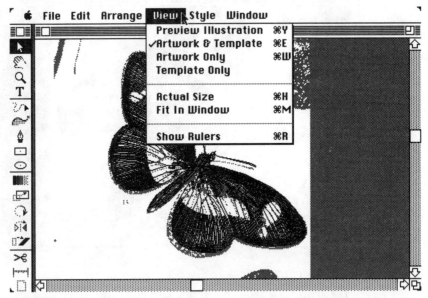

Figure 1-18.
Adobe Illustrator 88 offers a variety of viewing options.

select Artwork Only from the View menu (see Figure 1-20).

Adobe Illustrator 88 also provides a magnifying glass tool to "zoom into" the artwork and magnify your view to see the smallest possible detail. To zoom into (magnify) an area of the artwork, click on the zoom tool (the magnifying glass) in the toolbox palette, position the zoom tool over the area you want to inspect more closely, and click the mouse button (see Figure 1-21).

Each click of the mouse magnifies your view of the artwork and template by a factor of two. Zooming doesn't change the actual size of your artwork, just your view of it. In Figure 1-21 the mouse button was clicked twice, each time doubling in magnification. The + disappears from the magnifying glass when you have reached

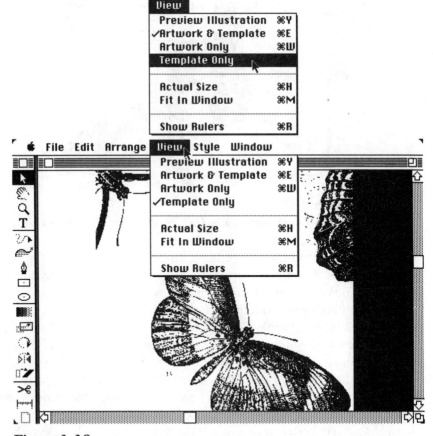

Figure 1-19.
You can view the template by itself in full black rather than gray, in order to see more detail.

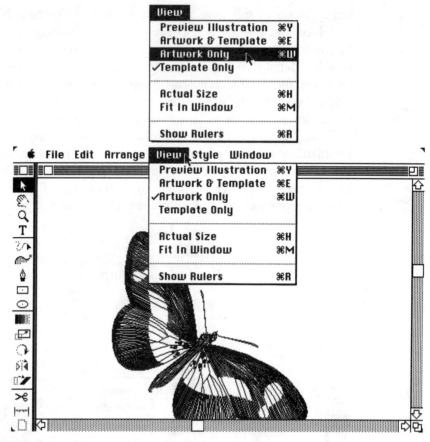

Figure 1-20.
Displaying the artwork by itself, without the background template.

the maximum enlargement. You can hold down the Option key and click the mouse button to zoom out (a - in the magnifying glass indicates you are zooming out to reduce the view). The program offers nine reduction or magnification levels.

The Artwork Only view displays the points, lines, and curves created with the Adobe Illustrator 88 program. These points, lines, and curves do not exactly match the printed artwork because the Artwork Only view — and the Artwork & Template view — do not display line weight, gray-scale values, color values, and other characteristics of the printed artwork.

To better approximate the printed artwork, select the Preview Illustration option from the View menu. However, even the Pre-

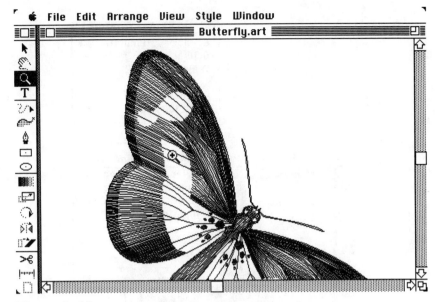

Figure 1-21a.
Using the zoom tool (magnifying glass) to enlarge your view to see more detail.

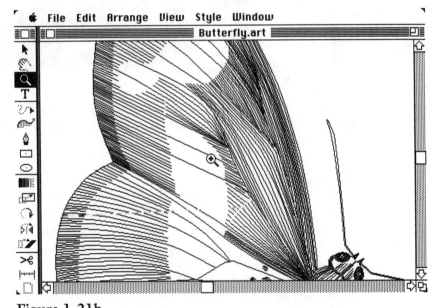

Figure 1-21b.
The zoom tool magnifies the image to be twice as large as before without changing the size of the graphics.

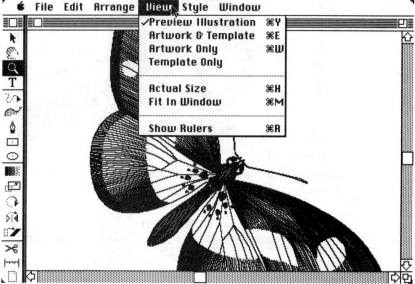

Figure 1-22.
The Preview Illustration display comes closer to showing how the printed output will appear, using actual line weights and patterns (and colors if you are using a color monitor).

view Illustration display is not exact. For an accurate view of the printed artwork, you must actually print it on a PostScript printer or imagesetter (laser typesetter). In Figure 1-22 the Preview Illustration option displays line weights different from the Artwork Only and Artwork & Template views; the heavy line weights were specified when the artwork was drawn.

Not only can you view the Illustrator document and template in a variety of ways, you can also view them in a variety of sizes. If you want to reduce the entire 14-by-14-inch Adobe Illustrator 88 document down in order to fit it in the active window, you can either select Fit In Window from the View menu (Figure 1-23), or you can point to the hand tool in the toolbox palette and double-

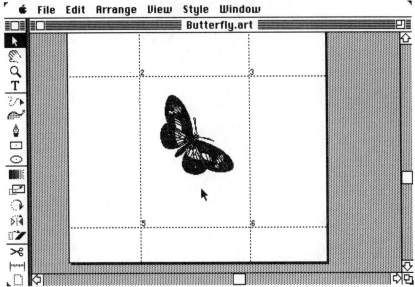

Figure 1-23.
The Fit In Window viewing option displays the entire artwork.

click the mouse button.

To end this quick tour of Adobe Illustrator 88, select Quit from the File menu to exit from the program. If any changes have been made since the last time the document was saved to disk, the program asks if you want to save the changes you made, and you can either save them or leave the artwork in its original state.

Examples in This Book

We interviewed several artists who created artwork using Adobe Illustrator 88 to gain insight on how the tools are used by professional illustrators. Chapters 2 through 4 describe how the artists used various tools and menu options to create special effects that are often difficult to achieve with other programs, or that would be difficult to duplicate with traditional art methods.

Chapters 5 and 6 comprise a reference section. Chapter 5 contains a complete description of each tool in the toolbox (from top to bottom) and all the selections and commands on the pull-down menu items (from right to left, top to bottom). Chapter 6 contains further information on using Adobe Illustrator 88 with PostScript.

When you return your Adobe Illustrator 88 registration card for a free subscription to Adobe's *Colophon*, you will receive more tips and techniques from artists using Adobe Illustrator 88. Adobe Systems offers the Gallery disks of artwork so that you can practice with examples.

2

Maps, Charts, and Clip Art

The best way to learn Adobe Illustrator 88 is to practice. Dean Dapkus, an artist from San Jose State University, knew nothing about computers when he started: "The rate with which you increase your efficiency is incredible. I began by doing simple symbols such as the men and women on bathroom doors and other international sign symbols. For my first drawing, I spent about three days doing a simple coffee cup.

"By the time I did the Gallery artwork, I was able to complete those drawings in 10 to 20 hours. By now, I could cut the time it took to do those images by half again. You build skills as you go along, and you can apply the techniques you learn to each new drawing."

Learning how to use Adobe Illustrator 88 is different than learning most computer programs because the program has so many features. The program can be difficult to learn at first, but it is not difficult to master if you know something about design. You learn how to become more productive with the program, and you find out that once you know how to do something, you don't have to keep reinventing the solution. Pat Coleman, a free lance graphic designer at Adobe Systems, is well adapted to using what is readily available: "Once you create an image, it can become a piece of clip art and you can borrow from it to create new images."

Although the freehand tool in Adobe Illustrator 88 is similar to the drawing tools found in other graphics programs, the curve manipulation tools are not the same. The pen tool does not draw lines — you use it to establish points for the program to draw with precision the line or curve segment to connect the points. The process of drawing with the pen tool is more like a connect-the-dots puzzle. You can switch from the pen tool to the selection tool in order to move the points, lines, and direction pointers to change the shape of a curve, then switch back to the pen and continue establishing more points.

The freehand tool creates a straight line or curve based on the actual movement of the mouse — you actually draw with the mouse as if it were a pencil or paintbrush, even though the shape of the mouse makes it very hard to draw with precision (as John Warnock, one of the inventors of Adobe Illustrator 88, described the process, "It's like drawing with a brick."). Illustrator's freehand tool can be adjusted to be less sensitive to variations in your hand movement so that sketching with a mouse can be a more natural activity than it usually is.

You can switch freely among the selection tool, the pen tool, and the freehand tool while drawing an object, making Adobe Illustrator 88 more powerful than most drawing programs.

Building Reusable Graphics

Besides drawing with the freehand tool and using the automatic tracing feature, you can build an illustration by establishing the points along a path with the pen tool, linking those points with straight lines (by clicking without dragging) or curves (by dragging).

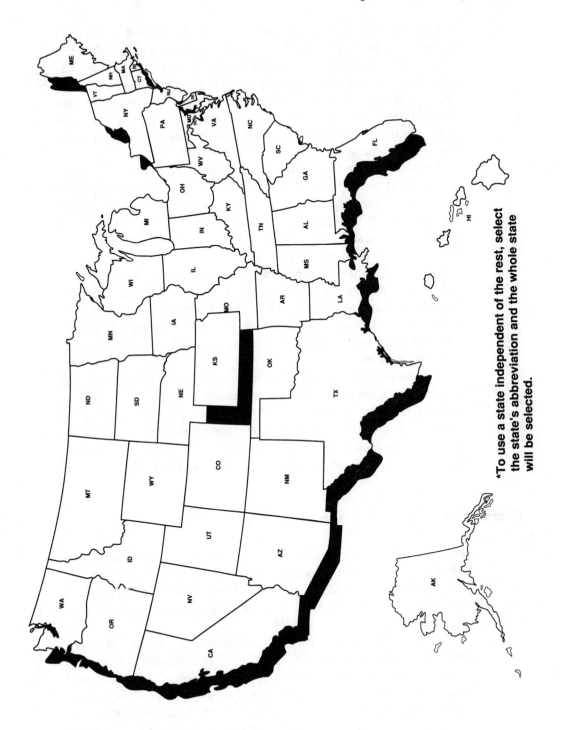

*To use a state independent of the rest, select the state's abbreviation and the whole state will be selected.

You can also draw rectangles and ovals (including perfect squares and circles) in much the same manner as other graphics programs — dragging the mouse to describe the area to be enclosed by the rectangle or oval. Other polygons and arbitrarily enclosed shapes are really just paths of points. The less points you use, the less choppy the shape appears because the program computes the smoothest curve. By adding more points you gain more control over the shape.

A map is an excellent example of a piece of line art that can be manipulated easily with Adobe Illustrator 88. You can quickly scale a complete map to any size and either keep the line weights the same (each line remains exactly the same width but changes length to accommodate the resizing), or let the line widths change with the same ratio as everything else.

A newspaper, for example, can take a large weather map and reduce it to use the map as a background for a four-day forecast, reducing the line weights as well so that the smaller versions of the map do not have heavy lines. The map could also be made very large (the size of a poster) but with all of the lines left at the same width as the actual size.

Maps or portions of maps can be reused for other purposes, and patterns (for example, rain and snow patterns) can be overlayed on top of a copy of the map to produce a different weather chart for each day. The benefit over manual methods is that once a state map is drawn, it never has to be drawn again — it can be scaled to any size and reused by itself or as part of the entire weather map.

Drawing Objects With Shared Borders

Pat Coleman drew the United States map found in Gallery Disk #1. Figure 2-1 shows the map template ready for use as a drawing aid, and Figure 2-2 shows how she drew more precise curves in areas where the template did not show enough detail (the drawing is magnified by the zoom tool).

To start drawing the map, Pat concentrated on each state and drew its outline separately. California, for example, combines curved segments with straight segments (Figure 2-3). Each state was drawn with segments that connect so that the state is one closed path (Figure 2-4). It takes a lot of small curved segments to draw the outline of the Bay Area, so she used the zoom tool to zoom

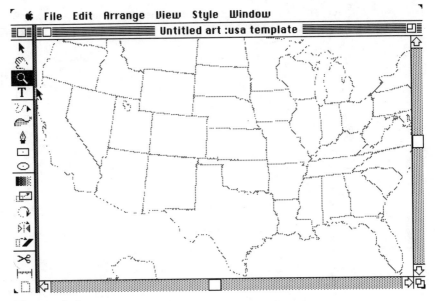

Figure 2-1.
A MacPaint file containing a scanned image is brought into Adobe Illustrator 88 as a template for drawing the U.S. map.

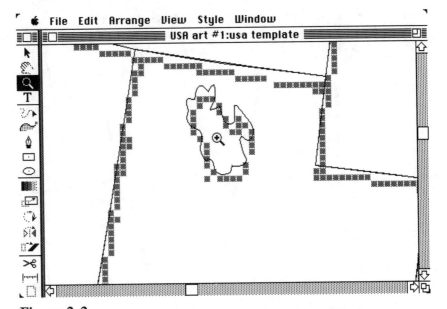

Figure 2-2.
The Great Salt Lake is a pattern a dots in the MacPaint template that can be dramatically improved by drawing precise curves with the pen tool after using the zoom tool to magnify the area of the image.

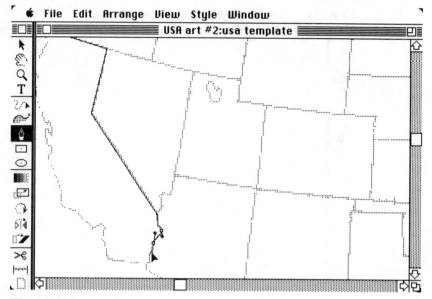

Figure 2-3.
You can use the pen tool to draw both straight line and curve segments to form a complete outline.

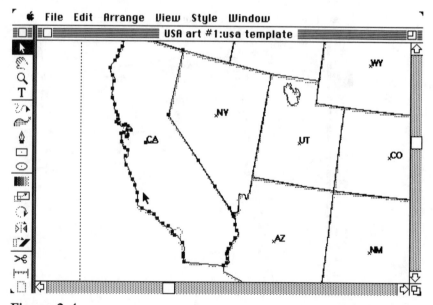

Figure 2-4.
Each state is drawn as a complete path that can be selected and moved or transformed without affecting other states.

into the area and see more detail (Figure 2-5). You can use the zoom tool to magnify the page to the largest magnification level and still use all of the other tools to draw very small segments.

To form a border where two states join (and thereby start the outline of the next state), Pat first selected the anchor points that defined the segments of the common border, and copied the segments to the Clipboard (Figure 2-6). Then she used the Paste In Front command, which placed the segments in the Clipboard in the same location and on top of the segments copied. She switched to the pen tool to continue drawing the rest of the state (Figure 2-7). "I used that technique for all of the common borders, so I had a head start in creating each new state, and it went fairly quickly."

Each state's border overlapped other state borders, so she made it easier to select a state by using the state's abbreviation as a handle. She typed the abbreviation with the Text tool, specifying the appropriate font, style, and size. Then she selected the outline path by holding down the Option key while pointing to a segment of the outline, and held down the Shift key to point at and include the state abbreviation in the selection. Finally she used the Group command in the Arrange menu to combine the selected items into

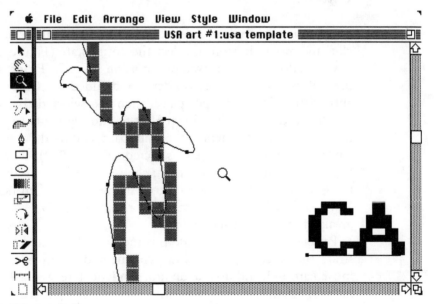

Figure 2-5.
Using the zoom tool to see more detail; the magnification can be as high as 1600 percent of the actual size.

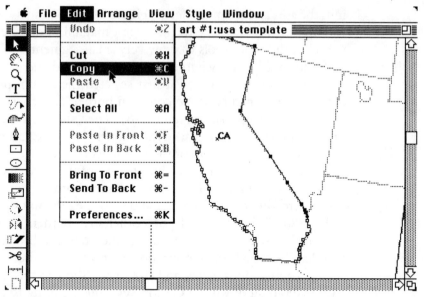

Figure 2-6.

To copy a state border, select the segments of the border (hold down the Shift key to include another segment in the selection), and Copy to the Clipboard.

one group. Anyone can now point at the state's abbreviation and click the mouse button to select the entire state (Figure 2-8).

Colorado is another example of using Paste In Front. First she drew all of the states that border it and added the Colorado state abbreviation in the proper place; then she selected the segments for the borders (holding down Shift to add segments to the selection), copied the borders to the Clipboard, and used Paste In Front while the borders were still selected (Figure 2-9). The borders joined to form an enclosed path; she selected it by holding down the Option key while pointing to a segment, and then held down Shift and selected the state abbreviation (CO), and finally grouped them to form one unit.

Pat explains why she chose this method: "I wanted to demonstrate that each state was independent and could be lifted out, moved around, and used as an independent state. So each state is a path by itself."

It is very convenient to select the state abbreviation and get the entire state. However, if you select a common border and get the neighboring state by accident, you can paste it behind the one you want by typing Command-B. (The key with the Apple logo or

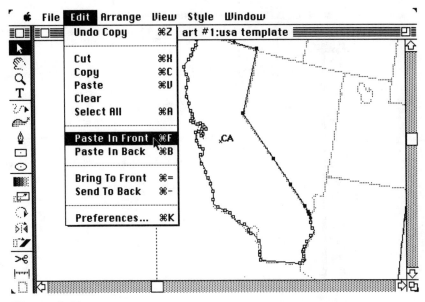

Figure 2-7.
After using the Paste In Front option to paste the copied border on top of the existing border, you can continue to draw the borders of the adjoining state.

cloverleaf design is also known as the Command key.) You can then select the state you want because it would be on top. You can always flip the order of the segments with this shortcut.

Important Tip: At any time during the process of creating the map, you can save your work so that if a power outage occurred you would not have to redo the work. Save the map continually while you work, but when it is finished and you want to edit a copy while leaving the original intact, use the Save As command to create a new illustration based on the original. The illustration's name changes to the new name (leaving the original name and illustration untouched), and subsequent Save commands save the work under the new name.

Adding Paint and Depth

To give the map a three-dimensional look, Pat Coleman added a shadow behind it, painted in gray. The outline of the entire country consisted of so many anchor points that the program could only move and duplicate the outline slowly. Thus, Pat decided to cut the

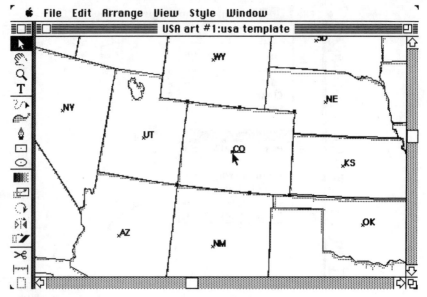

Figure 2-8.
Selecting the path for the entire state by selecting the state abbreviation, which is grouped to the path for the border outline of the state.

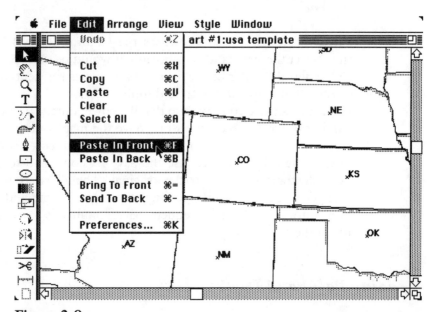

Figure 2-9.
Select the border of the other states and copy them to the Clipboard, then Paste In Front the contents of the Clipboard to make Colorado's border.

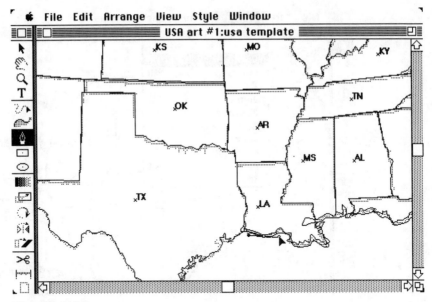

Figure 2-10.
Using the same template, the artist draws a separate outline of the entire country to be used as a shadow behind the map (this shadow outline has less detail than the state borders that form the regular outline).

shadow outline in half: one for the East Coast and one for the West. The outline is in two halves so that someone could use only half of the country for a map, or apply shading to only half of the country. It is also easy to dissect the partial outline and create regions, such as New England or the Midwest, if you want to use shading to differentiate them.

On the map there are many segments meticulously defining the coastlines, so Pat decided to draw another, less detailed outline using just the map's template. First she closed the artwork file and saved it, then she opened the template by itself, creating a new artwork file, and drew one outline around the West Coast, and one around the East Coast (Figure 2-10). To join the endpoints of the East Coast shadow (to keep it separate from the West Coast shadow), she clicked with the pen tool on a point on top of the first endpoint, and clicked on top of the other endpoint — Illustrator drew a straight line. She created the same type of line for the West Coast shadow by copying it to the Clipboard, then using the Paste In Front command to place the copy on top of the original line.

After finishing the outlines, she selected the first one by holding

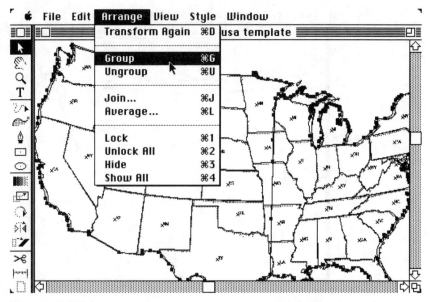

Figure 2-11.
The shadow outline consists of two paths; to combine them in a group, select one path with Option-click, and hold down the Shift key as well as the Option key to select the other path, and then choose the Group option from the Arrange menu.

down the Option key while selecting a segment (which selects an entire path); then while holding down the Shift and Option keys, she selected the other path. The Group command combined the two paths, defining the shape of the country into one unit (Figure 2-11). She was then ready to copy the entire group into the Clipboard, and save the new art file containing the U.S. profile.

Using the Open command, she opened the original U.S. art file without its template, and used the Paste In Back command to paste the group of paths from the Clipboard behind the U.S. map (Figure 2-12). The group remains selected, so she took the opportunity to specify the shadow using the Paint command in the Style menu — an 85% shade of black (dark gray) for the pattern, and no stroke (no outlining of the paths), as shown in Figure 2-13.

Returning to the art window, she started dragging the selected paths defining the shadow and then held down the Shift key while dragging. When she released the mouse and then released the Shift key, the shadow's outline had moved in a 45-degree angle below and to the right of the U.S. map (Figure 2-14).

The final step was to select a state, then hold down the Shift key

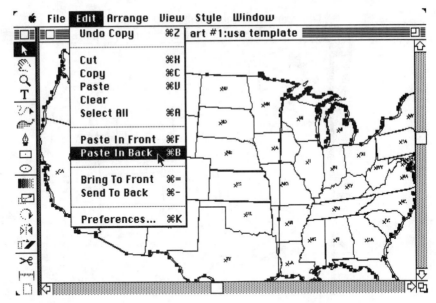

Figure 2-12.
Using the Paste In Back option to place the shadow outline (stored in the Clipboard) behind the map.

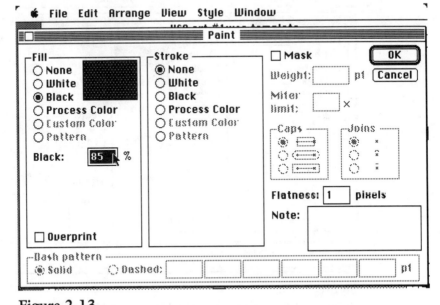

Figure 2-13.
Painting the selected closed path or group (in this case, the shadow outline) with 85 percent black for the fill , which is printed as a shade of gray. The Paint option is found in the Style menu.

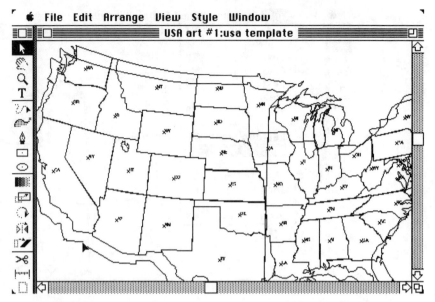

Figure 2-14.
Moving the grouped shadow outline paths by selecting and dragging.

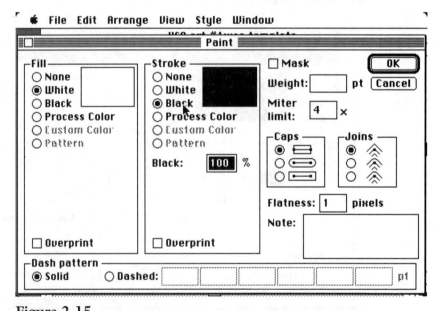

Figure 2-15.
Painting the selected states with white fill and black strokes so that the shadow outline does not show through the states.

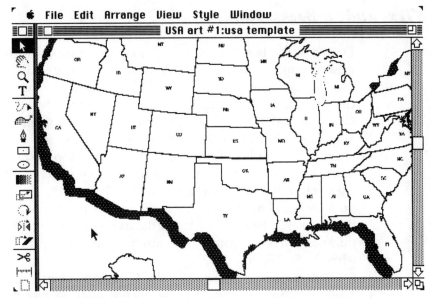

Figure 2-16.
Using the Preview Illustration option to see (as best as the screen can display) how the image will look when printed. Color monitors can display in color, and gray-scale or color monitors can display true gray scale.

and add all of the states to the selection, so that she could use the Paint menu again and apply the setting to all of the states at once. She switched the shade from black (the default setting) to white (Figure 2-15). The white shade makes the enclosed path white so that nothing underneath shows through.

To see what the map and shadow would look like if printed (and to see an approximation of the shadow's pattern), use the Preview Illustration option in the View menu (Figure 2-16). Preview Illustration displays the closest view of what the artwork will look like when printed, but takes some time to perform. You can't use the drawing or editing tools while using Preview — you must switch back to an artwork view to draw or edit the artwork. A better solution is to split the display screen so that one half displays the preview, and the other half displays an artwork view. Then, as you continue working on the artwork side of the screen, the updates will appear in the Preview half of the screen.

Text and Its Background

Dean Dapkus borrowed the U.S. map to create a weather chart. First he ungrouped each state and deleted the state's abbreviation; then he added small black circles and city names for the prominent cities in the country. The circles are easily drawn by selecting the ellipse tool, dragging from edge to edge, and holding down the Shift key to constrain the ellipse into a perfect circle.

Dean explains how he placed city names on top of state lines: "I wanted the black text of the city names to go over existing state lines, but rather than having a white box behind the name to cover the state line, I wanted a white outline of the text behind the text of the city name. To do this I typed the name of the city, gave it a line thickness of three, painted the stroke white, and painted the fill white." (See Figure 2-17.)

"I then copied the name to the Clipboard, then used Paste In Front to paste the copied name on top of the white name, and changed the copy to have no stroke and a black fill. I then had the city name in black, with a white outline around it. That's something you can't do with other graphics programs — they don't let you treat text as graphics."

Cloning and Rotating

Dean Dapkus also designed the curved weather front that overlays the weather chart. The curved weather front comprises a lot of small triangles whose baselines are matched to a long curve. Dean started the weather front by first making a triangle, then cloning it quickly. To make the triangle, Dean used the pen tool to define three points and link them with straight lines (Figure 2-18). The enclosed path is automatically filled with black as the default shade, and its stroke is also black.

To duplicate the triangle, Dean selected the first triangle by holding down the Option key while selecting a segment; this action selects the entire path. He started to drag the path, then held down the Option key so that he would create a copy (Figure 2-19), and held down the Shift key so that the movement would be constrained horizontally. When he had the second triangle next to the first and touching at the baseline, he let go of the mouse, then let go of the Option and Shift keys. He could then repeat the duplication many times by pressing Command-D (or selecting the Transform

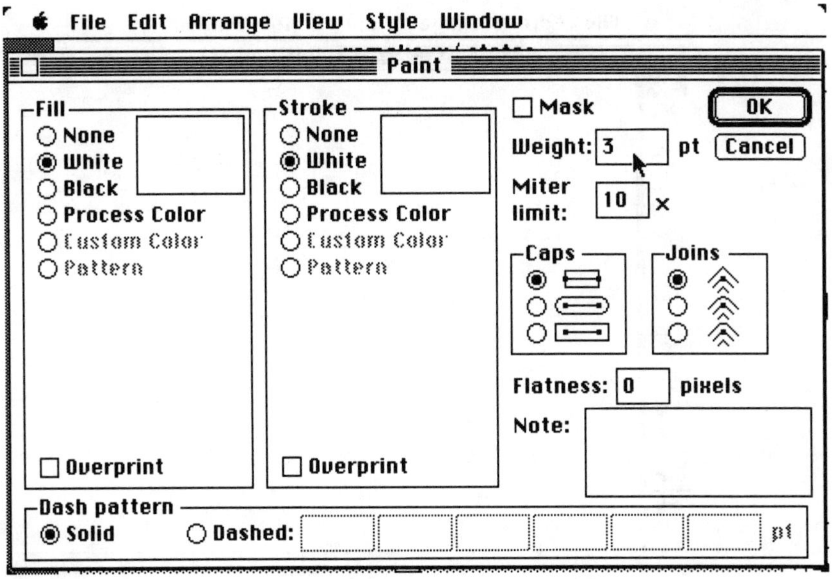

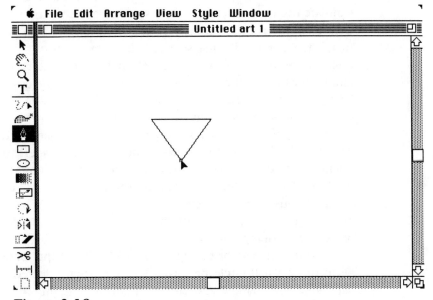

Figure 2-17.
Creating a white outline behind a word by assigning a white fill and thick stroke to the word, using Copy and Paste In Front to place a new version of the word on top of the white version, and painting the new version with a black fill and no stroke.

Figure 2-18.
Drawing a triangle path that will be cloned and rotated to form a weather front pattern to place on top of the map.

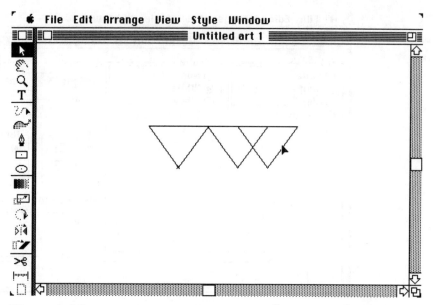

Figure 2-19.
Cloning the triangle to form a series of triangles.

Again command in the Arrange menu) for each duplication.

Dean had drawn a string of triangles, but they were in a straight line. To make curved weather-front graphics, Dean drew a curve to simulate the weather pattern, and selected all of the triangles. Dean then used the rotation tool to rotate the triangles into position to match the curve. He first selected the rotation tool, then clicked one end point of the first triangle to be the center of rotation (sometimes called the locus point), then dragged the corner of the baseline of any triangle up to the curve (Figure 2-20).

After releasing the mouse and finishing the rotation, Dean held down the Shift key and clicked a path of the first triangle to remove it from the selection of triangles to be rotated. This left the subsequent triangles still part of the selection, which could then be rotated into place (Figure 2-21), removed from the selection, and so on. "I just rotated every time I needed a curve," said Dean, explaining his technique for treating a group of paths as one object, and rotating it.

To draw the part of the weather front around the Great Lakes, Dean drew a half circle next to a triangle, then selected both the half circle and triangle and cloned them by dragging and holding down both the Shift and Option keys, as described above when

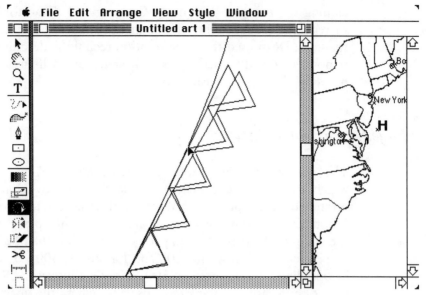

Figure 2-20.
Rotating the series of triangles so that each triangle aligns with a curve representing the weather front.

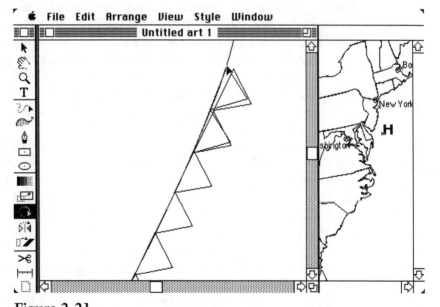

Figure 2-21.
As each triangle is aligned to the curve, you can deselect the triangle and continue rotating the rest of the series to match the next triangle.

cloning the triangle, then using Command-D (Transform Again) to repeat the duplication. To align the string of half circles and triangles, Dean used the same rotation technique described above, removing from the selection each triangle and half-circle that was properly aligned with each rotation.

Page Setup and Printing

The drawing area in Adobe Illustrator 88 is 14-by-14 inches, which is much larger than a standard 8 1/2-by-11-inch page printed by the Apple LaserWriter and other laser printers. The Linotype Linotronic typesetters, however, can typeset an image the width of the paper or film path — that is, less than 12 inches in one dimension (Linotronic 100 and Linotronic 300), or 18 inches in one direction (Linotronic 500). Adobe Illustrator 88 lets you control how large a page size to use, and where the image falls on the page or pages.

The program divides the drawing area into pages that match the dimensions you set for page size in the Page Setup dialog box (in the File menu). The program assumes you want a vertical page, also called portrait mode, where the longest edge of the page is vertical. Figure 2-22 shows the drawing area divided into pages that are the standard size for the LaserWriter. With the page tool (the last icon on the palette) you can move the page dividers to control how much of the image prints on each page. You can change the page orientation in the Page Setup dialog box to be horizontal, or landscape mode.

The weather chart would print vertically if Dean had just used the Print command, and only a portion of the chart would print on one page. Before printing, Dean opened the Page Setup dialog box to change the page orientation to horizontal (Figure 2-23), and then used the page tool in the Fit In Window view to fit the entire chart on one page (Figure 2-24).

Adobe Illustrator 88 numbers the pages (but does not print the page numbers) so that you can specify one page or a range of pages when printing. Although the corner areas do not display as full-sized pages, they are numbered so that page 1 is the top left corner, page 2 and 3 are the top center and top right, page 4 is the left middle edge, page 5 is the center of the 14-by-14-inch page (which holds the chart), and so on, up to page 9 at the bottom right corner. The program will print only those pages that contain part of the

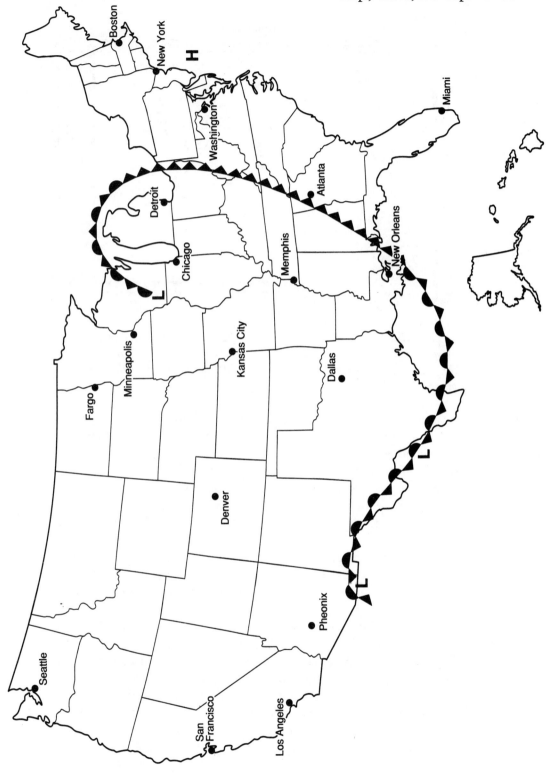

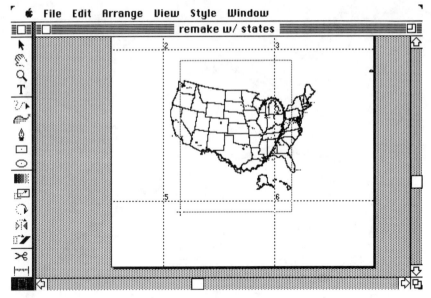

Figure 2-22.
The drawing area is divided into pages that are the standard size for most laser printers (including the Apple LaserWriter II). You can move the page boundary with the page tool to control how much of the image prints on each page.

graphic or its bounding box (the area that represents the smallest rectangle surrounding all points of the graphics). If your shape has curved edges, for instance, the bounding box that encloses the shape could extend across an extra page that will print as a blank page.

If a direction point extends across a page boundary, the printer could print a blank page for that reason. (The direction point determines the shape of a curve, and is connected to an anchor point.)

The LaserWriter Page Setup dialog box (see Figure 2-23) lets you specify a percentage reduction or enlargement. You can specify a percentage in the range of 25% reduction to 400% enlargement with a LaserWriter.

The LaserWriter prints only in an area that is 8.0-by-10.9-inches because the printer doesn't print all the way to the edge of the paper. The Linotronic typesetters do not have this limitation since you can run wide film or paper and print large images in landscape or portrait mode. Adobe Illustrator 88 ignores the smoothing effects for the LaserWriter, and font substitution does not affect appearance (Illustrator files are in PostScript).

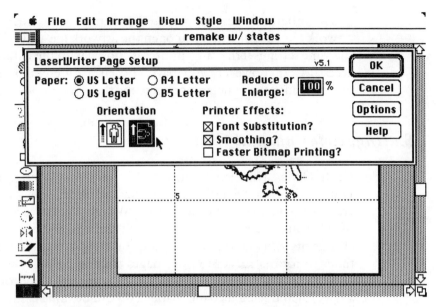

Figure 2-23.
Changing the page orientation to horizontal (landscape mode) in the Page Setup dialog box. You can also specify a percentage enlargement or reduction.

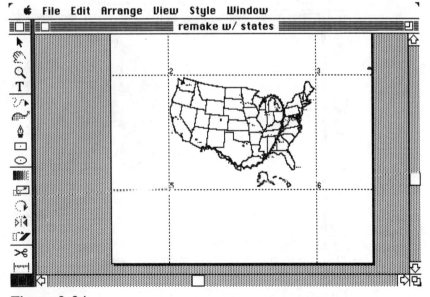

Figure 2-24.
After changing the artwork to landscape mode you can still adjust the page boundaries with the page tool.

The program saves the page setup settings you chose for your artwork file, so that when you open the artwork file again, it will use the same settings if the same printer is chosen with the Chooser desk accessory. If, however, you have chosen a different printer, the program adopts the default settings for that type of printer.

Scaling, Rotating, and Cloning

Keith Ohlfs, a freelance artist and a student at San Jose State University, drew "Skier" and "Horse and Rider," as well as several other pieces on the Gallery disks. We use "Skier" as an example of how you can take one image, change its shape and size by scaling, change its orientation by rotating, and then duplicate it many times to form a succession of images suggesting movement.

Keith started the skier illustration by scanning a photograph of a skier, then tracing its basic shape. This can be done easily with the automatic tracing feature (Figure 2-25). First select the auto trace tool, then click a starting point near the edge of the scanned shape to be traced. The program draws an outline around the shape and

Figure 2-25.
Using the automatic tracing tool to trace the outline of a scanned image of a skier.

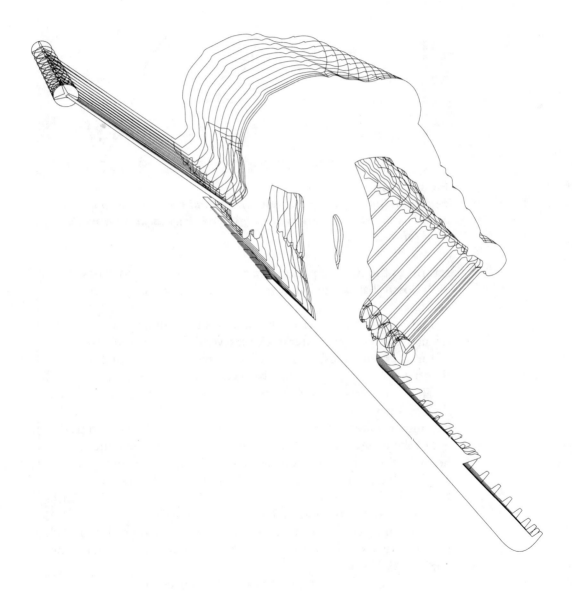

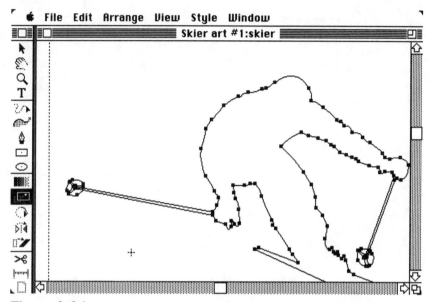

Figure 2-26.
After selecting the scaling tool, you click a focal point for scaling, then drag in a direction toward (reducing) or away (enlarging) from the focal point.

returns to the starting point. The automatic tracing tool works best with closed shapes, but it may treat a line as a closed shape rather than as a line.

Keith drew the spokes of the ski poles by zooming in to see the detail of the template. After drawing several paths to make the image of the skier and poles, he selected all of them and grouped them so that the rest of the operations worked on the entire group.

The image was too big for the LaserWriter page, so Keith used the scaling tool to manually rescale the artwork. He scaled it by clicking on a focal point for the reduction that was below and to the left of the image (Figure 2-26), and dragging to the left and down, holding the mouse button while watching the outline of the graphic change shape. He let go when he liked the way the image had been slightly stretched and contorted (Figure 2-27). Keith then selected the rotation tool, clicked on a focal point for the rotation, and dragged downward clockwise. He then changed his display to view artwork only, to touch up the curves and lines and make the image look better.

To create the first duplicate skier, he started dragging the selected group up and away from the original position, then held

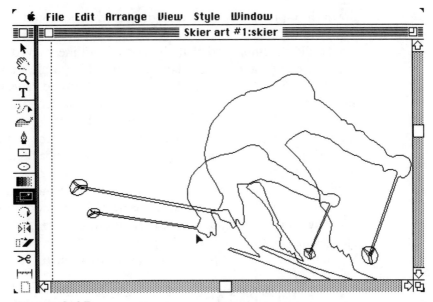

Figure 2-27.
You can stretch or compress an object with the scaling tool (or scale proportionately by holding down the Shift key).

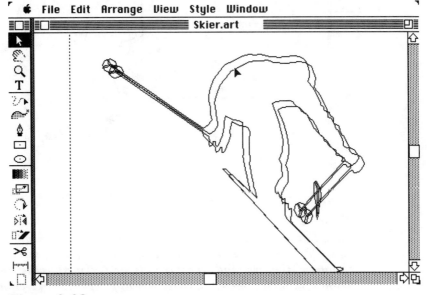

Figure 2-28.
Dragging the selected outline while holding down the Option key so that a duplicate is made that is offset from the original. This operation is a simple transformation.

down the Option key (while dragging) so that he would be moving a copy of the image, not the original. He also held down the Shift key (while dragging), so that the copied outline moved in a 45-degree angle (Figure 2-28). Having done this simple transformation (actually just a move and copy) once, he could repeat it over and over very quickly (Figure 2-29) by pressing Command-D or selecting the Transform Again command in the Arrange menu. The result is an image that simulates movement when the outlines are properly painted. The skier image and its copies are painted black by the default setting.

If you wanted to be more precise about the movement, you could hold down the Option key while using the selection tool (after selecting all of the segments of the outline), and bring up a Move dialog box (Figure 2-30) which lets you specify a measure of space in points (there are 72 points, or 6 picas, to an inch).

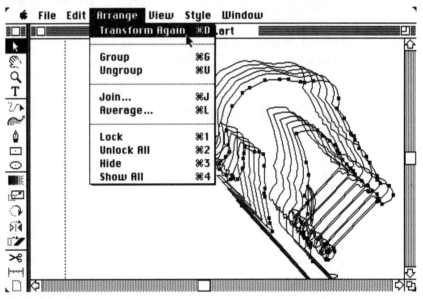

Figure 2-29.

Immediately after performing a transformation of any kind (such as the simple transformation in the previous figure), you can repeat the transformation over and over (to create many clones) by selecting the Transform Again command in the Arrange menu, or by typing the Command-D shortcut.

Shearing

"Horse and Rider" shows how you can create a slanted shadow of an object. You can slant an image along an x and y axes by using the shearing tool. "Horse and Rider" started as an automatic tracing of a template (Figure 2-31), which took only a few minutes.

To create the slanted shadow, Keith drew a marquee around the entire object by clicking the selection (arrow) tool and dragging from one corner of the object to the other corner (Figure 2-32). Everything inside the marquee's dotted lines is selected, even though the paths are not grouped. You can group the paths after they are selected by using the Group command in the Arrange menu.

Then Keith clicked the Shear tool, and the pointer turned into a crosshair. He moved the pointer to the horse's hind foot to define the intersection of the x and y axes for shearing (Figure 2-33). The

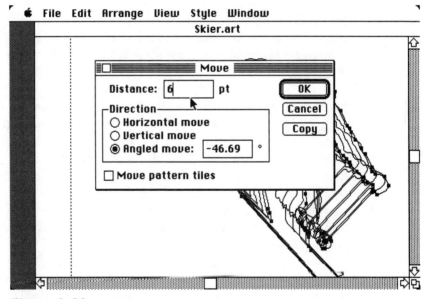

Figure 2-30.
After selecting the group of paths comprising the skier, hold down Option and click the selection tool to bring up the Move dialog box, which lets you enter precise measurements for distance and angle. The distance is in points because the measuring unit was set to picas/points in the Preferences dialog box (Edit menu).

Figure 2-31.
After clicking the automatic tracing tool and a starting point for tracing, the program takes a minute or less to trace the scanned image and displays a clock while tracing.

pointer changed from a crosshair to an arrowhead, and he then dragged in a horizontal direction away from the intersection of the x and y axes, and held down the mouse button to wait for the program to redraw the sheared image. He then held down the Option key to make a duplicate image for shearing (leaving the original image unsheared), and continued dragging back and forth slightly to adjust the shearing. When he had the image properly sheared, he released the mouse button, then released the Option key (Figure 2-34).

Shearing is best understood if you imagine that there is a horizontal (x) or vertical (y) axis that is either parallel to the sides of the window (the usual case), or angled from that position (if you've changed the axes with the Constrain command in the Arrange menu). You pick the intersection of the x and y axes, and you drag in either the horizontal (x) or vertical (y) direction (parallel to an axis) to shear the image in the direction of that axis. All points in the image that lie along the chosen axis do not move; all other points in the image move in the direction of that axis. So, as you drag horizontally, the image is slanted horizontally (along the x axis); as you drag vertically, the image is slanted vertically

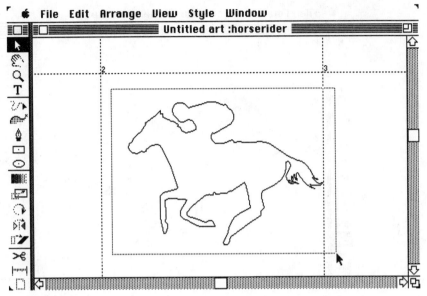

Figure 2-32.
*Selecting the entire object by drawing a selection marquee with the
selection (pointer) tool. Every point and segment inside the marquee's
dotted lines becomes part of the selection.*

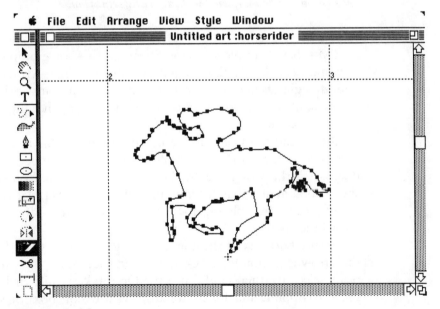

Figure 2-33.
*Clicking a focal point for the shearing tool to establish the x and y axes
for shearing.*

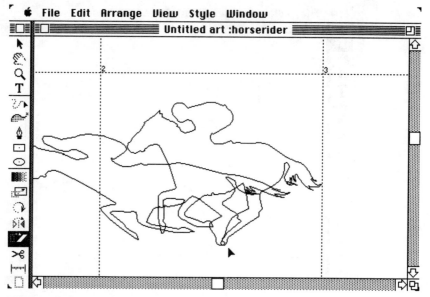

Figure 2-34.
Dragging horizontally shears the object along the x axis, and holding down the Option key creates a duplicate object for shearing, leaving the original unchanged. Remember to release the mouse button first, then the Option key, to complete the shear transformation.

(along the y axis).

If you have trouble with the Shear tool — for example, if the shearing is too drastic, flattening the image into a line — you can start your dragging farther away from the intersection point of the x and y axes, and have finer control over the shearing so that the changes are not so drastic.

After shearing in one direction, the pointer turns again into a crosshair so that you can establish another x-y intersection and drag along the x or y axis to shear the object again. You can also shear along angles that are multiples of 45 degrees (relative to the x and y axes) by holding down the Shift key while dragging the arrowhead pointer.

To specify the exact shear angle in degrees rather than dragging the arrowhead pointer, click the Shear tool (with the image already selected), then hold down the Option key while clicking the shear axis point, and Illustrator displays a dialog box for specifying the shear angle and the type of shear (horizontal, vertical, or angled by a specific degree (Figure 2-35). A positive shear angle

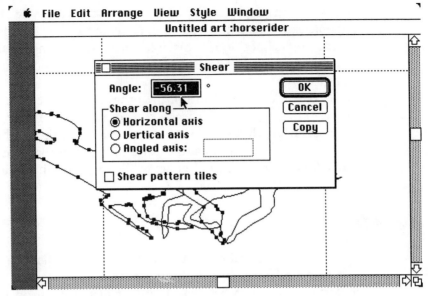

Figure 2-35.
*Specifying the shear angle in degrees rather than dragging (hold down
the Option key when clicking the shear tool's focal point).*

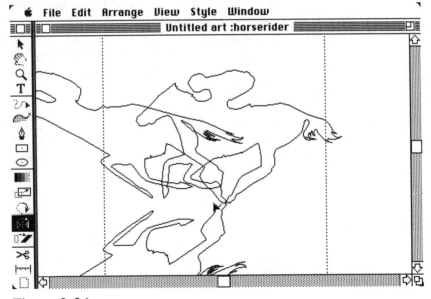

Figure 2-36.
*Using the reflection tool to make a reflection of the object; the focal point
for the reflection is the point where the objects touch.*

slants the image clockwise, and a negative shear angle slants the graphic counterclockwise (as in "Horse and Rider"), both relative to the original position. (This differs from other functions, such as rotation, where a positive angle produces a counterclockwise rotation.)

If you click the OK button, the program uses the specifications to perform the shear. To shear a copy of the image rather than the original image, click the Copy button rather than the OK button in the dialog box. (You can also shear a copy rather than the original by holding down the Option key while dragging the shear.)

Reflecting

For the final transformation, Keith used the reflection tool to produce a mirror image of the sheared copy. First he selected the reflection tool, then he clicked a point of reflection on the same hind foot that served as the point of shearing. Dragging downward away from the reflection point caused the image to be reflected into a shadow (Figure 2-36). In this case Keith did not hold down the Option key, since he was not making a duplicate image — he wanted to keep only the reflected version.

The "Horse and Rider" image and its sheared and reflected copy are both painted black, which is the default setting.

Reflection creates a mirror image across an invisible axis defined by clicking a focal point (Figure 2-37). You can reflect directly across a horizontal or vertical axis by first clicking the focal point (the crosshair turns into a pointer) and then clicking along another point on the invisible axis (Figure 2-38). Hold down the Option key while clicking to create a duplicate shape (Figure 2-39).

To reflect across a diagonal axis, click the focal point, then drag the invisible axis in order to rotate it at an angle (Figure 2-40). You can constrain this angle to 45-degree increments by holding down the Shift key. When you let go of the mouse button, the reflection is complete. You can also specify the angle of the axis by holding down the Option key while clicking the reflection tool's focal point (Figure 2-41).

The artist who drew the coffee cup clip art (from T/Maker's ClickArt EPS series) adjusted two mirror reflections in order to make a shadow effect appear on the coffee cup's saucer. When you

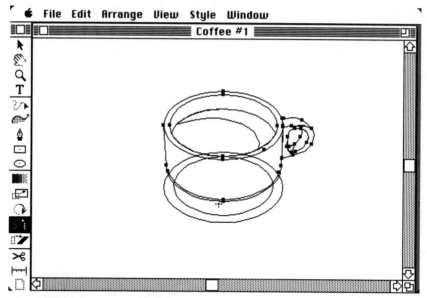

Figure 2-37.
Clicking a focal point for reflecting an object across a horizontal axis.

are adjusting objects and you want to know in advance how it will look (so that you can use the Undo option and experiment), first select the New Window option from the Window menu, which creates a second window on the artwork. You can resize this window to be on the right side of the display, and turn Preview Illustration on for the second window, then click in the first window and resize it to fit on the left side. The result is that you can adjust objects in the Artwork window and preview every move in the Preview Illustration window (Figure 2-42).

Blending

The blend tool creates a series of shapes between two objects. The tool works best if both objects use the same pattern (if any), but you can use different colors, gray scales, and stroke widths. The blend tool can blend process colors, gray scales, and stroke widths to achieve special effects such as an airbrush effect or a contour with different line weights.

For a simple example of blending, you could take a standard clip

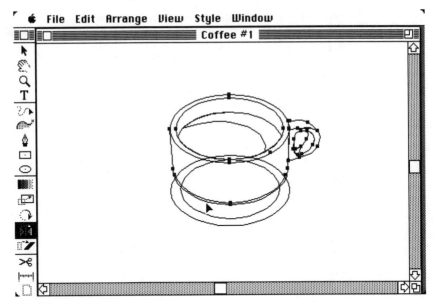

Figure 2-38.
Clicking along the invisible horizontal axis in order to reflect directly across the axis.

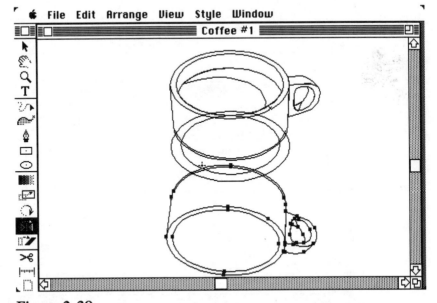

Figure 2-39.
The reflection tool creates a mirror image of the cup across the horizontal axis.

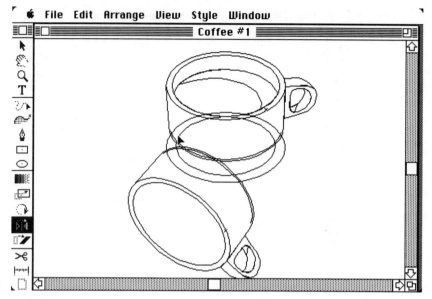

Figure 2-40.
After clicking the focal point, you can drag in order to rotate the invisible axis and reflect the object across a diagonal axis rather than a horizontal or vertical axis.

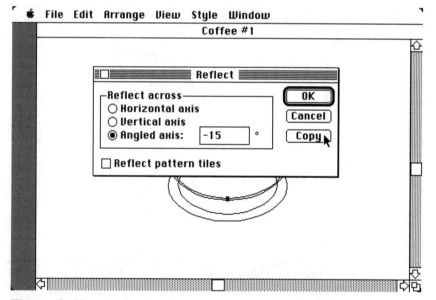

Figure 2-41.
Specifying a precise angle for the reflection axis by holding down the Option key while clicking the focal point.

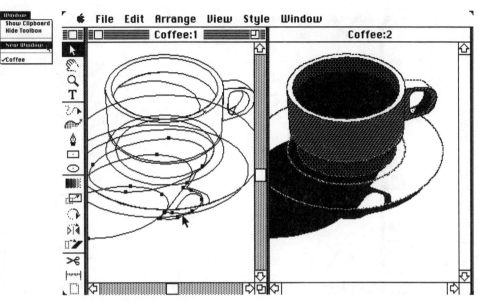

Figure 2-42.
After choosing New Window and resizing the two windows to fit side-by-side, you can set one window to be in Preview Illustration mode so that it shows a preview of every move.

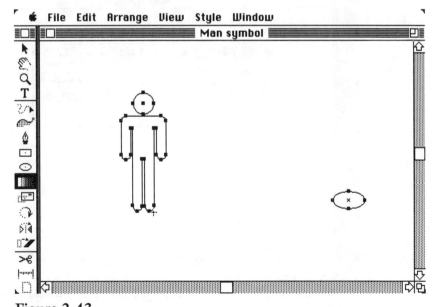

Figure 2-43.
After selecting two objects for a blending operation, select the blend tool and click a point on the first object.

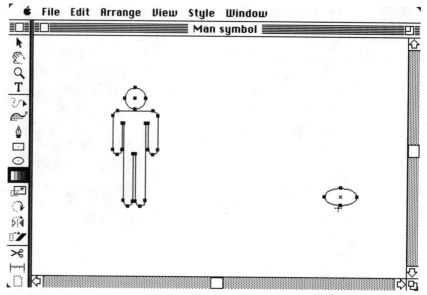

Figure 2-44.
Click a corresponding point on the second object for the blend operation.

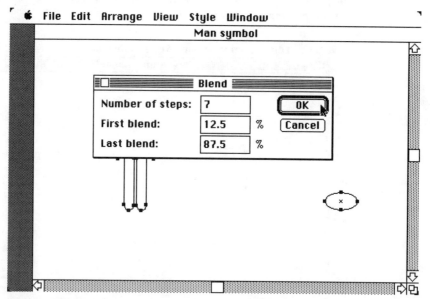

Figure 2-45.
The Blend dialog box appears, letting you specify the number of steps. The starting and ending percentages of the new steps are calculated for you, but you can change them.

art symbol (the man symbol from T/Maker's ClickArt EPS series) and blend it with another shape, such as an oval. First you select both objects, then choose the blend tool and click a point on the first object (Figure 2-43) and a corresponding point on the second object (Figure 2-44). The program displays the Blend dialog box, where you can specify the number of steps (Figure 2-45). The program calculates the first and last blend percentages, which you can change if you wish. For example, if you specify 19 steps, the first and last blends will be at five and 95 percent, which means that the first blend is at five percent of the starting object, and the last blend is at 95 percent.

When you click OK, the program performs the blending operation, creating a group of steps that are already selected (Figure 2-46). You can see the fill and stroke blend in the Preview Illustration window (Figure 2-47).

The blend tool interpolates between two points you select and calculates the steps. You can select more than two points (such as two entire paths) to have more control over the results. Paths must be ungrouped first before blending. To blend between open paths, select an endpoint on each path. You can create up to 1008 steps; the more steps you specify, the finer the gradation will be between the starting and ending shapes. For examples of blended process colors, see Plate 7 and Plate 8 in the color plates.

Drawing Freehand

Some artists prefer to draw images in a freehand style, then adjust and refine to get to the final result. Adobe Illustrator 88 provides a freehand tool for this purpose. First you select the freehand tool, then position the x marker to the place where you want to start drawing. As you drag, the marker turns into a pointer and leaves behind a dotted line. The faster you drag, the fewer dots are created.

The freehand tool responds to shakiness or other slight variations in your drawing motion, creating bumps. You can set the freehand tolerance level to reduce (or increase) the number of bumps by choosing the Preferences option from the Edit menu (Figure 2-48).

You can erase any part of the dotted line while you are drawing by holding down the Command key and redrawing back over the

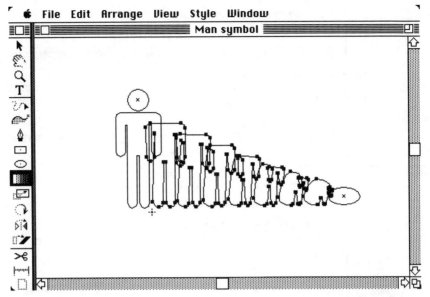

Figure 2-46.
The blend tool produces the steps grouped and preselected for further transformations.

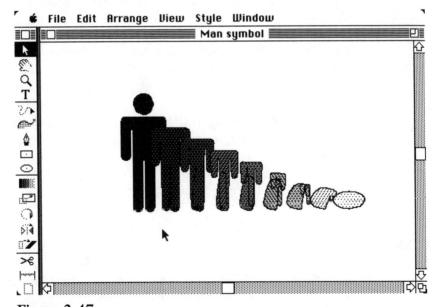

Figure 2-47.
The blending of patterns, fills, and strokes are shown in the Preview Illustration window.

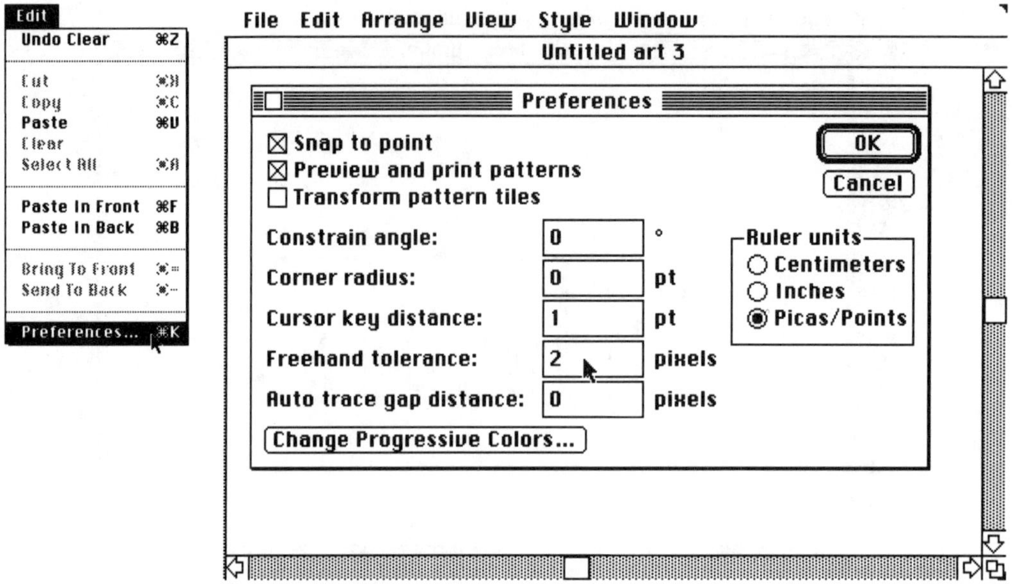

Figure 2-48.

The Preferences dialog box lets you specify, among other things, the freehand tolerance level to the number of pixels of variance in your drawing — more pixels means more bumps will be ignored by the freehand tool.

line (Figure 2-49). However, you can only erase the line if you have not yet released the mouse button. You can always delete a line or curve segment by selecting it and pressing the Delete or Backspace key.

You can stop drawing freehand at any point, and continue drawing freehand or using the pen tool to continue the path, by starting at the endpoint (Figure 2-50). To create a closed path, keep drawing with the freehand tool (or establishing points with the pen tool) until you reach the starting point of the path.

Summary

With "U.S. Map," Pat Coleman showed how to draw objects that have common borders; how to copy and paste a line and curve segment, path, and group of paths; and how to set up a shadow behind an object to make it appear three-dimensional. She also explained how she grouped the path outlining each state with the state's abbreviation, for easy selection of individual states. She

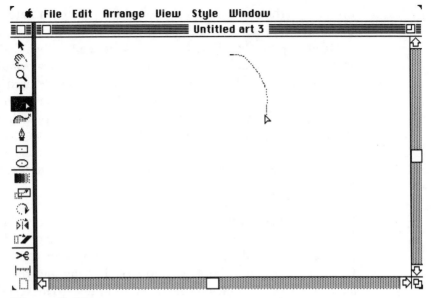

Figure 2-49.
With the freehand tool you can drag from a starting point and draw a shape; you can also hold down the Command key to go back over the shape and erase it.

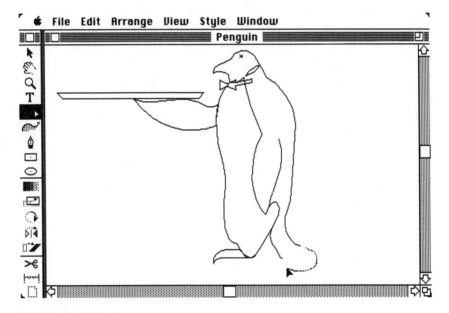

Figure 2-50.
Using the freehand tool to extend a path by starting at one of the endpoints of the path.

drew a map that could be used whole, or in part; each state or group of states could be used individually and with other artwork files.

Dean Dapkus took Pat's map and created a weather chart. Dean showed how he made clones of an object and used the rotation tool to form a weather front. He also explained how he used the text tool with a white stroke and fill to place text that extends over areas of the image. Dean changed the page setup to horizontal (landscape) in order to print the entire chart on one LaserWriter page, and discussed how you might scale a complete illustration by a percentage reduction or enlargement in the Page Setup dialog box.

Keith Ohlfs showed his technique for transforming and then cloning an image in the "Skier" illustration. Keith showed how you can repeat a duplication (or any transformation) over and over to achieve a special effect such as the skier that appears to be moving. Keith also showed a simple example of shearing and then reflecting a duplicate of an image (the horse and rider) to make a shadow.

The T/Maker ClickArt EPS graphics, stored in Encapsulated PostScript files, were manipulated by the reflection and blending tools, using two windows to show a preview window simultaneously with the artwork editing window.

A wide range of tools for creating graphics were described in this chapter; including tools for selecting, scaling, zooming, rotating, reflecting, and shearing an object. The Type and Paint dialog boxes, and the pen, freehand, and oval-drawing tools were also shown. The chapter introduced the Open, Save, Save As, Print, and Page Setup commands in the File menu; the Cut, Copy, Paste, Paste In Front, Paste In Back, and Preferences commands in the Edit menu; the Transform Again, Group, and Ungroup commands in the Arrange menu; the Preview Illustration and other display modes in the View menu, the New Window command in the Window menu, and the Paint and Type commands in the Style menu.

CHAPTER

3

Graphic Design and Illustration

The largest category of artwork produced using Adobe Illustrator 88 is graphic design and illustration. Andy Warhol is one artist who would have especially liked the program; his Campbell Soup cans would have been an excellent project. He could have outlined the cans quickly, added text for the label, and specified exact shades of gray and process colors.

Adobe Illustrator 88 gives you a better chance of getting high-quality results because it is a versatile program for cloning, scaling, and transforming graphic objects to form illustrations. The effects take some time to create, but once they are created, they can be reused over and over, and modified very quickly for custom work. Keith Ohlfs, a freelance artist who drew many of the Gallery pieces, compared the use of Adobe Illustrator 88 for the images he drew with conventional methods: "These effects could be done in an ink drawing, but Illustrator makes them much easier, and you can vary copies of them again and again for use in other drawings, which saves a lot of time and effort."

Starting a Large Illustration

"The Golfer," by Luanne Seymour Cohen, a graphic designer for Adobe Systems, is an excellent example of the type of commercial art that is easily rendered by using Adobe Illustrator 88. Luanne started with a scanned image of a photocopy of an old advertising poster. She scanned a photocopy because the original, which was in color, scanned too dark. The goal was to get as much detail out of the poster as possible, and not to worry about the quality of the scanned image (Figure 3-1).

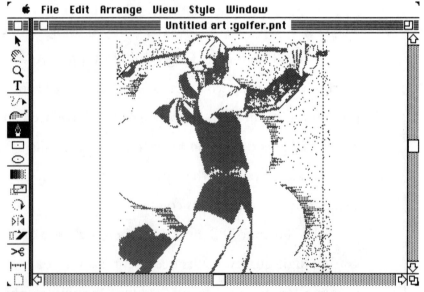

Figure 3-1.
Starting with a low-quality scanned photocopy may be better for tracing than a direct scan of the color image because the contrast is sharper in the photocopy.

ARTWORK CREATED USING ADOBE ILLUSTRATOR. ADOBE ILLUSTRATOR IS A TRADEMARK OF ADOBE SYSTEMS INCORPORATED.

Luanne started the artwork by drawing the background because, she says, "I think of [Illustrator artwork] as layers of paper." She drew the background square first, then the circles for the clouds, then the lines on top of the circles, then the golfer's clothing, and finally the overlays, such as the golfer's bracelet. She worked on the face before the hair because she knew the hair would cover the head and therefore she didn't have to draw a perfect head shape (Figure 3-2).

Luanne explains how she drew the face: "When it was scanned, a lot of detail disappeared. I wanted the golfer to have a modern face, so I sketched my office mate, but changed her hair." Figure 3-3 shows that although the scanned image has very little facial and hairstyle detail, Luanne used the image as a guide to help draw a new face and hairstyle. "There was no eye, or any facial detail in the scanned image, so I drew the eye from a sketch, and moved it around by selecting until I had it where I thought it should be." The selection tool lets you draw a marquee by dragging; you can drag the marquee around the part of the image you want to select, and the program selects any path intersected by the marquee (Figure 3-4).

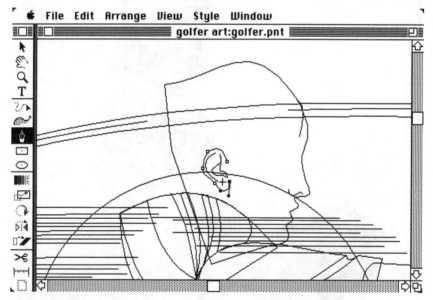

Figure 3-2.
Drawing the front part of the head without regard to the back part since the back part will be covered by an object representing hair. Layers in a drawing are like painted paper or completely transparent.

Transformations

To draw the belt, Luanne drew one square and sheared it into a diamond shape by using the shear tool. To shear, she clicked a point defining the x and y axes for the shear on the lower left corner of the square, and dragged upwards along the y axis (Figure 3-5). The axes point and the vertical drag keeps the left side of the rectangle from moving as the other points of the shape are sheared into a diamond.

Luanne created a copy of the shape by holding down the Option key while dragging, then using the rotation tool to rotate the copy slightly (Figure 3-6). She repeated the copy with several Command-D (Transform Again) commands, and moved them into place using the selection tool and then the rotation tool.

Strokes and Fills

To draw the folds in the tunic, Luanne drew lines and turned their strokes to white (Figure 3-7). She drew them last so that they would be placed on top of the 100% black tunic (she could also

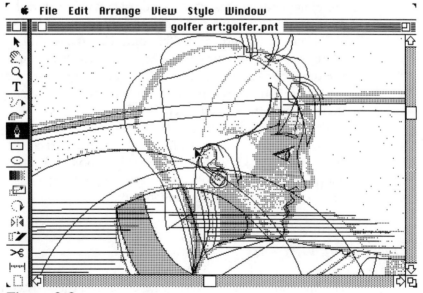

Figure 3-3.
Drawing a new face and hair using the scanned image as a template.

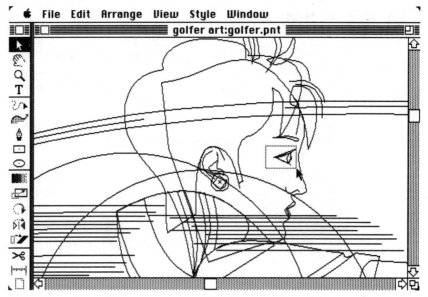

Figure 3-4.
Selecting the eye object by dragging a selection marquee.

have used Copy and then Paste In Front to place the line in front of the selected objects). To get the soft fold in the golfer's skirt, she drew lines with strokes set to a shade of gray. However, the white line on the bracelet is a white-shaded shape, not just a line.

The cloud behind the golfer comprised many circles filled with white that have no stroke, so they blend together without seams. She drew one circle and set the Paint attributes (white, no stroke), then those attributes were used automatically for the shapes drawn afterwards (until she changed the Paint settings).

The white circles are drawn on top of a large rectangle for the entire page, which is set to have a 10% black screen (gray), and a 100% black stroke whose weight is one point. Another box was drawn on top of the gray box with the same dimensions, but with a heavier line (three points) and no fill.

Overlaying Graphics

The lines on the clouds were drawn first, and then pasted in back of the clouds (first she copied the lines to the Clipboard, then she selected the clouds, then used the Paste In Back command). Luanne

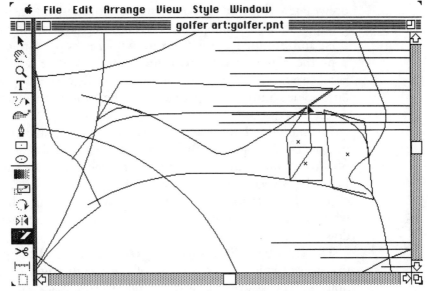

Figure 3-5.
Shearing a square into a diamond shape by selecting the shear tool,
clicking a point to define the x and y axes for shearing, and dragging
upward along the y axis.

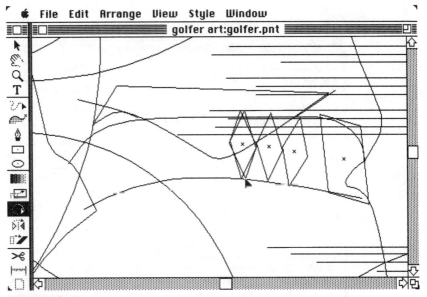

Figure 3-6.
Drawing the belt by cloning the diamond shape and rotating each clone
to fit the belt outline.

drew a few lines of random length, moved them into position, grouped them, then copied the group, moved the copy into position, and grouped the first group with the copy. She could then copy the bigger group, move this copy into place, and form one large group. When she was finished, she had seemingly random lines joined into a group that could be moved anywhere on the page.

Luanne added the sailboats on top of the sea pattern at the bottom of the page by drawing one sailboat, painting it white with no stroke, and copying it while scaling the copy to a smaller size. First she selected the sailboat and the scaling tool, then she clicked the scale focal point (Figure 3-8), and finally she dragged while holding down the Option key to make a clone that is scaled down (Figure 3-9).

The last object drawn to complete the figure of the golfer was the sleeve, which covered some of the rough edges of the other objects. The sleeve was given a fill of 20% black (gray) with a 100% black stroke with a weight of 0.2 points. The fill makes it a solid shape; no fill would have made it transparent. "I really think of drawing with Illustrator as layers of paper," says Luanne, "perhaps a collage of objects. I think about things as being in front,

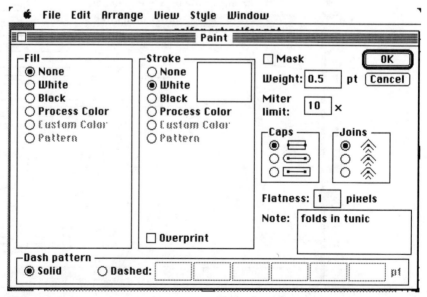

Figure 3-7.
Painting strokes white to represent folds in the golfer's tunic.

or behind... When you are working with a complex drawing with a lot of lines and pieces, you might not be able to keep track of what's in front and what's behind. You can use Cut and Paste In Front or Paste In Back to move things behind or in front of other selected objects. There are times when even if you know the order to draw things, circumstances dictate that you can't follow that order. I have to draw the golf club in front of her head, but I can cut and paste to layer it in the correct order."

Techniques For Calligraphy

Adobe Illustrator 88 can turn the skill of calligraphy into a piece of cake. The original calligraphy for the Artifactory logo was drawn by hand using calligraphy techniques by Sumner Stone. Pat Coleman scanned the hand-drawn image to use as a template for drawing (Figure 3-10). Although she could have used the automatic tracing tool, she wanted to draw them so that she would have more control over the creation of line and curve segments.

To get the thick and thin lines of calligraphy, Pat treated each pen stroke as an enclosed polygon, not as a single pen stroke, and

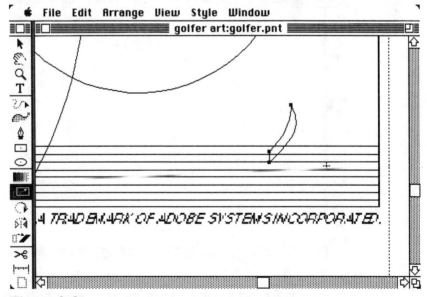

Figure 3-8.
Clicking a focal point for the scale tool to reduce the sailboat shape.

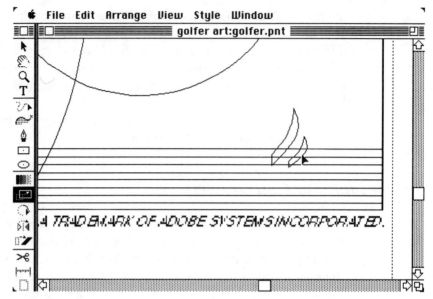

Figure 3-9.

Cloning the sailboat while reducing it by holding down the Option key while dragging with the rotate tool.

Figure 3-10.

Starting with a scanned sketch of the logo as a template, the artist drew outlines of the characters to represent calligraphy strokes.

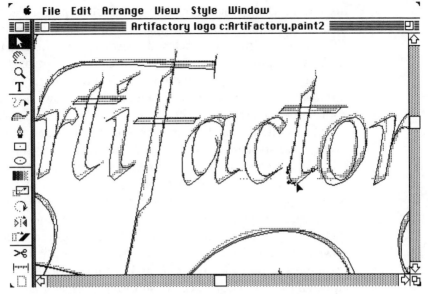

Figure 3-11.
After using the zoom tool to increase magnification, you can adjust the strokes and points to make smoother or sharper characters.

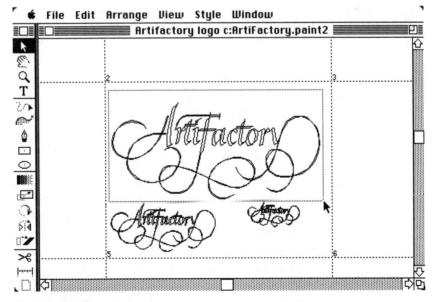

Figure 3-12.
Selecting the entire logo (comprised of many individual paths) by dragging the selection marquee.

drew around the characters to get the filled paths. Pat described how Adobe Illustrator 88 compares to a calligraphy pen or brush: "The program fills any enclosed space. It's a different technique than calligraphy, but you actually have more control than with a calligraphy brush or pen, and you can zoom in to get the thick and thinness of each stroke exact." (Figure 3-11 shows how she could zoom into the artwork and work on the serifs and strokes.)

Pat cloned an already-drawn pen stroke and used the copies to make other strokes, making the strokes consistent. She could also point to a stroke and adjust its direction points to change the curve.

To create the reduced versions, Pat selected all of the paths in the logo by using the selection tool and drawing a marquee around the image (Figure 3-12). She then selected the scaling tool, clicked a focal point for the scale (upper right corner to scale downwards), and dragged down and to the right in a diagonal. "Scaling is another feature that makes Illustrator useful for calligraphy and logos. The image doesn't lose quality when it's reduced, and it doesn't fill in and get muddy, like bit-mapped graphics do when they are reduced."

Gradation, Shadow, and Airbrush Effects

Keith Ohlfs' "Grapes" shows how you can create a gray or color gradation and airbrush effect. Keith created one grape using concentric circles on the grape to simulate gradations in shading. Although he could have used the blend tool to create the steps for the gradations, Keith drew the concentric circles by drawing one circle, selecting the scaling tool, clicking the edge of the circle as the focal point for scaling, and holding down the Option key while dragging the circle. This transformation created a second circle that still touched the first circle at the focal point. He repeated this transformation (cloning and scaling) by typing Command-D (or selecting Transform Again). He then went back to adjust each circle for positioning.

Each circle has no stroke and a fill of a percentage of black (or of a color) relative to its position on the grape; for example, the middle circle (Figure 3-13) has a fill of 50% black and no stroke (Figure 3-14), which makes it easier to blend the circles into a pattern. The innermost circle is white.

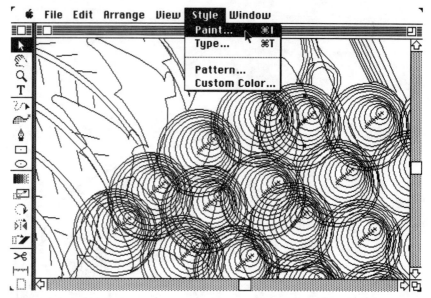

Figure 3-13.

Selecting the middle oval in the grape to display or change its paint attributes.

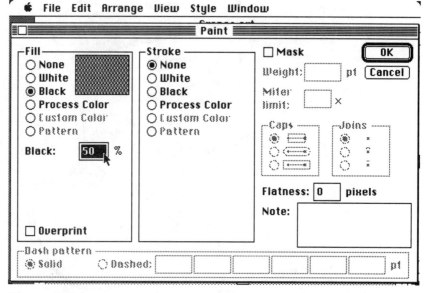

Figure 3-14.

The paint attributes of the oval selected in the previous figure: 50 percent black fill (gray), and no stroke (so that each oval blends into the adjoining oval without a visible line).

After creating one grape, Keith cloned it by using Copy and Paste In Front or Paste In Back, so that some grapes were overlapping others.

To create the more pronounced gradations of gray in the branch (Figure 3-15), Keith painted the branch path with a 10% gray fill, then drew white-stroked and black-stroked lines and white shapes on top to intersperse white and black in the gray pattern.

Keith saved a grape in a separate file by using Copy, then selecting a New file, then using Paste. The new file could then be opened whenever he needed a group of concentric circles with a gradation of shades. Eventually Keith had made several of these files containing pieces of graphics with well-defined gray scales. He could then use these pieces to make new illustrations simply by transforming them into new shapes.

To see how the artwork will look when printed, at the same time that you are editing the overlaid graphics, create another window display of the same artwork with the New Window command in the Window menu, then select the Preview Illustration command to

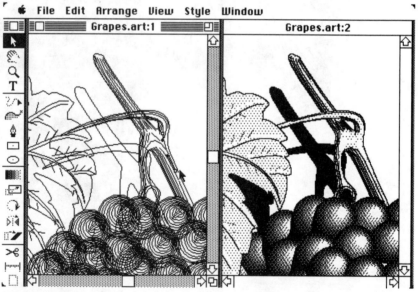

Figure 3-15.
The branch was painted with a 10 percent black (gray) fill, then white-stroked and black-stroked lines and white shapes were drawn on top to make shadows and highlights (the second Preview window was created by using the New Window and Preview Illustration commands, then resizing both the preview and artwork windows to fit the screen).

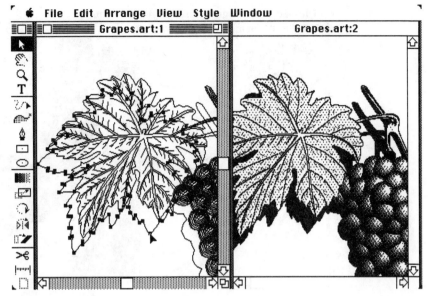

Figure 3-16.
Adjusting the leaf shadow using two views: an artwork-only window and a preview window.

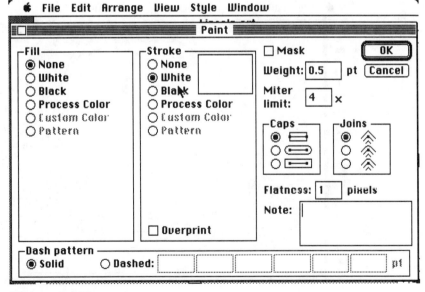

Figure 3-17.
Changing the default paint attributes in the Paint dialog box to make paths with no fill and with very thin white strokes (line weight at 0.5 points).

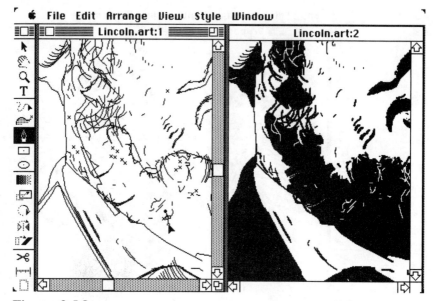

Figure 3-18.
Drawing white-stroked curve segments in the black silhouette of Lincoln's beard.

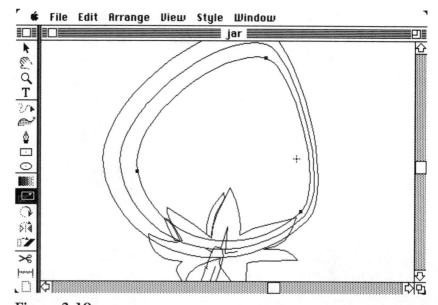

Figure 3-19.
Each strawberry in "Jar of Preserves" is a series of scaled clones of a basic shape, with the scale focal point set to make the cloned shapes closer to the basic shape on one edge.

make the new (active) window the preview. You can resize both windows to fit side by side on the screen (see Figures 3-15 and 3-16), and either window can be the preview window.

Using the New Window and Preview Illustration commands, Keith set up two windows in order to adjust the background shadow (Figure 3-16). To create the leaf shadow, Keith selected the path of the outline of the leaf, and held down the Option key while dragging it, to create a duplicate outline. Keith then painted the duplicate 100% black, cut it from the artwork, selected the path of the outline of the leaf again, and used the Paste In Back command to place the 100% black outline behind the leaf. The branches and the grapes were just as easy to create.

Dean Dapkus' "Abe Lincoln" is an example of an image that would ordinarily be drawn with a paint-type graphics program because it has so much irregular detail that could only be drawn with dots. (Paint-type graphics are called "bit-mapped graphics" because they comprise many single pixels of the display, which correspond to specific dots on paper when printed.) However, since paint-type graphics cannot change in resolution (the number of pixels and the number of dots per inch can't be reduced to achieve higher resolution), artists have always wanted a program that could be as precise and flexible as Adobe Illustrator 88 for defining very tiny line and curve segments that are independent of the screen's resolution.

Dean drew "Abe Lincoln" using large black silhouette shapes. He then magnified areas and drew segments with very thin line weights and white strokes. First he drew one segment and changed the default paint specifications (with the Paint command in the Style menu, or Command-I) to have no fill, a white stroke, and a thin line weight (Figure 3-17). After clicking OK, those specifications were used for drawing subsequent segments until he changed them again with the Paint command.

Figure 3-18 shows a magnified view of segments Dean drew in Lincoln's beard. Dean explains: "This technique is similar to one that a lot of artists are familiar with, called scratchboard. You start with a black artboard, and you scratch or etch in white shapes."

The effect of a simulated halftone with gray shades can be done by drawing paths close together and using increments of gray shading for fills (for example, 5%), and no strokes.

The strawberries in the label of "Jar of Preserves" (by Gail Blumberg, a graphic designer for Adobe, and Keith Ohlfs) were

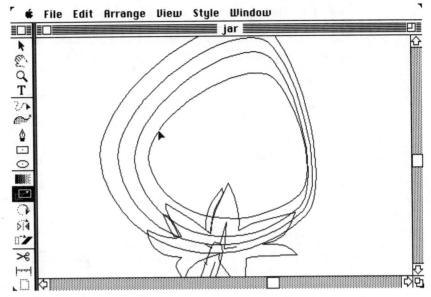

Figure 3-20.
Cloning and scaling the shape by holding down the Option key while dragging with the scale tool. Repeat this transformation with the Transform Again option or Command-D.

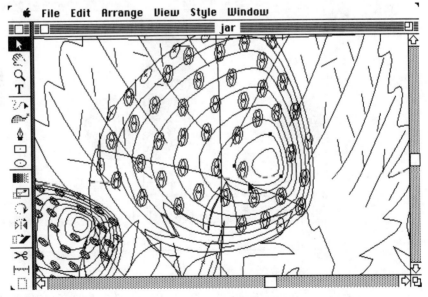

Figure 3-21.
Selecting one of the shapes to paint it with a shade of gray.

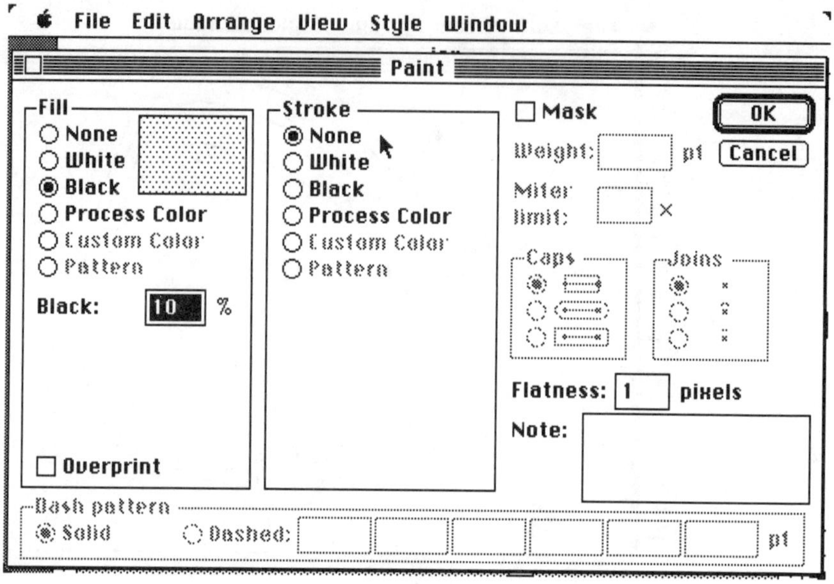

Figure 3-22.
Each scaled shape is filled with a different percentage of black (gray) and has no stroke so that the gray shades blend together.

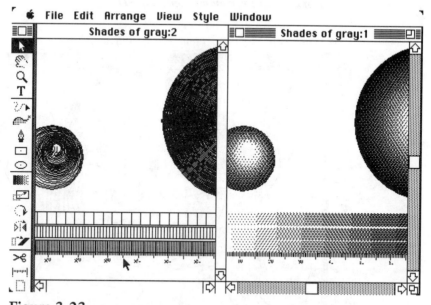

Figure 3-23.
A file of standard shapes that can be copied and pasted into other documents and adjusted to fill different shapes.

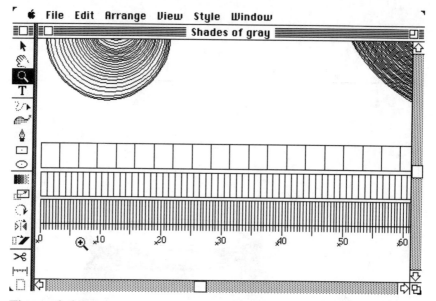

Figure 3-24.

The gray shade bands are designed for use with the 300-dpi LaserWriter (top), the Linotronic 100 at 1270 dpi (middle), and the Linotronic 300 at 2540 dpi (bottom).

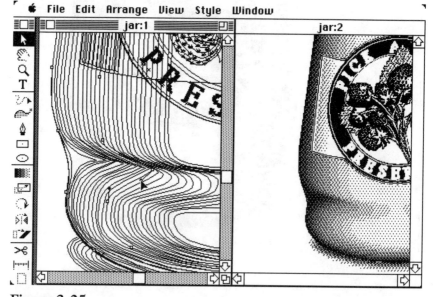

Figure 3-25.

Adjusting direction and anchor points to fit gray shaded paths in the shape of the artwork.

drawn with one basic shape (Figure 3-19) that was cloned and scaled (Figure 3-20). You can quickly clone and scale an object by repeating the first clone-and-scale transformation with Command-D or Transform Again.

The artists assigned a different percentage of black (gray) to fill each shape, and set no stroke (Figures 3-21 and 3-22). Small ovals were drawn to look like seeds on top of the layers of gray.

Keith created a file of standard gray shaded objects that can be scaled in any direction and used for filling areas of other illustrations (Figure 3-23). The shaded circle and the top gray-scale band are designed for 300 dpi laser printers (such as the LaserWriter) and have 33 steps, each with a different percentage of black to simulate a gray shade (Figure 3-24). The middle band is designed for 1270 dpi imagesetters (such as the Linotype Linotronic 100), and has 100 steps. The bottom one is designed for 2540 dpi imagesetters (such as the Linotype Linotronic 300) and has 200 steps. "Although each one takes up a lot of disk space," says Keith, "when I want to have an airbrush effect, I can copy and paste the appropriate shape and then stretch it to whatever size I need."

The shaded objects can be adjusted properly because they consist of grouped paths — Keith could select anywhere on the object and get the entire object. He used Copy and Paste to copy the shade to another document, where he could drag direction and anchor points until the shades (Figure 3-25) lined up with the shape, then use the reflection tool to mirror it to the other side of the jar. He added points to segments with the scissors tool in order to bend them. "Using the shades reference saves a lot of time," he says, because he can use them over and over in many different illustrations, no matter what the final shape is.

Rotating Text

To add the text to the label of the jar of strawberry preserves, Gail used the text tool and clicked a starting point for the first letter, typed the letter, and set its type characteristics (Figure 3-26). Then she selected the rotation tool, clicked the point of rotation at the center of the label (Figure 3-27), and dragged with the Option key to create a rotated copy of the first letter (Figure 3-28). To rotate more letters to form a word, she repeated the transformation by pressing Command-D (Transform Again).

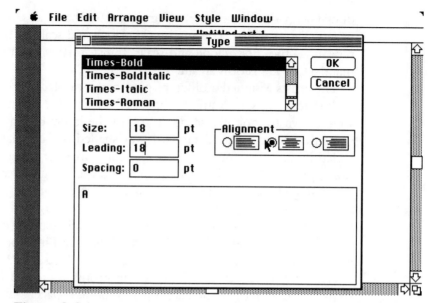

Figure 3-26.
After clicking a starting point with the text tool, you can set the text's typesetting attributes in the Type dialog box (in the Style menu).

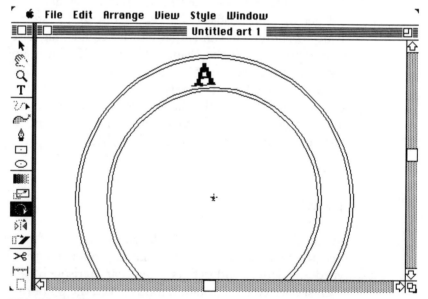

Figure 3-27.
Clicking a focal point for rotating characters in the "Jar of Preserves" illustration.

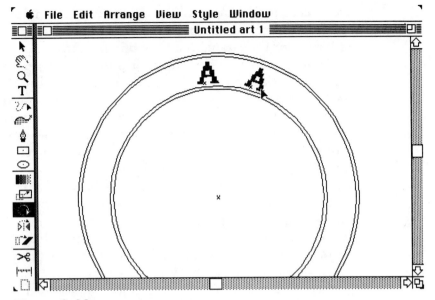

Figure 3-28.
Dragging with the scale tool (and the Option key) to clone the characters and rotate at the same time. Command-D or Transform Again can repeat the transformation to form more characters (you can type the correct letter afterwards in the Type dialog box).

After rotating the same letter around the label into the positions she wanted, she went back and selected each letter with the pointer tool and used the Type command in the Style menu (Command-T) to change the letter to the appropriate letter for that word.

Through careful use of the Paste In Back and Paste In Front commands, Gail was able to place the strawberries in front of the text on the label, while the stems of the berries are behind the label, providing the illusion of three dimensions. It is helpful to work with two views (Figure 3-29) when overlaying complex images.

Painting With Color

Adobe Illustrator 88 lets you assign custom colors to paths in an image whether or not you are using a color display. You need a color display to see the color assignments, but you don't need a color display to print the image, nor do you need it to produce color separations for publishing. However, to be able to predict the results better, a color display is most helpful, as is a knowledge of how color is reproduced on the printing press.

If you are not familiar with color printing and separations, we recommend that you consult with the print shop or printer whose press will be used for your publication. This is because there may be major differences in appearance between the colors you assigned and the color inks that are printed, and you may want to take certain factors into consideration and adjust your color assignments before producing a color separation.

A color rarely appears in print in exactly the same way as it appears on film or on the video display. In addition, no two displays are exactly alike, and the appearance of the same color on the same screen can be different depending on factors such as the ambient lighting of the room and the presence of other objects that are within your vision while you are looking at the display.

There is also a disparity in the color models used in printing presses and displaying devices. For displays, video monitors use the red, green, and blue (RGB) primary additive colors that are combined with direct light to form any color on the screen. Print-

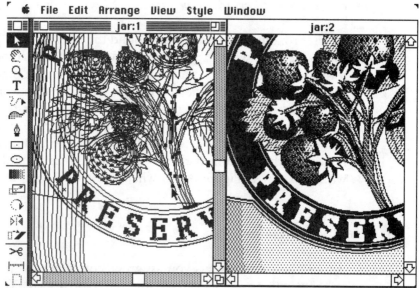

Figure 3-29.
Using the Paste In Front and Paste In Back options (with the help of a preview window) to paste strawberries in front of the label and paste stems behind for a three-dimensional effect.

ing presses use cyan, yellow, and magenta (CYM) primary subtractive colors in inks that can be applied to a white surface and combined with black ink. This color model, referred to as CYMK (for cyan, yellow, magenta, and black), corresponds to the process color inks available with all printing presses.

Although some Macintosh programs let you specify colors using the RGB model, publishing on paper requires that you convert these specifications to the CYMK model so that you can choose proper ink mixes. Adobe Illustrator 88 lets you directly assign percentages of CYMK to the image so that color assignments closely reflect process color inks. The program automatically displays your CYMK assignments using the proper RGB values so that you don't have to make wild guesses about how the colors will appear. Illustrator 88 also lets you adjust this conversion from time to time for your particular display, so that colors will appear the same under different lighting conditions.

Adobe Illustrator 88 also offers the ability to assign more than 700 PANTONE printing inks which are also available with all printing presses. The premixed PANTONE colors are chosen by consulting the PANTONE MATCHING SYSTEM, developed by

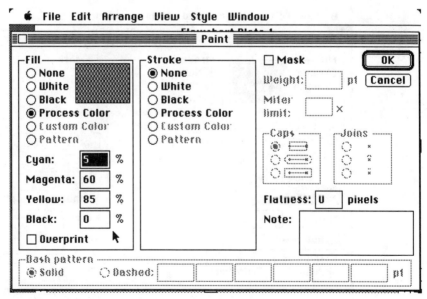

Figure 3-30.
Assigning 5 percent cyan, 60 percent magenta, and 85 percent yellow to make a bright orange shadow for the flowchart (Plate 1). Colors appear as patterns on black and white monitors.

Pantone, Inc. You specify a specific PANTONE color and the printing press uses an ink formula provided by Pantone, Inc. Unlike process colors, which can be mixed by yourself to make different shades of color, PANTONE colors can't be mixed — you simply select one that looks right.

There are two kinds of color you can assign to artwork: a mix of the process colors (cyan, yellow, and magenta), or premixed PANTONE colors. Process colors are specified by percentages in the Paint dialog box (Figure 3-30), and PANTONE colors are specified by clicking the Custom Color button to display a scrolling list of color names (Figure 3-31). As you select a color, it appears in the rectangle next to the None, White, and Black buttons. You can select a different color for an object's stroke.

To see the list of PANTONE colors, you must also have open a document with PANTONE colors already specified; Adobe Systems provides two documents containing all of the PANTONE colors for both coated and uncoated paper stock. You can open one of these documents and leave it open while coloring objects in other documents.

As you assign a PANTONE color to an object in a document,

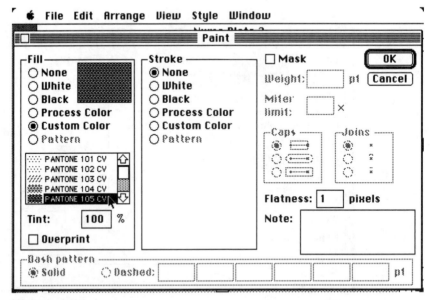

Figure 3-31.
Assigning a PANTONE color (a document containing PANTONE color assignments, such as the supplied documents for coated and uncoated paper, must already be open).

that particular color name is saved with the document, appearing whenever you open that document. You can also create custom mixes of process colors that can also be listed by name along with the PANTONE colors in this scroll box. First create the custom color with the Custom Color option in the Style menu. You can simply create a custom name for a PANTONE color (Figure 3-32), or mix process colors into custom color that you can use by name (Figure 3-33).

As you begin to use colors regularly, you will want to create custom color mixes using familiar names, and perhaps have specific PANTONE colors ready for use in any new document. To make it easy to call up these colors, create a document that contains all of these colors. As long as this document is open, you can assign those colors to objects in any other documents.

PANTONE colors are often used for spot color that highlights a graphic image, and the use of PANTONE ink is usually in addition to process color inks in order to achieve a color effect not possible with the current mix of process colors. It is helpful to consult with your printer before choosing PANTONE colors, since they can add to the cost of your press run. You may want to

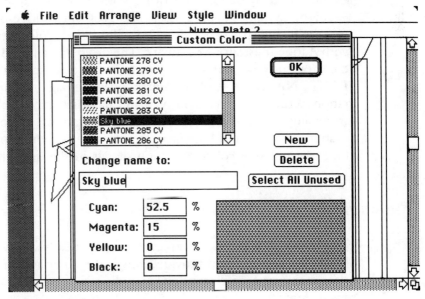

Figure 3-32.
Using the Custom Color option (in the Style menu) to change the name of a PANTONE color as it will appear in the Custom Color list in the Paint dialog box.

simulate a PANTONE color by mixing process colors precisely, following a guideline such as the PANTONE *Process Color Simulator* available from Pantone, Inc. Color charts are also provided in the back of the *Adobe Illustrator 88 Color Guide.*

The color plates included in this book were produced entirely with process colors. "The Nurse" (Plate 2) began as a black and white sketch and then was colorized in the Roy Lichtenstein comic book style, with strong primary colors — red lips of 100% magenta, with 80% yellow added to produce the warm ruby red, and hot spots of white light to make them look wet (Figure 3-34). The fingernails are 30% magenta with 25% yellow, producing the effect of a comic book pink color, with warm red dots. The skin of the hands and face colored 10% red to achieve the palest pink, which enhances the white tear in the eye. Also, to enhance the white tear, the background is painted darkly in 100% cyan, giving the effect of nighttime. Her blouse and hat stripe are 80% cyan to distinguish them from the background.

You can print color images in color on the QMS ColorScript color printer or similar PostScript color printing or recording device. You can also make films for color separations using black-printing Linotronic imagesetters and other high-resolution devices.

Adobe Systems supplies a separate program, Adobe Separator, for producing professional-quality film-based color separations with Adobe Illustrator 88 artwork. The program can produce four-color or custom-color separations (such as a separation for each PANTONE color). It offers control over the page size and orientation, settings for emulsion type and halftone screen ruling, and the ability to produce custom color separations or to convert custom colors to the four process colors for a four-color separation. We describe color separation details in the next chapter.

Summary

This chapter showed examples of using nearly every tool in Illustrator's arsenal and provided tips and techniques for drawing almost any type of illustration, including the use of gray shades and color.

"The Golfer" started with a photocopy scan as a template and Luanne Seymour Cohen, the artist, used numerous overlaying

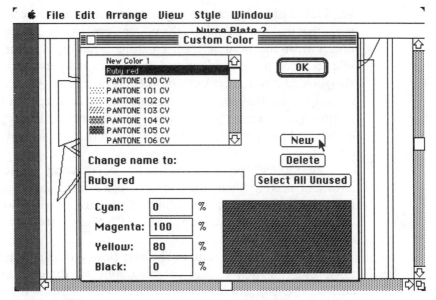

Figure 3-33.
Using Custom Color to premix process colors under a name that will appear in the Custom Color list in the Paint dialog box.

Figure 3-34.
White hot spots are added to ruby red lips to make them appear wet (see Plate 2).

graphics to hide all the rough spots. She was able to select all of the paths that make up an object (the golfer's eye) by dragging across the object with the pointer tool, creating a marquee rectangle that selected everything inside it and every path it intersected. Luanne also showed how to perform simple transformations — shearing and rotating — to draw the diamond-shaped belt. To repeat a transformation, you can use the Transform Again command or type Command-D. She used the scale tool to transform several sailboat images.

"The Golfer" provided examples of drawing white-stroked lines and pasting them on top of a black-filled shape using the Paste In Front command. White-filled circles (with no stroke) were used to simulate clouds, and a 10% black screen was applied to the background.

The "Artifactory" example showed how you can simulate the thick and thin pen strokes of calligraphy by drawing lines that enclose the pen strokes to form individual shapes that can be manipulated to simulate the thick and thin of the calligraphy stroke. The zoom tool comes in handy for working on details. The example also demonstrated how an image that has been worked into perfection can be copied and used for other areas in the artwork. Illustrator calligraphy can be reduced or enlarged without any loss in quality.

The "Grapes" artwork demonstrates an airbrush effect you can achieve by drawing one shape, scaling it slightly, and using Transform Again (Command-D) to repeat the transformation many times, then assigning to the shapes a gradual range of percentages of black or color (and no stroke, for smoothness). By drawing paths closer together and using a more gradual range of percentages of black or color for fills, you can make the airbrush effect smoother.

You can also draw white-stroked lines to place on top of black areas, or black-stroked lines and white shapes on top to intersperse white and black in the gray pattern. To see two views of the artwork while working — a preview and a view of the artwork only — you can use the New Window command.

The "Abe Lincoln" portrait was drawn by mimicking a conventional process called scratchboard, where an artist scratches or etches white shapes on a black artboard. After setting up white strokes for lines with a certain line weight, those specifications are used for drawing subsequent segments until changed again with the Paint command.

"Jar of Preserves" demonstrates many features, from quickly performed successive transformations to the use of Paste In Front and Paste In Back to simulate three-dimensional graphics. The artist (Gail Blumberg) also used the rotation tool with individual letters to rotate them around the jar's label.

The example also includes the use of a file of standard gray shaded images that can be scaled in any direction and used for filling areas of other illustrations. Gray shading was accomplished with a one-time use of the airbrush technique with finer gradations used in gray-shade templates designed for the Laser-Writer printer and the Linotronic 100 and 300 typesetters.

Painting with color is introduced at the end of this chapter, with descriptions of "Flowchart" (Plate 1) and "The Nurse" (Plate 2) by artists at Adobe Systems. Adobe Illustrator 88 can show colors on a color monitor, which can be adjusted for room lighting and individual characteristics to match printed colors (see Preferences, Edit menu, in Chapter 5). On black and white monitors, the program displays different colors as patterns. You can use either type of monitor to assign colors to paths. Process colors can be freely mixed, or you can select a PANTONE color if you open a document that has PANTONE color assignments (such as the supplied documents for coated and uncoated paper). You can also premix process colors under a new name to be listed in the Custom Color list, and rename PANTONE colors for this list.

For more on color separations, trapping, and printer preparations, read on through Chapter 4.

4

Advanced Techniques

Adobe Illustrator 88 can make art departments and publishing efforts far more productive than they have ever been. In addition to the power to trace scanned images, the program also provides the flexibility to incorporate pieces or entire drawings in other drawings, to produce color separations, and to make the archival recording of drawings routine and therefore less prone to casualties.

Artists can start with an automatic trace or use the freehand tool, then transform shapes with the mouse or with the precision of the dialog boxes. When specifying a uniform scale for the artwork, you have the option of scaling or preserving the line weights of strokes.

Combine these capabilities with the ability to trace templates that can be scanned images or sketches, and the ability to add formatted text in fonts and perform PostScript effects, and you have a fantastic tool for artists, designers, and illustrators.

Technical publications departments will especially like the feature of automatically tracing scanned images, because this method may be the best way to convert old images into Illustrator graphics. All of the previous examples were based on scanned templates. However, you can also draw without using a template simply by measuring points in your sketch or original image and using the ruler to precisely place those points.

Dean Dapkus drew "Eyeball" from thumbnail sketches derived from biology texts. "Once you know how to use the zoom tool to analyze and edit details, and the shortcuts for drawing [the reflection, rotation, shearing, and scaling tools], there isn't anything difficult about working without a template."

Scaling or Preserving Line Weights

In traditional technical art drawing, artists have to draw diagrams and illustrations at a large scale and then reduce the art photographically. Line weights are automatically scaled with the rest of the art. This means that you have to take the final reduction percentage into consideration before drawing a single line.

With Adobe Illustrator 88, you can scale either one path, a group of paths forming an object (or part of an object), or an entire illustration, and have the choice of scaling or preserving the line weights. Artists especially appreciate the choice of preserving line weights on drawings with hairlines so that when the art is reduced, the lines don't disappear. On the other hand, with a finished drawing that looks good the way it is, scaling the line weight with the art will preserve the look of the drawing.

When you drag to scale, the line weights are preserved (not scaled). To get the option of scaling or preserving line weights, you must use the Scaling dialog box rather than the drag method of scaling. After selecting the scaling tool, hold down the Option key while clicking a scale origin point. The dialog box for scaling requires a scale factor as a percentage for uniform scaling (scaling in proportion), and the choice of preserving or scaling line weights by the same percentage. You can't scale line weights with non-uniform scaling, in

The Eye

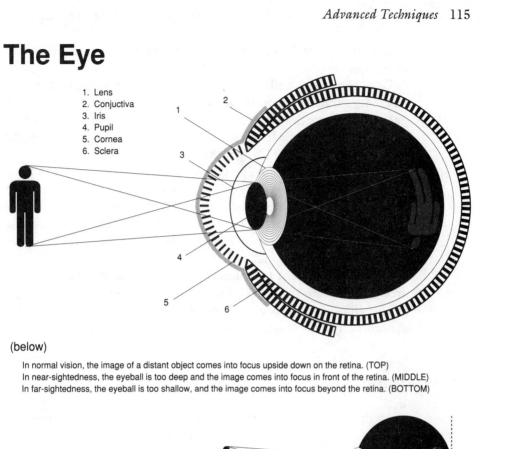

1. Lens
2. Conjuctiva
3. Iris
4. Pupil
5. Cornea
6. Sclera

(below)

In normal vision, the image of a distant object comes into focus upside down on the retina. (TOP)
In near-sightedness, the eyeball is too deep and the image comes into focus in front of the retina. (MIDDLE)
In far-sightedness, the eyeball is too shallow, and the image comes into focus beyond the retina. (BOTTOM)

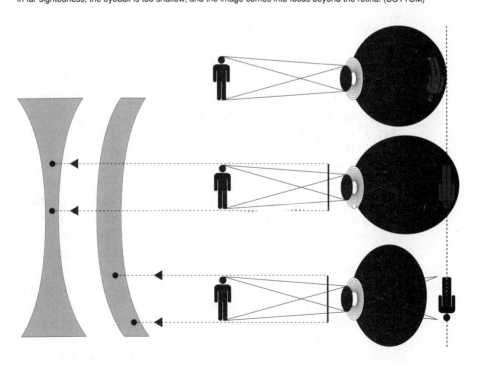

which the image is scaled in uneven proportion for deliberate distortion.

Dean Dapkus started "Eyeball" by drawing concentric circles, and repeating a transformation that used a precise scale percentage. First he used the circle drawing tool to draw a circle, then he selected that circle, clicked the scale tool, and held down Option while clicking the focal point (Figure 4-1) to get the Scale dialog box.

In the Scale dialog box, he typed a percentage under 100% for a uniform reduction (Figure 4-2), and clicked the option to preserve the line weights. He then clicked Copy to produce a reduced copy and preserve the first circle. The reduction percentage was consistent for the remaining circles, so Dean could use Command-D to repeat the transformation to make each subsequent circle.

Dean used the same technique to draw the lens of the eye: first he drew an ellipse for the outer edge of the lens, then he reduced a copy of the ellipse and repeatedly pressed Command-D to draw the concentric ellipses (Figure 4-3).

Line Caps and Joins

Dean drew the human symbol based on the American Institute of Graphic Arts (AIGA) symbol used by the Department of Transportation for men's bathrooms and other signs. (The Man symbol is included in T/Maker's ClickArt EPS Series.) He used round line caps and joins which can be set in the Paint dialog box (Figure 4-4).

The line cap choices affect the endpoints of open paths and dashed lines. The line join choices affect the corners of paths that are stroked (it has no effect on nonstroked paths or points where paths intersect). Figures 4-5 and 4-6 show examples.

The default setting for line cap is the butt cap (at the top). If you don't change it, the butt line cap uses squared-off ends perpendicular to the path. The middle choice, round cap, creates a half-moon cap in which the diameter equals the line width. The projecting cap (bottom) offers square ends that extend half of the line width beyond the end of the line.

The default line join is a miter join (at top), in which the edges of the intersecting strokes are extended until they meet in a point. The middle choice is the round join, which connects corners in a circular arc with a diameter equal to the line width. You would use both round caps and round joins because round joins do not fit well with

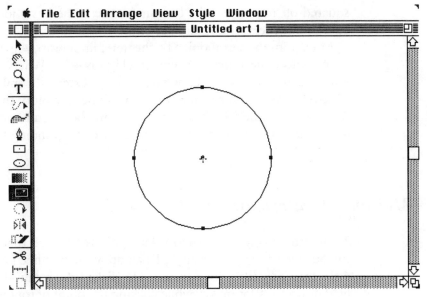

Figure 4-1.
Clicking the focal point for the scale operation, while simultaneously holding down Option to get the Scale dialog box (next figure).

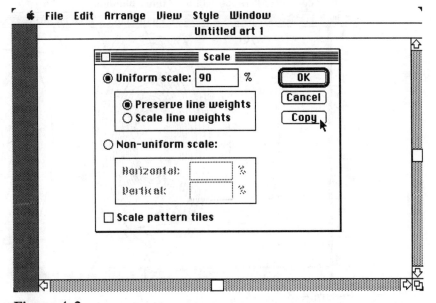

Figure 4-2.
Scaling precisely with the Scale dialog box, which provides the option to scale or preserve line weights (default settings are shown, with a change in the scale percentage).

squared-off butt caps. The bottom choice is the bevel join, which connects corners with triangular ends.

Miter joins can be modified by the miter limit ratio, which is active if you select the miter join choice (Figure 4-7). When two lines intersect at a sharp angle, a miter corner extends a spike that is controlled by the miter limit ratio. The higher the ratio, the sharper the corner (Figure 4-8). You can select a ratio between 1 and 10, with 4 corresponding to a square corner and 1 corresponding to a bevel corner.

Multiple Transformations

To draw the many lines that look like spokes of a wheel that make up the outside edge of the eyeball, Dean drew the first line (see Figure 4-9), then selected it for rotation. He clicked the rotation tool and held down the Option key while clicking the point of rotation at the center of the concentric circles.

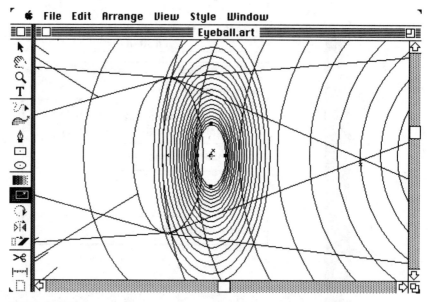

Figure 4-3.
The lens of the eye is made up of many concentric ellipses drawn using Transform Again to repeat a scaling and cloning operation.

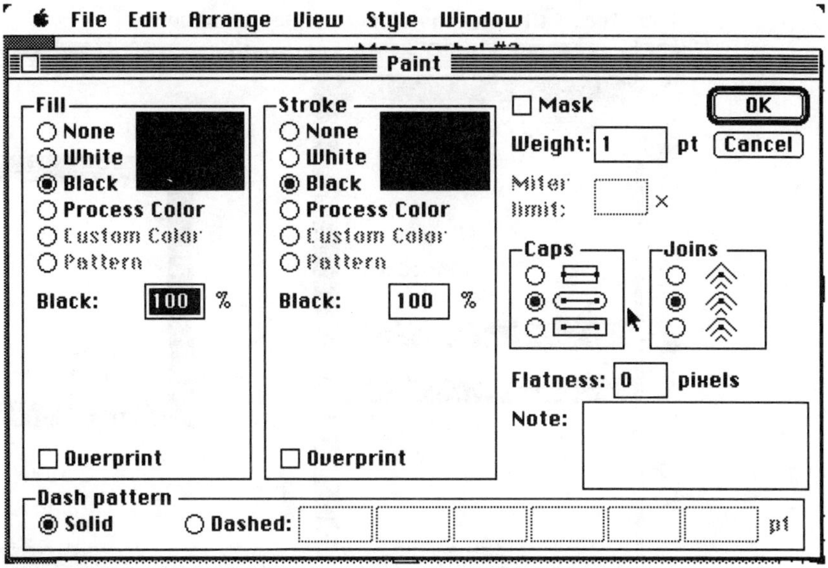

⌘ File Edit Arrange View Style Window

Paint

Fill
- ○ None
- ○ White
- ● Black
- ○ Process Color
- ○ Custom Color
- ○ Pattern

Black: [100] %

Stroke
- ○ None
- ○ White
- ● Black
- ○ Process Color
- ○ Custom Color
- ○ Pattern

Black: [100] %

☐ Mask

Weight: [1] pt   [Cancel]

[OK]

Miter limit: [   ] ×

Caps   **Joins**

Flatness: [0] pixels

Note: [   ]

☐ Overprint   ☐ Overprint

Dash pattern
- ● Solid   ○ Dashed: [   ][   ][   ][   ][   ] pt

Figure 4-4.
The line cap and join styles are set to round for the human icon.

⌘ File Edit Arrange View Style Window

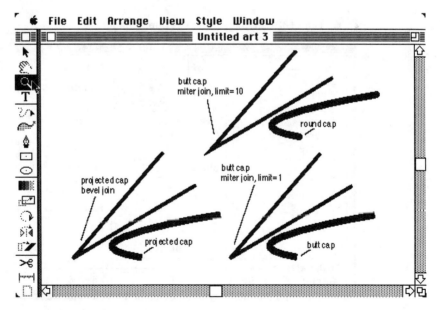

Figure 4-5.
Examples of line cap and join styles.

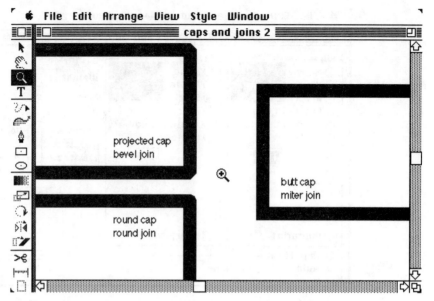

Figure 4-6.
Bevel joins with projected caps work best with rectangular corners.

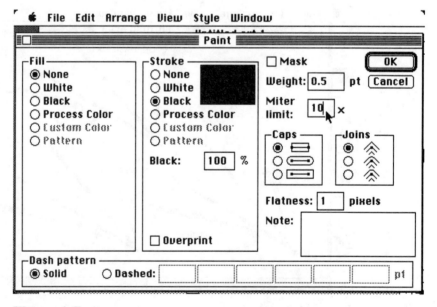

Figure 4-7.
After selecting a miter join, you can set the miter limit to 10, which is the sharpest miter limit ratio.

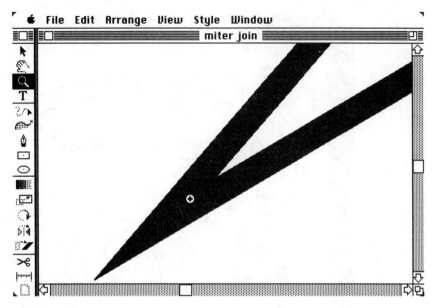

Figure 4-8.
A preview of a miter corner with two four-point lines and a miter limit ratio of ten.

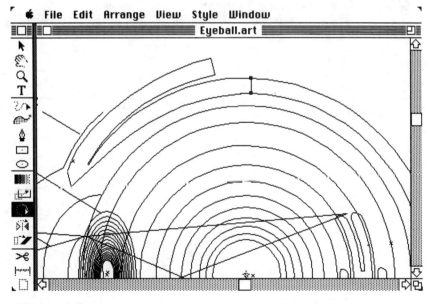

Figure 4-9.
The first line to clone and rotate to make the outer edge of the eyeball.

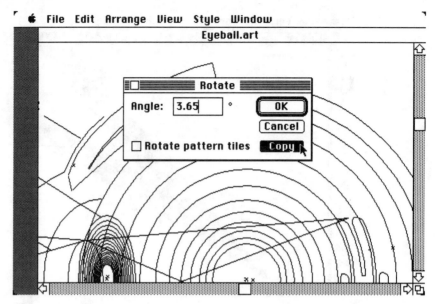

Figure 4-10.
The Rotate dialog box lets you specify a precise angle, and the Copy button creates a clone as part of the transformation.

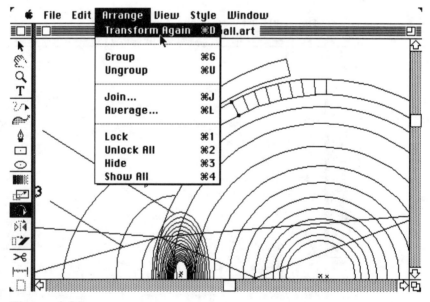

Figure 4-11.
Repeating the transformation with Transform Again (Command-D) to create the outer layer.

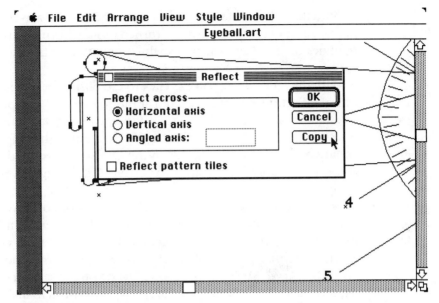

Figure 4-12.
The Reflect dialog box appears if you hold down Option while clicking the focal point with the reflect tool, and lets you specify a horizontal, vertical, or angled axis of reflection as well as the option to reflect pattern tiles.

In the Rotation dialog box (Figure 4-10), he specified a fractional percentage based on the number of lines divided into the 360 degrees total. He left the "Rotate pattern tiles" option alone since he was not using a pattern. This option lets you specify whether or not the pattern tiles (if any) used in a shape should also be rotated. We describe pattern tiles later in this chapter.

Dean clicked the Copy button to produce a duplicate while rotating and preserve the first line. The result was a duplicate line rotated slightly to the left (counterclockwise) of the first line. Positive-degree rotations are counterclockwise; to specify a clockwise rotation, subtract the degree of rotation from 360 degrees and use this figure as the degree of rotation.

After clicking the Copy button, the program remembered the transformation so that Dean could repeat it quickly by pressing Command-D (Figure 4-11). After pressing Command-D about one hundred times, Dean had completed the ring of lines.

To bend the human icon to fit the curves of the concentric circles,

Dean reflected the shape directly across a horizontal axis to create a mirror clone of the shape that was turned upside down, then changed the lines of the shape to curves while moving points to adjust the curves.

With the reflect tool, you can click to establish a focal point on the axis of reflection, or drag in a circular motion around the focal point to establish an area in which the program can calculate the axes by bisecting the angle between the starting position of the drag and the ending position. By holding down the Option key while dragging, you create a clone that is a mirror image of the original, reflected along the axis.

You can also reflect an image quickly over a horizontal or vertical axis, or an axis defined as a degree relative to the current x and y axes. After selecting the image to reflect, click the reflect tool, and hold down the Option key while clicking the focal point. The Reflect dialog box then appears (Figure 4-12), and you can select a horizontal, vertical, or angled axis, and click the Copy button to make a copy of the reflected image. You can also specify whether or not the pattern tiles (if any) used in the shape should also be reflected. We describe pattern tiles later in this chapter.

The reflection does not change the shape. To bend the human icon shape to the curves of the concentric circles, Dean had to replace line segments with curved segments. Fortunately his method of drawing the human icon made this editing change very easy. "I tried to use as few points as possible to draw the human icon. With the exception of the head, hands and balls of his feet, and his shoulders, he was made of straight lines, and each of these lines had two definition points. I made the straight reflected image, then selected the straight lines, and drew them over as curves."

Figure 4-13 shows the reflected human shape placed in the inner eye image. Dean first selected the line segment, then deleted it and drew the segment as a curve. Figure 4-14 shows how he fine-tuned the curves to match the curves of the concentric circles — by dragging the direction points.

Drawing With Perspective

Normally when you draw shapes such as rectangles and circles, you are drawing along standard x and y axes parallel to the sides of your display. By holding down the Shift key, you can move or transform

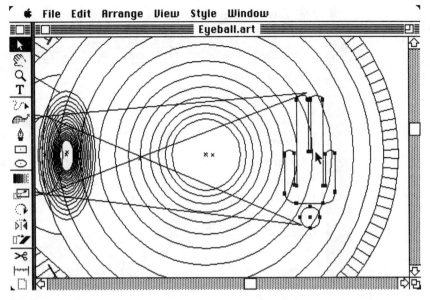

Figure 4-13

The human icon shape after the reflection, placed in the inner eye before editing.

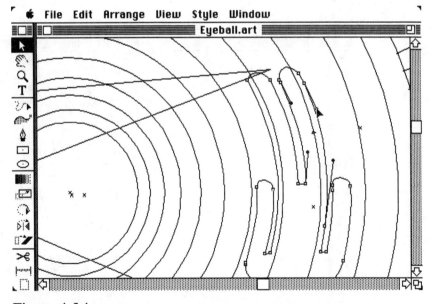

Figure 4-14.

The human icon shape, composed of straight lines, is edited to be composed of curves that are adjusted to the concentric circles.

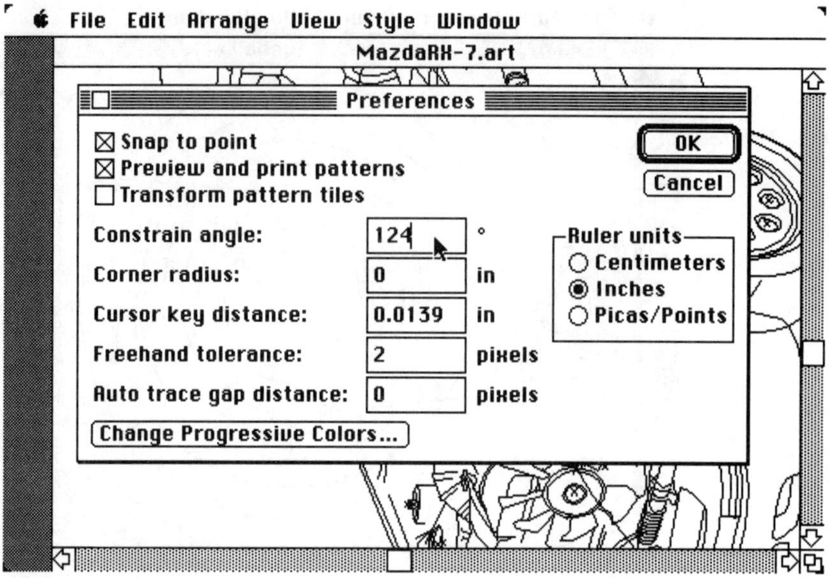

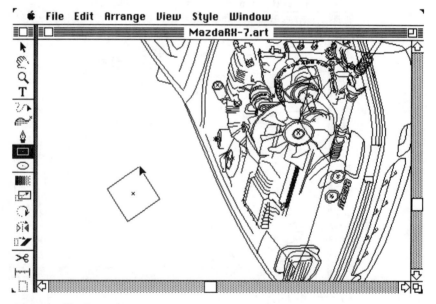

Figure 4-15.
Changing the constrain axes counterclockwise from the standard x and y axes, so that all constrained drawing and movement (activated by holding down Shift while dragging) follows the new constrain axes.

Figure 4-16.
Drawing a rectangle with the new constrain axes.

shapes straight up or down, sideways, or constrained to increments of 45 degrees — these are based on the standard x and y axes.

However, you can also change the axes orientation that determines these angles by changing the constrain angle in the Preferences dialog box, available in the Edit menu. The horizontal and vertical (x and y) axes are usually parallel to the sides of your window, but you can change them to any orientation, then constrain all movements to that orientation. For example, you can rotate the axes so that when you draw rectangles and circles, and when you constrain movements or transformations, the result is angled according to the new axes.

To add to the "Mazda" artwork, Keith Ohlfs changed the constraining axes with the Preferences options (available from the Edit menu, or Command-K), which displays a dialog box in which he could specify an angle that is counterclockwise from the standard x and y axes (Figure 4-15). He could then draw a rectangular shape constrained along the new axes (Figure 4-16), and shear it to match the shape already used in the drawing (Figure 4-17).

Plate 6 ("The Car") shows extensive use of constraining for perspective drawing, which helped the artist draw the lines in the seat cushions, the lines defining the car body, the shapes for the open car doors (changing the constraining axes to change the perspective), and drawing the ovals for the tires.

By using slanted constraining axes you can draw a complex image to perspective and keep your geometric shapes accurate. You can also use the shear tool to slant the image along different axes. The constraining axes also affect the angle of the baseline of text typed with the text tool.

Drawing in Layers

When an illustration has a lot of detail and cut-away views of interior construction, as with Keith Ohlfs' "Mazda," you have to dissect the image into layered objects. "You begin to think of things as all being layered on top of each other," says Keith about starting a complex illustration, "so you draw the background first, then draw the layers you want to be on top."

PostScript automatically masks objects that overlap one another, so that the part of an object that is underneath another object does not print. It is like painting with non-transparent pieces of paper for each shape (even though the shapes in the artwork view are transpar-

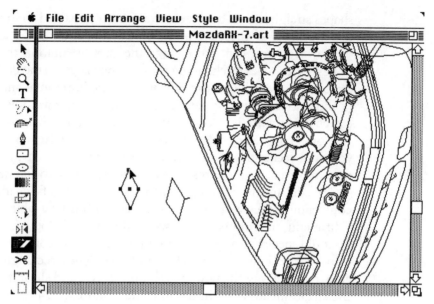

Figure 4-17.
Shearing the rectangle with the Shift key to use the new constrain axes for control.

ent). If you ever have any doubt that two shapes overlap, choose the Preview Illustration option to see what will happen when the illustration is printed.

Technical illustrators usually have to choose a line weight that will be scaled when the entire image is scaled, but Keith discovered that he could draw the entire "Mazda" artwork using one line weight (and no fill). He then fine-tuned the image and changed some of the lines, such as the outer edges of the car body, to a thicker line weight. "It was really simple [to change line weights], and it's a great example of how a technical illustration can be done without worrying about line weights."

Keith found it easier to work on "Mazda" in sections, then join the sections as the last step. He started with the background detail, and the last object he drew was the outline. To work out the detail, Keith used the zoom tool to magnify the drawing. "You can zoom in [to the artwork] to make a little, very complicated part of a drawing almost a drawing by itself."

The "Mazda" artwork took about 12 to 16 hours to finish (using an earlier version of Adobe Illustrator). Although this may seem a long time, it would take a lot longer using conventional methods. It

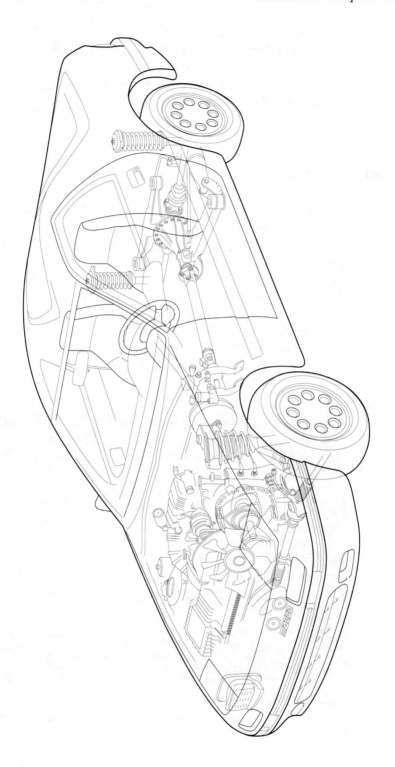

may take a while to learn all the tricks and techniques of using Adobe Illustrator 88, but these techniques can be utilized over and over, and pieces of the artwork can be reused, without worrying about scaling line weights. As Keith described his efforts, "I would never try to do these illustrations with a pen and ink. Only Illustrator makes it possible to do them."

Color Separations

Adobe Illustrator 88 files can be separated by the Adobe Separator program (supplied on the Tutorial/Utilities disk). You can produce four-color and custom separations, and choose various options including the page size, orientation, type of emulsion, positive or negative, and the halftone screen ruling in lines per inch. Adobe Systems provides PostScript Printer Description (PPD) files for various printers and imagesetters so that separations are produced with the best possible control settings.

When designing color artwork, you first need to understand the printing process you will use, so that your artwork can be properly

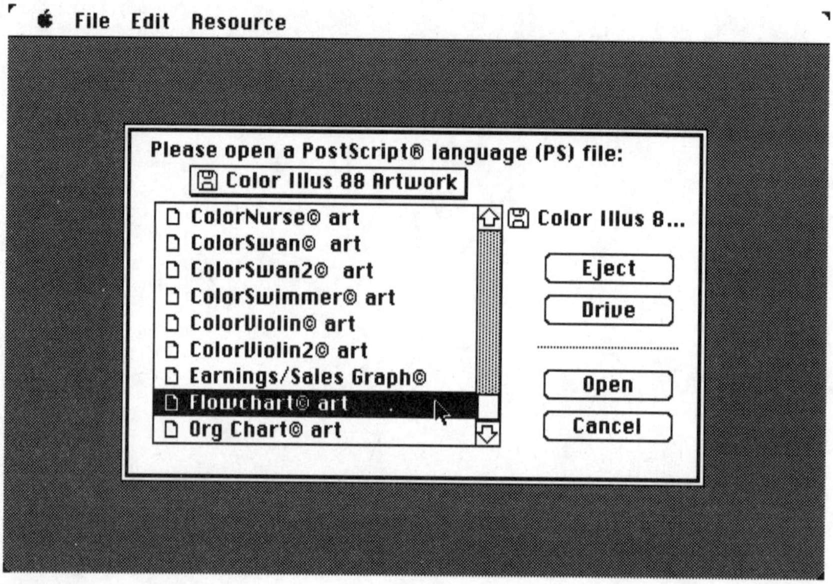

Figure 4-18.
Opening a PostScript file (an Illustrator document) with the Adobe Separator program.

reproduced by a printing press. To assure success before producing final film, ask your printer to look at a color proof and tell you whether the piece can be reproduced without problems on press. The benefit of using Adobe Illustrator 88 is that if your printer tells you the artwork won't reproduce well and describes the changes needed (such as larger or bold type), you can quickly modify the artwork before producing the negatives, and the final art will print properly, saving time, money and aggravation.

For Plate 1 ("Flowchart") a separation consisting of four pieces of film (one for each process color) was produced by the Adobe Separator program. Each piece of film contained the necessary elements that ensure proper registration and color control on press.

When you start Adobe Separator, a dialog box asks for the name of a PostScript file (Figure 4-18). Illustrations saved by Adobe Illustrator 88 are PostScript files, and you can also select PostScript files from other applications.

After choosing the PostScript file, the program displays the dimensions of the artwork's bounding box (Figure 4-19). The bounding box is defined in PostScript units (points), and represents

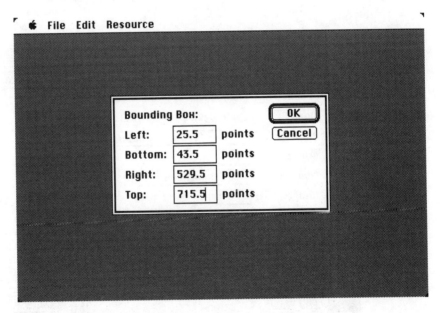

Figure 4-19.
Changing the bounding box dimensions that describe the smallest rectangle that could fit around the entire illustration; outside this box are printed the trim marks and registration targets.

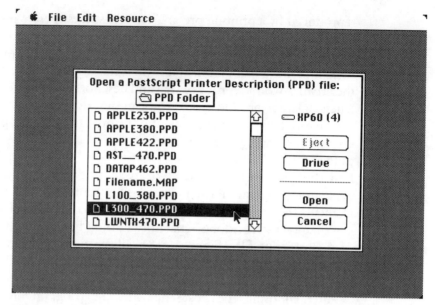

Figure 4-20.
Choosing a PostScript Printer Description file for the device you are using to create the separations (Linotronic 300 chosen).

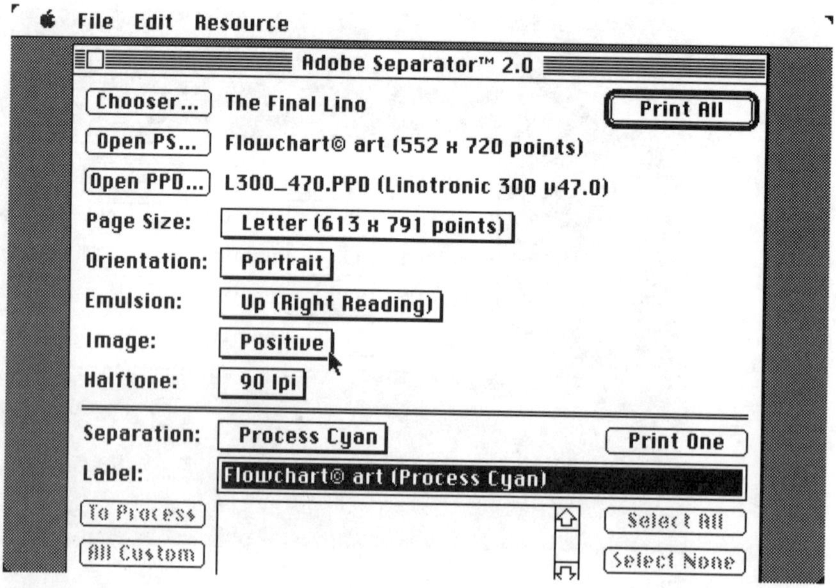

Figure 4-21.
The Adobe Separator dialog box lets you activate the Chooser, change your PostScript and PPD file, and set various options for output (Linotronic 300 defaults shown).

the outside dimensions of an illustration (the smallest rectangle that could be dragged over all printing pieces of the artwork).

The trim marks and registration symbols (target symbols) are printed just outside the bounding box so that printers can align the pieces of film and position the image on the page. Trim marks and registration targets, which are always outside the trim area and therefore not laser printed if your page and printer are letter-sized, are required by most print shops and should be left on the film (the marks are included inside the image area in Plate 1 on purpose, by adjusting the bounding box for a custom separation of the illustration).

After clicking OK for the bounding box dimensions, the program asks for a PostScript Printer Description file (Figure 4-20). The PPD file contains specific device information for Adobe Separator including the resolution, available page sizes, color support, and acceptable screen rulings. You should always use the appropriate PPD file for the device you are using.

The Adobe Separator program displays its dialog box (see Figure 4-21) containing specific choices for the output device in pop-up menus. You can switch PPD and PostScript files for convenience in producing multiple separations. You can also activate the Chooser desk accessory from this dialog box in order to choose an output device by name.

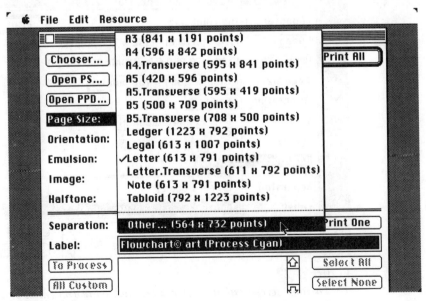

Figure 4-22.
Changing the page size in the Adobe Separator dialog box.

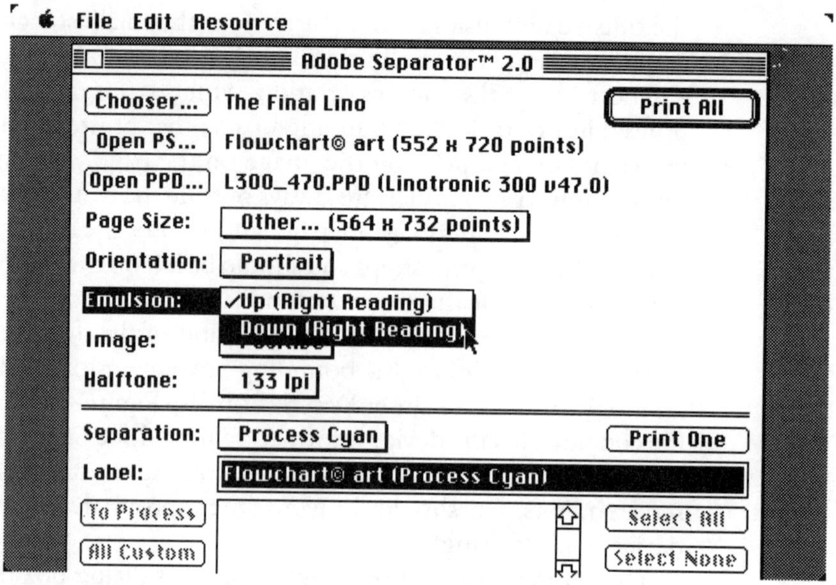

Figure 4-23.
Adobe Separator offers two emulsion choices for Linotronic 300 film separations: emulsion side up or down (both right reading).

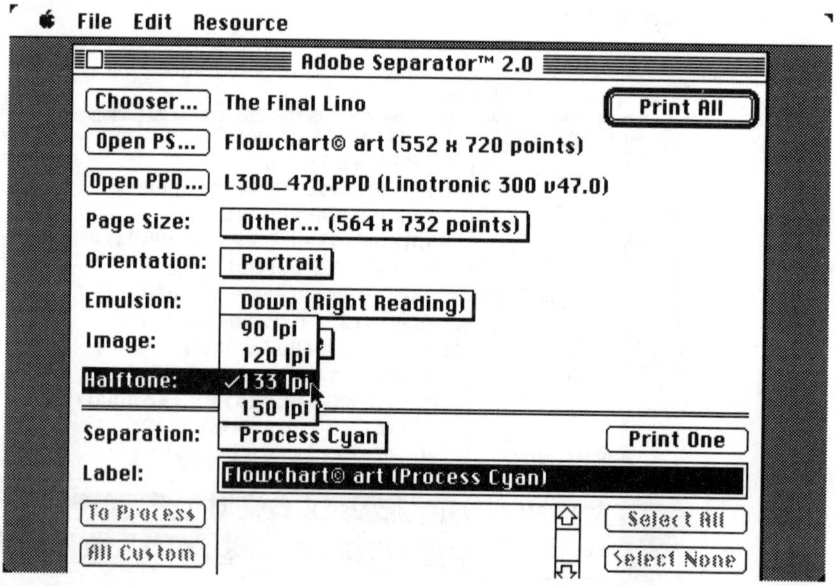

Figure 4-24.
The halftone screen ruling in lines per inch set to 133 (most print shops can't print rulings finer than 150 lpi).

The page size option includes the dimensions (in points) of the page (Figure 4-22). Page sizes are listed by name or by dimensions, which define the printable area for the separation (including space for trim marks and registration targets). For some devices you can specify a custom page size and an offset to move the page away from the right edge of the printed sheet. The maximum page size you can use depends on the resolution setting of the device used. For example, the Linotronic 300, can accommodate a larger page size if the resolution is lowered.

The page orientation can be set to Portrait or Landscape. Portrait is the usual setting for illustrations in which the top should be parallel with the short side. Landscape orientation prints the illustration's top in parallel with the long side.

The emulsion type you choose (Figure 4-23) depends on your printer's requirements. Emulsion, the sensitive layer on film or paper, can be up (readable when facing at you) or down (readable when facing away from you). Illustrations printed on paper are usually set to have emulsion side up, and film separations are usually set to have emulsion side down. You can also choose to print a positive or negative image (usually set to negative for film separations). If you need to produce separations, you should use film since it cuts out one step in the production process and avoids image degradation problems that may occur by shooting screened images.

The halftone screen ruling (Figure 4-24) defines the number of halftone dots per inch, referred to as lines per inch (lpi). A higher screen ruling usually produces a better separation but requires a high resolution device such as a Linotronic 300 set to 2540 dpi.

If you are connected to a Linotronic 300 you will also see screen angles for the process colors and custom colors listed in parentheses in this order: cyan, magenta, yellow, black, and custom. Colors are set at different screen angles so that they don't directly overlap each other.

Adobe Separator lets you print all of the process color separations in one operation, or separately, or as a color comp to a color printer, or color comps are translated to grays (Figure 4-25). The Print All button lets you print separations for all four process colors and one for each custom color. Alternatively, custom colors and PANTONE colors can be converted into percentages of process colors automatically and included in the separations for the four process colors.

To convert a custom or PANTONE color to appropriate process color percentages, select the color's name in the list of custom and

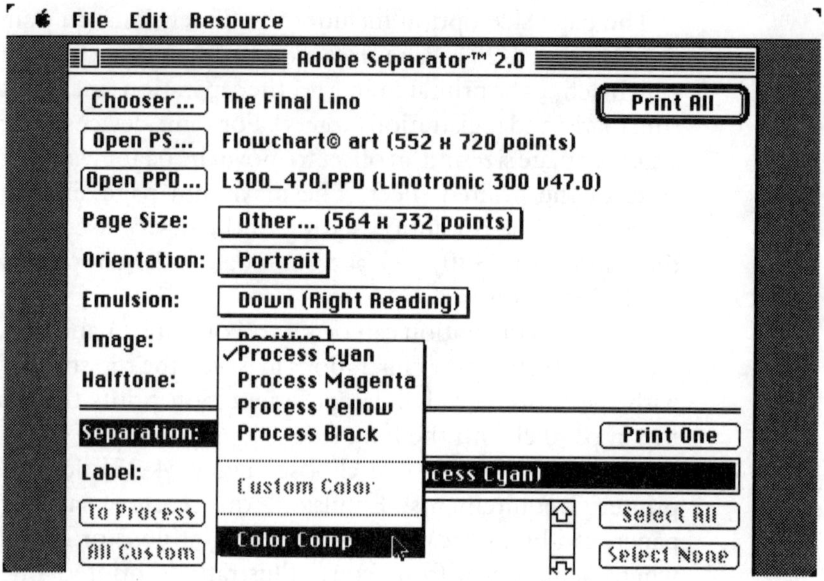

Figure 4-25.
You can choose to produce a color comp on a color printer (converted to grays for black printers), otherwise you should select one separation for each process color plus one separation for each custom color.

PANTONE colors, and click the To Process button. The program automatically converts the custom or PANTONE color into process color percentages; to reverse the process (reverse previously converted custom or PANTONE colors), click the All Custom button.

Although custom colors should be converted since they are comprised of process colors, PANTONE colors may not appear the same after conversion to process colors, since process colors can only approximate PANTONE colors. Since the results differ depending on the image-setting device, you must experiment or use a custom separation for each PANTONE color.

Setting Type in Color

Many of the registration problems that occur with color separations are related to the fact that fast presses sometimes print slightly off-register. Type can be a problem if it is too thin. Black type prints best (sharp and crisp) on any type of press, and is usually the best choice for small type sizes and for thin-stroked characters. However, web offset presses have a problem trying to register type that is too fine.

Plate 1 ("Flowchart") has black type for the copyright notice and bold blue type in the flowchart boxes. It also has type (for "yes," "no," and "maybe") reversed-out from the background color which is larger than the copyright notice, and set in bold. Reversed type should be large and bold enough to avoid printing problems, such as characters breaking up or plugging up. Bold type is also easier to register on press and to read when the type or the background of reversed type is composed of more than one process ink color.

Plate 5 ("Organizational Chart" by Laura Lamar) also shows the use of colored text. The title, "ORGANIZATIONAL CHART," is not stroked (outlined), but is filled with color — 50 percent yellow, 35 percent magenta, and 90 percent cyan (Figure 4-26). The font is set to 12 point Helvetica Bold with 20 points of leading, aligned left, with a spacing value set to five points (Figure 4-27).

The extra spacing is inserted between the characters to space them further apart than the default setting of zero points (which uses the

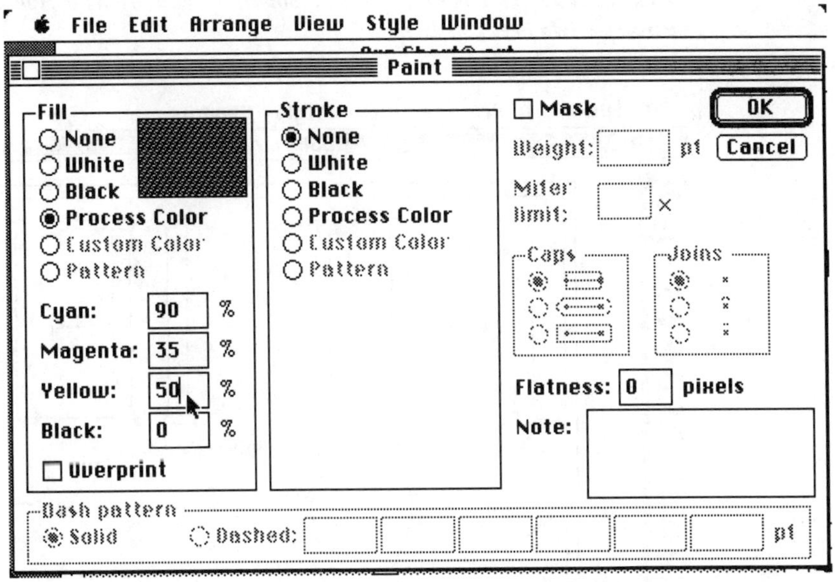

Figure 4-26.
The Paint dialog box for the text "Organizational Chart" for Plate 5, set to 90 percent cyan, 35 percent magenta, and 50 percent yellow for its fill and no stroke.

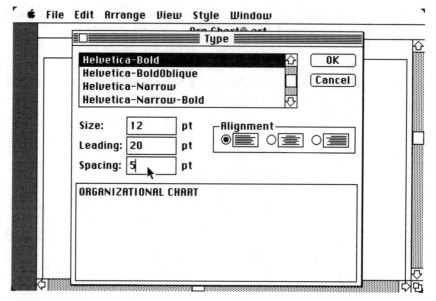

Figure 4-27.
The Type dialog box for the text "Organizational Chart" for Plate 5, set to 12 point Helvetica Bold with 20 points of leading and five points of extra spacing between letters.

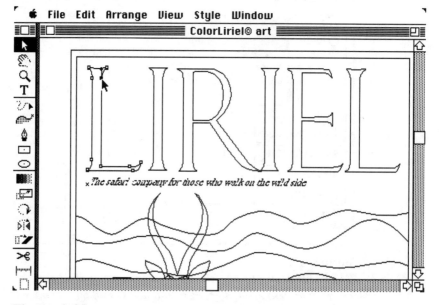

Figure 4-28.
The title "Liriel" (Plate 4) was drawn rather than typed so that the characters have a unique shape.

font's standard setting for spacing). You can specify a negative number for spacing to move characters closer together (similar to tracking or automatic kerning functions in page makeup programs). Type attributes can be set before typing text and changed after typing text, and you can set attributes for several blocks of type simultaneously (if they are all selected). You can't vary the type attributes within one block of type.

If your type requires a special look or modification to its shape or serif, you should draw the characters with the pen or freehand tool, perhaps starting with an automatic trace of scanned characters. Plate 4 ("Liriel" by Luanne Seymour Cohen) has a title composed of characters that were drawn rather than typed (Figure 4-28). The path created for each character has a fill of 40 percent magenta and 100 percent yellow and no stroke. Another reason for drawing text characters rather than typing the text with the text tool is that drawn character shapes can blend into other shapes, but you can't use the blend tool with typed characters. A set of drawn characters are provided in the *Adobe Collector's Edition I* available from Adobe Systems.

You don't have to draw the characters if you want to perform transformations such as rotating, scaling, shearing, or reflecting.

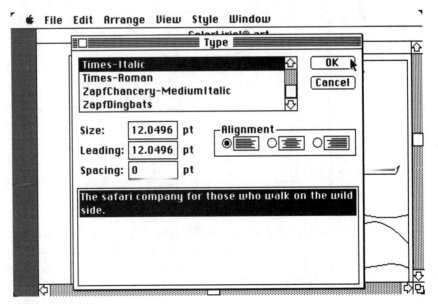

Figure 4-29.
Typed text can be scaled along with the rest of an illustration, and the actual point size may be fractional.

Text typed with the text tool can be transformed, and its baseline will conform to whatever the x and y axes are set to in the constrain field of the Preferences dialog box. You can also change the line cap and join styles in the Paint dialog box for typed text. If you get long, sharp corner points with letters such as "M," "A," "V," and "W," change the join style to something other than a miter join, or lower the miter limit.

The white text below the title of "Liriel" was typed with the text tool, set to a specific point size and leading, and painted with a white fill and stroke. When "Liriel" was scaled down for color separations, the entire illustration was uniformly scaled, and the size of the type was also scaled. As a result, the type font size is defined in fractional points (Figure 4-29). If your illustrations will be scaled before printing them, choose text and line weights that will still print well after the image has been scaled.

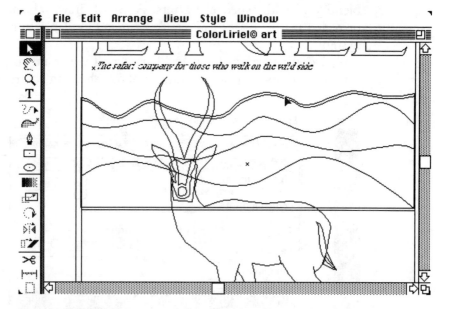

Figure 4-30.
The bright red path in "Liriel" (Plate 4) extends behind other paths colored to be reddish-purple and purple. When colored paths overlap, the color of the path on top is the color printed and displayed, unless you use the overprint feature.

Trap and Overprinting

Adobe Illustrator 88 provides precise control over the coloration of paths and strokes so that you can fine-tune images for print jobs on different presses. There are a host of problems that can occur in a press run, including registration problems in which the dots of ink do not fall precisely where they should and cause white to appear between two colors. Illustrator's overprint feature and black strokes can be used to "create trap" and prevent some of these problems.

When you draw painted objects that will overlap each other, you should draw the background first, then draw the layers you want to be on top. Alternatively you can draw the layers in any order, then use the Paste In Front and Paste In Back options to place layers on top of or underneath other layers.

PostScript automatically masks painted objects that overlap one another, so that the color that is underneath another color does not print. Plate 4 ("Liriel" by Luanne Seymour Cohen) shows how colors do not mix when they overlap. The path for the bright red hilltops (Figure 4-30) extends behind other colored paths (the reddish-purple and purple areas), which are on top of the bright red path. The bright red does not mix with the colors of the other path unless you use the overprint feature, but in most cases you will not want to mix the colors of two or more paths.

When there is a high probability that registration problems will occur and cause white to appear between two colors, you can use several different techniques to "create trap" to compensate for anticipated registration problems. One way is to apply a stroke with a heavy weight, as shown in "The Swan" (Plate 7) around the swan figures. Whenever colors meet at solid black lines, Adobe Separator automatically creates the necessary trap. "The Swimmer" (Plate 3) is one interesting way to ensure trap with black lines: the basic swimmer shape is a path (Figure 4-31) that is stroked and filled with 100 percent black, then colored shapes are pasted in front of the swimmer shape.

Without black lines, you ensure trap by providing a bit of overlap. To create trap for a shape within another shape, specify a stroke for the inner shape in the same color as its fill. Usually a stroke line weight between 0.8 and 1.4 points is useful for creating trap. Then click the

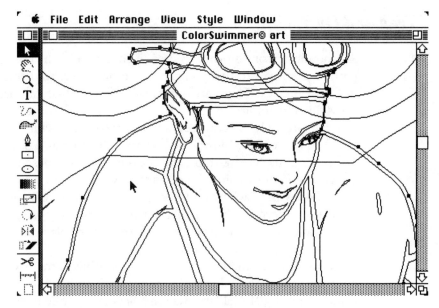

Figure 4-31.
The swimmer shape (Plate 3) is stroked and filled with black, with color-filled shapes placed in front. Trap is automatically created between shapes due to the solid black lines.

Overprint box in the Stroke part of the dialog box (be careful — there is another Overprint box in the Fill part of the dialog box that you should *not* click).

Although nothing appears different in the preview display, the overprint option allows color underneath the object to mix with the color of the object, thus creating a color somewhere between the two for the overlapping area. An overprinting stroke mixes its color with the color beneath it, preventing any separation between the two objects in print even if the registration is slightly off.

If two colored objects meet flush along a straight line, you can select the top-most object and check the Overprint option in the fill part of the Paint dialog box, then stretch the topmost object slightly so that it overlaps the other object. If the objects don't meet in a straight line, you can create trap by specifying a stroke with overprint. If, however, an object needs trap only on a segment that overlaps another object, use the masking feature described later.

You don't need to use the overprint feature for 100 percent black lines because Adobe Illustrator automatically overprints black. However, tints of black must be overprinted if used for trapping.

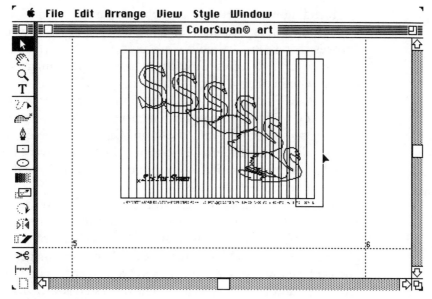

Figure 4-32.
The color gradation background for "The Swan" (Plate 7) was created by blending the process colors of two rectangles; the "S" was blended into the swan shape and their colors were also blended.

When a colored object is overprinted, the process colors that are common to it and the objects behind it are not affected and print normally; only the colors that are not in common are mixed.

Shapes that are 100 percent black are automatically overprinted by Adobe Separator over all other colors. If a large black area has two or more different colors behind it, you should add 15 to 30 percent cyan, magenta, and yellow to the black area. When two objects contain all four process colors, overprint does not affect them, but trapping is usually not necessary with such objects. In fact, when you have two objects that contain the the same color, you probably don't need to create trap between them. When a lightly-colored object overlaps a darker object, create trap using the lighter object.

Blending Colors and Tints

Adobe Illustrator 88 can blend colors and tints as well as shapes. Plates 7 and 8 are examples of color and tint blending as well as shape blending, all created with the blend tool.

Blending works between two objects painted with process colors or custom colors, and between a PANTONE or custom color and a process color. Process colors are used for all intermediate shapes between any two colors. Tints are blended by percentage in the same color, whether it is a process, custom, or PANTONE color.

In Plate 7 ("The Swan"), the outline "S" (from the Adobe Collector's Edition of non-text characters and other PostScript clip art objects) is blended into the swan shape. Both object shape and color (fill) were blended. The outline of the letter has a beak shape overlaying its upper serif to correspond to the beak shape that appears at the other end of the blend.

The outline's fill is 100 percent cyan, 90 percent magenta, and 20 percent yellow, and it blends in four intermediate steps to a swan shape with seven percent cyan and no other colors. The first intermediate step is 81.4 percent cyan, 72 percent magenta, and 16 percent yellow, and the next is 62.8 percent cyan, 54 percent magenta, and 12 percent yellow. The third step is 44.2 percent cyan, 36 percent magenta, and eight percent yellow, and the fourth and last intermediate step is 25.6 percent cyan, 18 percent magenta, and four percent yellow.

The blend tool was also used to create the gradual color blend from left to right behind the "S" and the swan. In 20 steps, an ungrouped rectangle (Figure 4-32), painted 30 percent cyan, 40 percent magenta, and 50 percent yellow, was blended to another rectangle at the other end of the illustration painted with 1.4 percent cyan, 13.8 percent magenta, and 50 percent yellow (the yellow stayed at 50 percent for all intermediate steps).

The number of steps you specify in the Blend dialog box determines the color and tint blending percentages. You can also change the percentages of the first and last intermediate steps in order to fine-tune the blending or produce special effects.

Custom Patterns

Adobe Illustrator 88 lets you fill and stroke paths with a custom pattern. You can even stroke and fill type with a custom pattern. A pattern can be transformed with the shape, transformed separately, or remain the same while the shape is transformed. You can also move a shape and have the pattern move with it or have the pattern stay in the same place while the shape moves (as if the shape was a window exposing the stationary pattern).

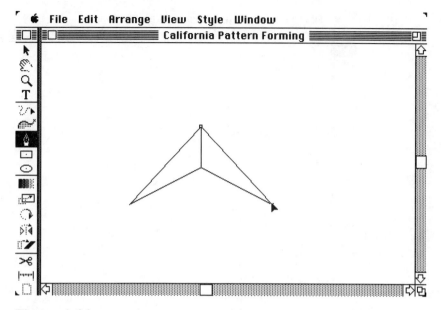

Figure 4-33.
Creating an element of a custom pattern just as you would create any other artwork. It is painted with a green fill and no stroke.

A pattern is available for a document if it has been defined in that document or in another document that is open at the same time. A custom pattern is always stored with the document in which is was defined and in any document that uses the pattern as a fill or stroke. You can see the list of custom patterns stored with the documents that are currently open by choosing the Paint dialog box and clicking the Pattern button for either the fill or stroke. You can also see the pattern list by choosing the Pattern option from the Styles menu.

Any pattern in the list can be used in any open document. If a pattern you want is not in the list, open a document that uses it, leaving your other document or documents open at the same time. The pattern name should appear in the list if it was saved with the newly opened document. For example, if you want to use the pattern Meadow 1 in the "Pennsylvania" document, but Meadow 1 is so far saved only in the "California" document, simply open both documents and assign the Meadow 1 pattern to a shape in the "Pennsylvania" document. The result is that Meadow 1 is stored in both documents.

To manage the use of many different patterns, it may help to create a document that contains all patterns (perhaps called "Patterns"), that you can leave open while opening other documents and applying

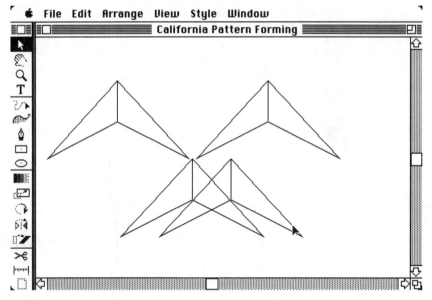

Figure 4-34.
Cloning the pattern element and placing the clones in appropriate places to create a custom pattern.

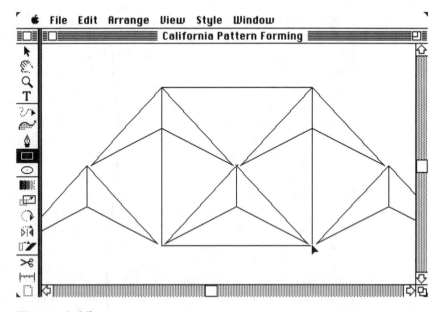

Figure 4-35.
Drawing the pattern tile rectangle to define the custom pattern; this rectangle acts like a masking object that shows only what is inside it.

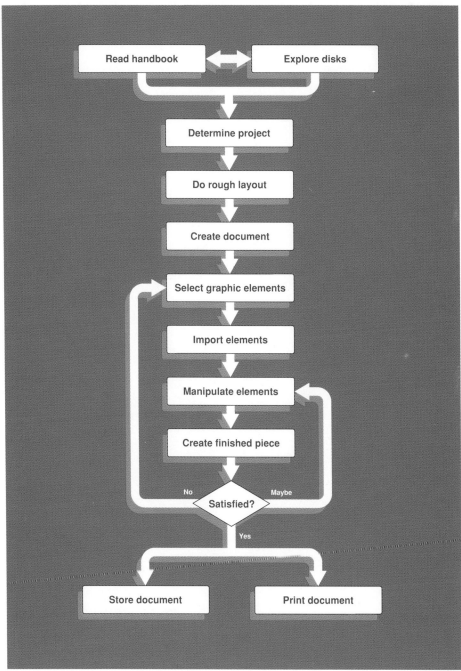

LIRIEL

The safari company for those who walk on the wild side.

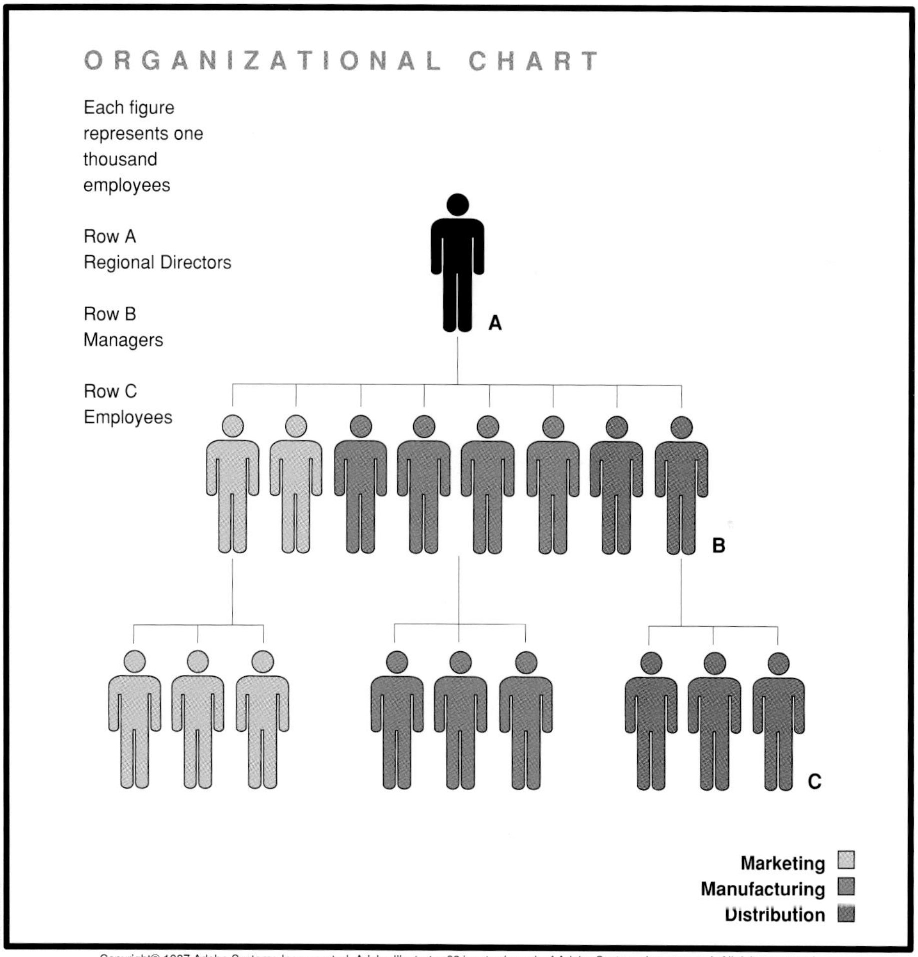

ORGANIZATIONAL CHART

Each figure
represents one
thousand
employees

Row A
Regional Directors

Row B
Managers

Row C
Employees

A

B

C

Marketing
Manufacturing
Distribution

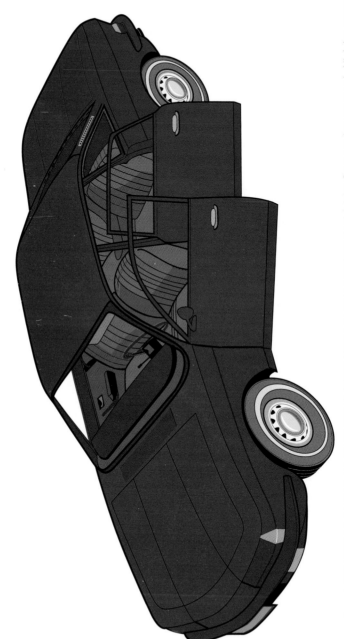

S is for Swan

V is for Violin

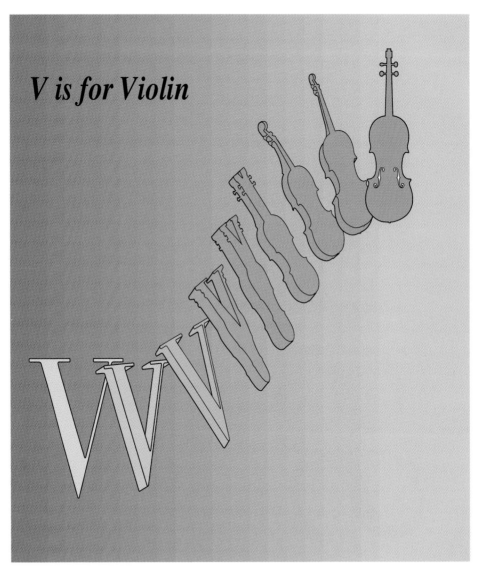

patterns. Patterns remain stored with a document unless they are explicitly deleted in the Pattern option's dialog box.

To create a pattern, simply draw an element of the pattern using Adobe Illustrator 88 in a document (Figure 4-33). Paint the element as you would like it to appear in the pattern — we used 80 percent cyan and 90 percent yellow for the fill (a strong green), and no stroke.

Next, clone the element several times and place the clones in appropriate places (Figure 4-34). The placement of these elements is critical for achieving a uniform pattern — you may want to use the Shift key to constrain the movement of clones so that the clones are at specific angles from the main element. You can draw these elements at any size, then scale them later when you decide how large the pattern elements should be.

The next step is to define the *pattern tile* with a rectangle. The pattern tile acts as a masking object (more on masking later) that shows only the part of the pattern that is inside it. The rectangle must have perpendicular corners (be sure that the corner radius is zero in the Preferences dialog box). You can draw the rectangle with the rectangle tool or with the pen tool as long as the constraint angle set in the Preferences dialog box is set to zero.

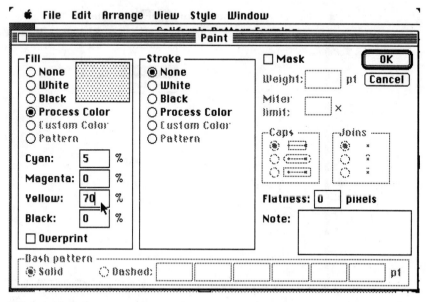

Figure 4-36.
Painting the pattern tile rectangle to have a slight yellow-green tint for a fill and no stroke; this becomes the background fill for the pattern.

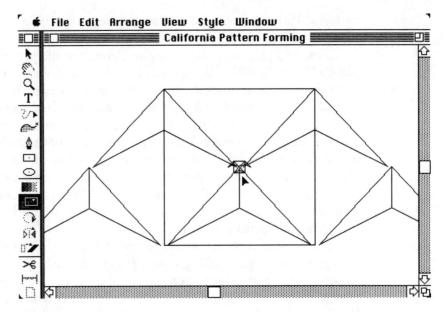

Figure 4-37.
Scaling the pattern tile and pattern elements at once to the size they should appear when defined as a pattern.

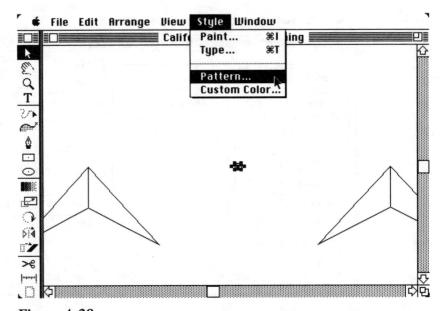

Figure 4-38.
With the pattern tile and elements still selected (after scaling them down to actual pattern size), choose the Pattern option from the Style menu.

Pattern tiles are placed next to each other in the pattern, so draw a pattern tile rectangle so that the edges will match smoothly. You should make the pattern tile as small as possible to contain a few carefully placed elements (Figure 4-35). When you are drawing the pattern tile rectangle, imagine how the pattern will appear if the tiles are placed next to each other and in rows above and below it.

The pattern tile rectangle must be behind the other objects in the pattern, so after drawing the rectangle, Cut it and use the Paste In Back option to paste it in back of the other objects. You should also paint the rectangle — whatever fill you apply to the rectangle becomes the pattern's background. If you specify no fill, the background will have no fill. You should always specify no stroke for the pattern tile rectangle unless you want the pattern tile lines to be visible in the pattern.

We painted our pattern tile rectangle to have a slight yellow-green tint (the elements themselves are painted green) and no stroke (Figure 4-36). This fill becomes the color of the background of the pattern. We then Cut the rectangle and use Paste In Back to paste it behind the pattern elements.

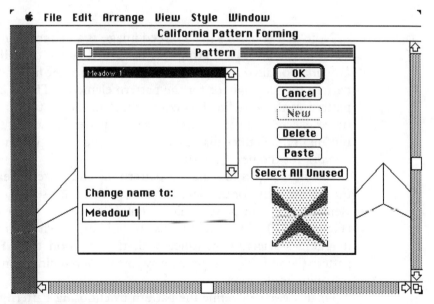

Figure 4-39.
After clicking the New button in the Pattern dialog box, the New Pattern 1 name appears, which you can change by typing over a new name. A preview of the pattern appears at the bottom right.

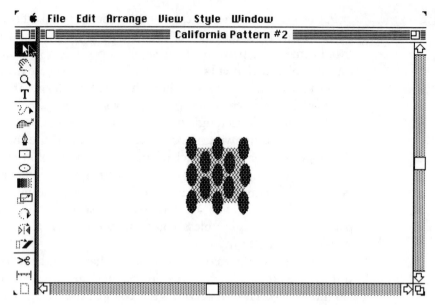

Figure 4-40.
Using Preview Illustration to preview new artwork to be defined as a pattern (the pattern tile rectangle is behind the pattern elements).

Note that you can't use a placed image as a pattern element, nor can you use a masked group (as described later): only Illustrator artwork. You also can't specify another pattern as the fill for either the pattern tile rectangle or for the pattern elements. This is because a pattern can't be defined as containing another pattern. You can, however, create a pattern using another pattern by using the Paste button in the Pattern dialog box to paste the other pattern into the artwork for the new pattern.

The next step is to scale our pattern tile and pattern elements to the size we want for the defined pattern. You must select all pattern elements and the pattern tile rectangle and scale them together (Figure 4-37). You can do this by holding down Option while dragging a selection marquee with the selection tool. Scale the pattern tile and elements in any way you like, stretching, condensing, or scaling uniformly.

Finally, you can define the pattern by choosing Pattern from the Style menu (Figure 4-38), and click the New button. The name New Pattern 1 appears in the pattern list and in the change name field, and you can rename it by typing over this name (Figure 4-39). A preview of the pattern appears in the Pattern dialog box.

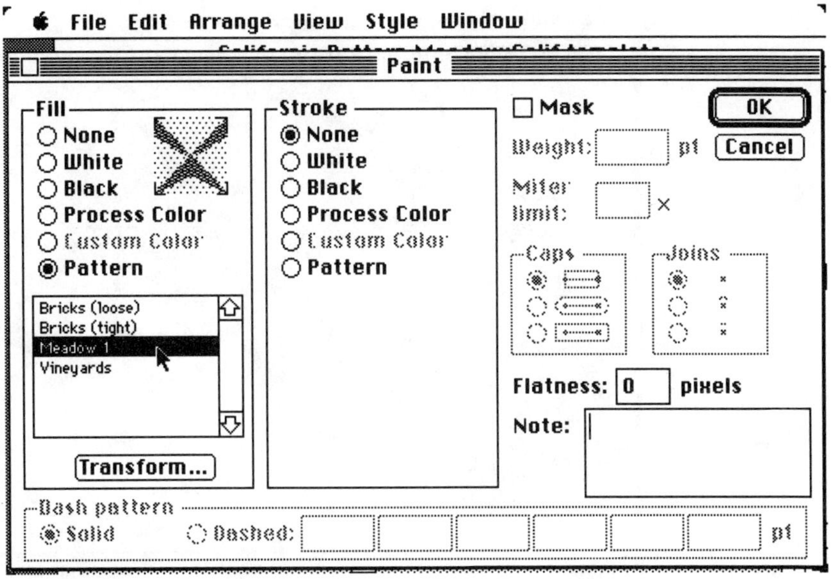

Figure 4-41.
*Assigning a pattern to an object's fill by clicking the Pattern button in
the Paint dialog box and selecting a pattern; a preview of the pattern
appears in the fill preview window.*

It sometimes helps to preview the artwork before scaling or before
defining the artwork as a pattern. We drew another custom pattern
of ovals and used the Preview Illustration option to see how they
would appear in a pattern tile before defining the pattern (Figure 4-
40). If you intend to use a lot of patterns, it helps to define them in
one document which can be left open while opening other documents and applying patterns.

When you have defined a pattern, you can paste it into another
document so that it is treated as regular artwork, not as a pattern. Use
the Paste button in the Pattern dialog box after selecting a pattern by
name. You can then use the artwork to create another pattern.

To assign a pattern to an object's fill, click the Pattern button in
the Paint dialog box (in the fill area) and click on the name of a
pattern (Figure 4-41). A preview of the pattern appears in the
preview window. You can also choose a pattern for an object's stroke.
The pattern appears in the artwork when you choose the Preview
Illustration option (Figure 4-42). The pattern itself starts at the
current ruler origin, which is at the lower left corner of page 5 (usually
the center page of the drawing area). You can change the ruler origin

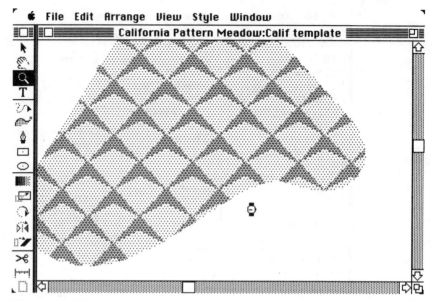

Figure 4-42.
The pattern is printed and displayed with the Preview Illustration view.

(the point where zero appears on both rulers) by moving the ruler intersection square to the new position. You can alternatively move the pattern itself, as described later.

An object painted with a pattern fill can be transformed (that is, moved, scaled, rotated, reflected, and sheared) and the pattern can either be transformed in the same fashion, or left alone. You can also transform the pattern itself without transforming the object.

When moving or transforming an object with a pattern, if you drag to move or transform (and you haven't checked the Transform pattern tiles box in the Preferences dialog box, or in the Move or transformation dialog box), the pattern is not moved or transformed with the object. If, however, you check this box in the Preferences dialog box (Figure 4-43), the pattern tiles are always moved or transformed with the object when you drag to move or transform the object (Figure 4-44).

You can also choose to transform (or not to transform) the pattern tiles in a transformation dialog box, such as the Rotate dialog box (Figure 4-45). Whenever you turn this option on or off, it automatically updates the Preferences dialog box to your latest choice. Each transformation dialog box has an option to transform the pattern tiles, and the Move dialog box has an option to move the pattern tiles.

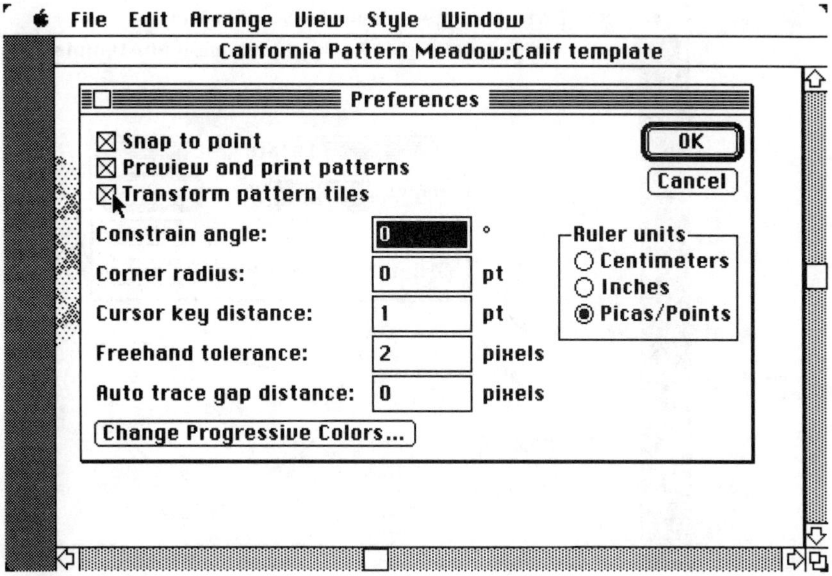

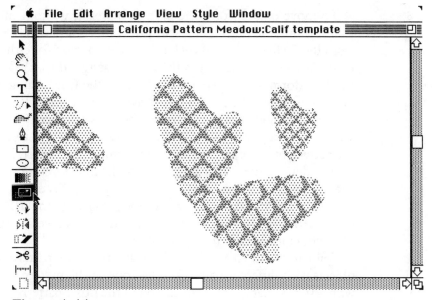

É File Edit Arrange View Style Window

California Pattern Meadow:Calif template

Preferences

☒ Snap to point
☒ Preview and print patterns
☒ Transform pattern tiles

[OK]
[Cancel]

Constrain angle: [0] °

Corner radius: [0] pt

Cursor key distance: [1] pt

Freehand tolerance: [2] pixels

Auto trace gap distance: [0] pixels

─Ruler units─
○ Centimeters
○ Inches
◉ Picas/Points

[Change Progressive Colors...]

Figure 4-43.
Checking the option in the Preferences dialog box to always move or transform pattern tiles along with the object. This box is checked automatically if you choose to transform pattern tiles from the Move dialog box or any transformation dialog box.

É File Edit Arrange View Style Window

California Pattern Meadow:Calif template

Figure 4-44.
Transformed objects are filled with patterns that are also transformed.

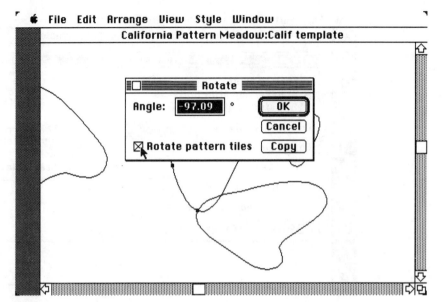

Figure 4-45.
The Rotate pattern tiles box is already checked because the Transform pattern tiles box was checked in the Preferences dialog box. Turning this option on or off (in any dialog box) automatically turns the Transform pattern tiles box off in the Preferences dialog box.

To move or transform the pattern by itself, without moving or transforming the object, first select the object or path, choose Paint from the Style menu, and click the Pattern button for either the fill or the stroke (whichever has the pattern assigned to it). Then click the Transform button (see Figure 4-41 for the Paint dialog box with pattern list), and the program displays the Transform Pattern Style dialog box (Figure 4-46). This dialog box lets you specify movement, scaling, rotating, reflecting, and shearing information to transform the pattern of an object without transforming the object. No matter what order you specify the information, the transformations occur in order: moving, scaling, rotating, reflecting, and shearing. When you transform a pattern, the operation doesn't change the definition of the pattern, nor does it change the pattern as it is used in other parts of the document or other documents.

You can blend two objects that have the same pattern, but not objects with different patterns unless one of the patterns is defined with artwork that is a transformation of the other pattern (the blend produces intermediate shapes with intermediate transformations of the pattern).

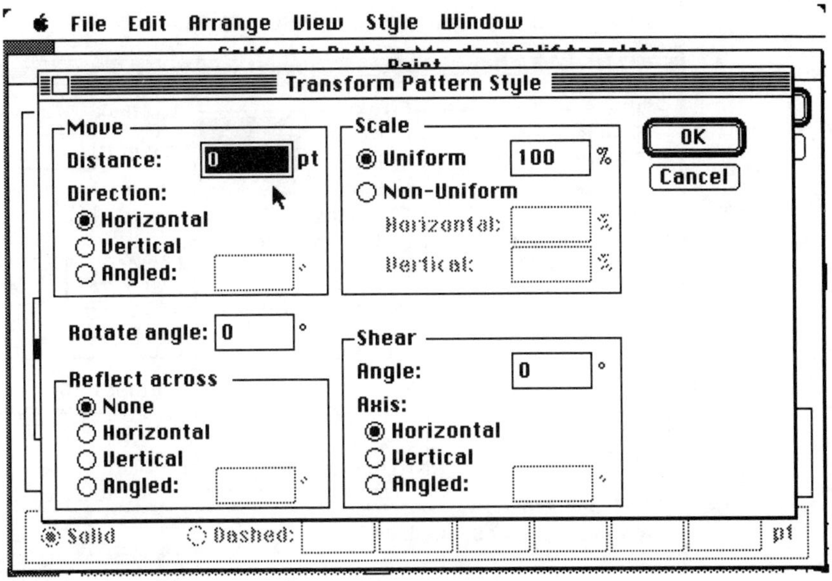

Figure 4-46.
The Transform Pattern Style dialog box, activated from the Paint dialog box (in the Patterns window of either fill or stroke), lets you specify movement, scaling, reflecting, rotating, and shearing information to transform only the pattern of an object.

Masking

You can prepare an object so that it is filled with whatever artwork lies in front of it. The object in back, called the *masking object*, defines the boundaries and treats everything it touches (that is pasted in front of it) as part of a pattern for the masking object. With this neat trick you can compose an object that looks like a window on top of a piece of art. You can also use masking to create trap between two irregularly-shaped objects where stroke-style trapping would be noticed in inappropriate areas of the artwork.

To create a masking object, draw and select the path and be sure it is ungrouped. You should use a single object for a masking object, and one masking object per set of objects to be masked. You can't use a blend as a masking object (although each intermediate step could be a masking object for a set of masked objects). Then choose Paint from the Style menu, set the paint and stroke attributes, and click the Mask check box to turn on masking for this object (Figure 4-47). The Mask option stays on until you group the masking object with the masked objects.

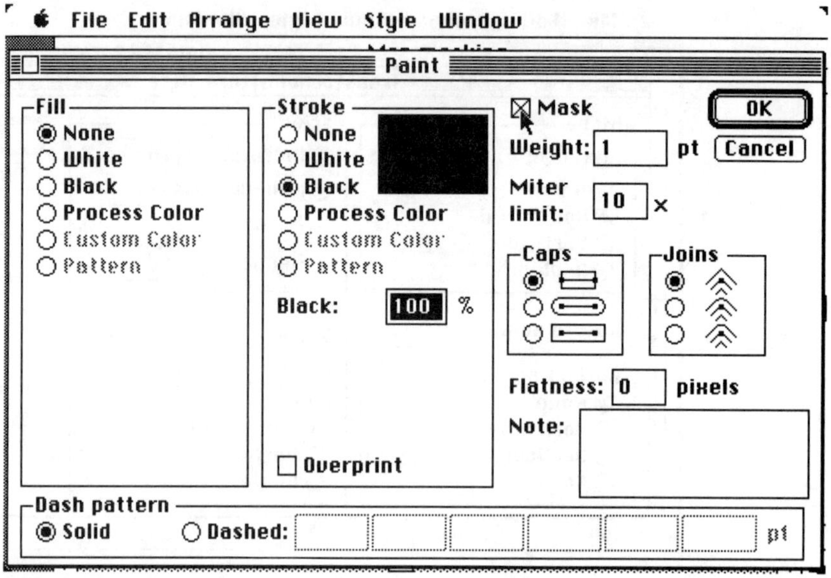

Figure 4-47.
To prepare a masking object, select the object, choose the Paint option, set its paint and stroke attributes, and click the Mask option, which stays on until you group the masking object with the masked objects.

The next step is to paste or drag artwork to be on top of the masking object, which in this case is the Man icon from T/Maker's ClickArt EPS Series of PostScript clip art. The artwork to be masked is "The Rose" which is supplied in the Adobe Illustrator 88 Tutorial folder. After selecting both objects (and checking that the masking object — the Man icon — is behind the masked objects, choose the Group option from the Arrange menu (Figure 4-48). The Mask option automatically turns off when you group the masking object with the masked objects. This completes the masking operation, and the Preview Illustration option shows the result (Figure 4-49).

You can use the blend tool to create a blend that could be used as a set of masked objects. With the combination of the blend tool and masking, you can mask a gradation of colors or shades of gray.

For example, we blended two rectangles shaded at five percent and 95 percent black with 99 intermediate steps, and used the Paste In Back option to paste the Man icon as a masking object behind the blend (Figure 4-50). The Preview Illustration window shows how the masked blend appears in print.

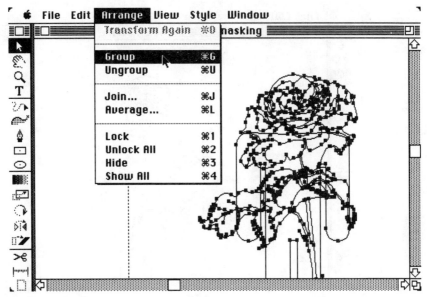

Figure 4-48.
After placing the objects to be masked ("The Rose") on top of the masking object ("Man" icon), and selecting both, choose the Group option to complete the masking operation.

Another use of the masking feature is to set trap for a colored object that overlaps another colored object (only partially enclosed). In such cases, a heavy stroke would be noticed in the areas where the trap is not needed. However, a masking object limits the exposure of the objects in front that are grouped to it. You can set the object on top to be a masking object, and clone the other object and place the clone on top of the masking object, and paint the clone with no fill and a stroke that is heavy enough to act as a trap (usually 0.8 to 1.4 points). The masking object limits the exposure of the clone's stroke to the area within the masking object, which is the area where trap is needed.

If you inadvertently set the mask attribute for a small object (a line, single anchor point, or very small shape), it can cause all the objects in front of it to be masked and not appear in your preview window. This can happen if you set the mask attribute to the center point of an oval or rectangle. You should first select and ungroup (Command-U) an oval or rectangle and delete its center point before using it as a mask.

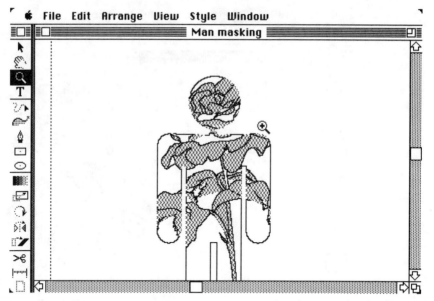

Figure 4-49.
Preview Illustration shows the result of masking the flower with the man icon as the masking object.

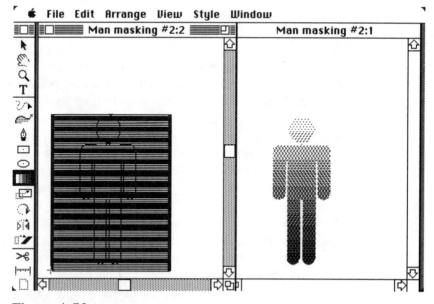

Figure 4-50.
Masking a blend of gray shades with the man icon, and a Preview Illustration window showing the result.

Summary

Professional illustrators gain productivity by using the automatic tracing feature, the blending feature, constraining, multiple transformations, patterns, masks, and measuring tools and rulers.

Adobe Illustrator 88 lets you scale either one path, a group of paths forming an object, or an entire illustration, and have the choice of scaling or preserving the line weights. This choice comes only with the use of the Scale dialog box and uniform scaling — after selecting the scaling tool, hold down the Option key while clicking a scale focal point. If you drag to scale, the line weights are preserved (not scaled). The line weights are also preserved (never scaled) with non-uniform scaling. The Scale dialog box lets you type a percentage for a uniform scale (scaling in proportion), with the choice of preserving or scaling line weights by the same percentage, or for a non-uniform scale.

The "Eyeball" illustration demonstrated the use of multiple rotation transformations, the use of the reflect tool to create an upside-down image, the use of alternate line caps and joins, and the techniques for editing lines into curves.

The "Mazda" illustration showed how you can change the axes for constraining drawing and movement in the Preferences dialog box. You can draw a complex illustration in perspective with accurate geometric shapes, and use the shear tool to slant the artwork along an angled axes. The axes also constrains the angle of the baseline of text typed with the text tool.

When an illustration has a lot of detail and cut-away views of interior construction, as with "Mazda," you have to dissect the image into layered objects. PostScript automatically masks objects that overlap one another, so that the part of an object that is underneath another object does not print.

To produce color separations, use the Adobe Separator program (supplied on the Tutorial/Utilities disk), which can produce four-color and custom separations. You can change the page size, orientation, emulsion type, positive or negative, and the halftone screen ruling in lines per inch. PostScript Printer Description (PPD) files supply information for various printers and imagesetters. You should always use the appropriate PPD file for the device you are using.

To assure success before producing final film, ask your printer to look at a color proof and tell you whether the piece can be reproduced without problems on press. You can use Adobe Illustrator 88 to change things like stroke weights, type point sizes, and process color percentages to adjust your illustration for specific press conditions.

Adobe Separator can print all process color separations in one operation, or separately, or as a color comp to a color printer. Custom colors and PANTONE colors can be converted into percentages of process colors automatically and included in the separations for the four process colors, or you can specify custom separations.

Plate 1 ("Flowchart") shows how you can reverse type out from the background color as long as the type is large and bold enough to avoid printing problems. Plate 5 ("Organizational Chart") also shows the use of colored text and the use of the spacing value for spacing out type characters. Plate 4 ("Liriel" by Luanne Seymour Cohen) has a title composed of characters that were drawn rather than typed.

Illustrator's overprint feature and black strokes can be used to create trap between colored objects and prevent registration problems on high-speed presses. Whenever colors meet at solid black lines, Adobe Separator automatically creates the necessary trap (Plates 3 and 7). Without black lines, you ensure trap by providing a bit of overlap and using the overprint feature. The overprint option allows color underneath the object to mix with the color of the object, thus creating a color somewhere between the two for the overlapping area. Shapes that are 100 percent black are automatically overprinted by Adobe Separator over all other colors.

You can blend between two objects painted with process colors or custom colors, and between a PANTONE or custom color and a process color. Process colors are used for all intermediate shapes, and tints are blended by percentage in the same color (Plates 7 and 8).

The program lets you fill and stroke paths and type with a custom pattern. A pattern can be transformed with the shape, transformed separately, or remain the same while the shape is transformed. Patterns are created as regular artwork, then defined with a pattern tile using the Pattern option. Patterns are painted in fills and strokes using the Paint option. A custom pattern is always stored with the document in which is was defined and in any document that uses the pattern as a fill or stroke.

Finally, this chapter covered the masking feature. You can select an object to be a masking object that defines a boundary of exposure for printing (and previewing) any artwork that lies in front of it and is grouped to it. You can use this feature to create a window on top of a piece of art, to put a gradation of color or gray shapes inside an object, and to create trap between two objects where a partial stroke is required.

The next chapter takes Adobe Illustrator 88 apart and describes every tool and menu option. You can use it as a handy reference to the program's features.

C H A P T E R

5

Adobe Illustrator 88 Dissected

This chapter provides a complete description of each Adobe Illustrator 88 tool, then each menu item, including dialog boxes and keyboard command shortcuts.

The tools are discussed in sequence (from the top to the bottom of the toolbox); the margin of each page shows the selected tool in the toolbox. Each tool description is followed by a list of tool actions and keyboard command options.

The menus are then discussed in sequence. Dialog boxes and keyboard command shortcuts are included in the descriptions of the menu items.

Using the Mouse

The arrow cursor is also referred to as the pointer. You move the pointer by dragging the mouse, and you click the mouse button to select menu items, dialog box options, objects, line segments, and so on. The mouse can also move and resize windows. Moving the mouse (or any other input device such as a trackball, graphics tablet stylus, etc.) moves the pointer around so that you can point to things on the screen for the purpose of selecting or manipulating them. The ratio between the amount the pointer moves and the amount the mouse moves can be adjusted in the Control Panel (see Figure 5-1).

There are basically five actions to perform with a mouse:

Point. When you move the mouse, a pointer moves across the display.

Click. You click a point on the display by quickly pressing and releasing the mouse button. You do this to establish a point in an illustration, or to select an option in a dialog box (such as a check box or button).

Double-click. You double-click a point (such as a file or program icon) by quickly pressing and releasing the mouse button twice. By double-clicking a file or application program, you automatically run the program associated with that file.

Drag. You drag something (such as a graphic object or icon) by pointing the mouse, holding down the mouse button, and moving the mouse so that the pointer (or object) moves to a new position. Then you release the mouse button.

Select. To select a menu option or command, drag down a menu (which drops down to show you the options or commands) until the command or option you want is highlighted, then release the mouse button.

The Macintosh employs drag-down menus and displays dialog boxes after you select a command or option. In the dialog boxes you can select items by clicking boxes or buttons displayed on the screen, and sometimes there are scroll bars for scrolling items in a small window. To operate the scroll bar, click below the white box in the gray area, or click the up or down arrow, or drag the white box up or down. Dialog boxes often have text boxes for typing numbers or text, and every dialog box has an OK and a Cancel button.

Whenever any pointer is moved outside the active window, it changes into the arrow pointer in order to let you select tools, issue commands, or move windows.

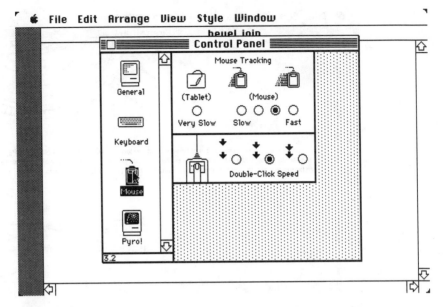

Figure 5-1.
Adjusting the mouse tracking option will change the ratio between the amount the pointer moves and the amount the mouse moves.

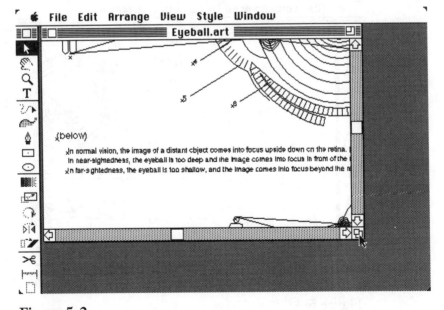

Figure 5-2.
In the bottom right corner of the active window is the size box; drag it with the mouse to change the window size.

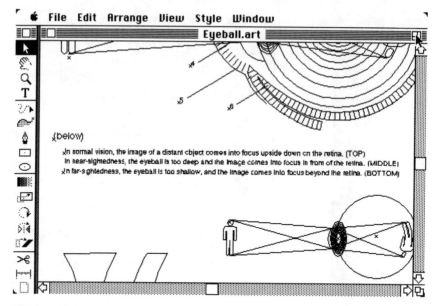

Figure 5-3.
The title bar contains the name of the document (and template, if any).
At the left end is the close box, and at the right end is the zoom box.

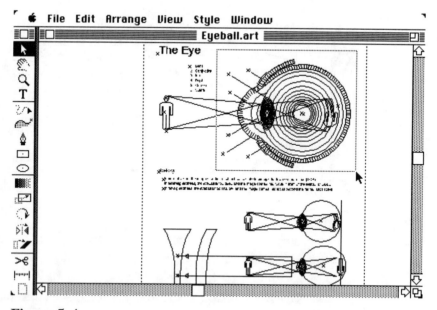

Figure 5-4.
Dragging the selection marquee around a group of objects to select
everything inside the marquee.

Resizing, Zooming, and Moving Windows

You can move and change the size of Adobe Illustrator 88 windows. For example, to change the size of a window, point to the window's size box (see Figure 5-2), hold down the mouse button, and drag with the mouse until the window is the size and shape you want it to be. When you release the mouse button, the window will change size.

A shortcut for enlarging the window is to point to the zoom box in the window's title bar (Figure 5-3). The zoom box is located in the upper right-hand corner of the window. Click the zoom box, and the window will enlarge until it fills up the Macintosh's screen. Click it again and it returns to the size it was before.

If you want to move the window, point to any place on the window's title bar (except the close box at the left end of the bar and the zoom box at the right end of the bar), hold down the mouse button, and drag the window to a new location on the Macintosh's screen (or onto an additional monitor if you are using two monitors that work together). If you move a window with this technique, it will become active if it was previously inactive.

If you want to move an inactive window and have the window remain inactive after it is moved, use the previous technique except hold down the Command key while dragging the window to its new location.

On the other hand, to make an active window inactive, point to the title bar of the window, hold down the Command key, and click the mouse button; this will deactivate the window and send it to the back, behind any other windows that are displayed. Similarly, you can point to the title bar of an active window and drag it to a new location while holding down the Command key in order to move it and deactivate it at the same time.

Selection Tool

The arrow icon in the top slot of the toolbox is the selection tool. To get the selection tool you can either click on the selection tool in the toolbox or use the tool temporarily by holding down the Command key while using another tool. (If your view is set to Preview Illustration, the pointer will remain an arrow, but you can't select objects in the Preview Illustration view. You can select objects only

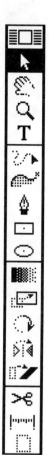

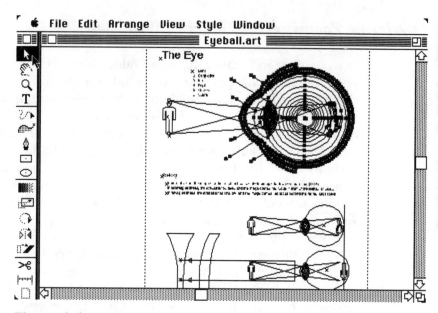

Figure 5-5.
One or more objects are selected, you can activate the Move dialog box by holding down the Option key while clicking the selection tool.

in the Artwork and Template view, or the Artwork Only view; selected from the View menu.)

Once you have drawn a path, you can use the selection tool to move the path to a new location, or to manipulate the path to change its shape. To move an object without changing it, the entire object (and all its connecting lines and points) must be selected; otherwise you may accidentally alter the artwork, since moving any anchor points, direction points, lines, or curves without moving all of them can change the shape of the paths.

To prevent objects from being changed when you move them, use the Group command on the Arrange menu to group the points, lines, and curves in the object into a single unified object. The grouped object is not only resistant to accidental changes, it is also easier to select, because pointing and clicking anywhere on the object selects the entire object.

To select an ungrouped object to move, you select all the items that comprise the object. You can select all the items by dragging a selection marquee (see Figure 5-4) completely around an object, being careful not to include any other objects. To select an entire path, point to any location on the path and click while holding down

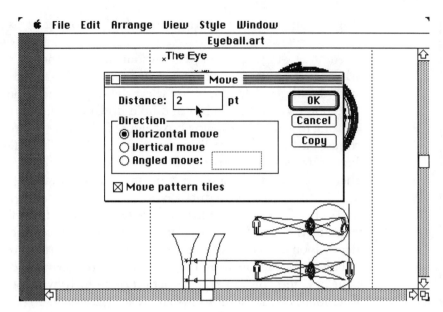

Figure 5-6.
The Move dialog box lets you specify in points (or other measures) how far to move the selected object or objects; you can choose a horizontal, vertical, or angled move and specify the angle in degrees. You can also click Copy to create a clone.

the Option key. If you hold down Option while dragging the marquee, the marquee selects all paths that intersect it.

Alternatively you can select one component of an object by pointing to it and clicking (or by using the selection marquee), and then select another component by pointing and clicking while holding down the Shift key. If you hold down the Shift key before you click on or drag over an item, the item is added to the group of selected objects. If you hold down the Shift key after you start dragging, the program constrains movement of the arrow to increments of 45 degrees. Constraining movement with the Shift key makes it easier to move objects vertically, horizontally, or diagonally at a 45 degree angle.

If there are several objects on top of each other, you can select the top object by pointing to it, holding down the Option key, and clicking the mouse. You can then move it by releasing the Option key and dragging the object to a new location. If you hold down the Option key while you drag an object, it will create a duplicate of the object for moving, and the original will be left in its place. This

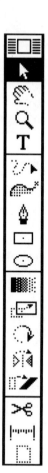

duplication technique is extremely useful for cloning items to reuse in your artwork.

Another way to move objects without changing them is to use the Move dialog box to specify movement precisely. To move an object with the Move dialog box, first select the object, then point to the selection tool in the toolbox and hold down the Option key while clicking to activate the dialog box (Figure 5-5). After you release the mouse button, the Move dialog box appears (Figure 5-6). The dialog box contains the values of the last move that took place, if any, during the current program session; if no move has yet taken place, the values are set to a move distance of zero and horizontally.

To specify the distance to move the selected object(s), click in the box after the word "Distance:" and type in the distance. The measure depends on the measurement chosen for the rulers in the Preferences dialog box (available from the Edit menu). By default the measure is inches, and you can type a fraction of an inch by using decimal notation. You may want to switch the measurements to points (one point = 1/72 of an inch).

Next, specify the direction of the movement by clicking the radio button next to either "Horizontal move," "Vertical move," or "Angled move." If you choose the Angled move option, you also need to specify the angle in degrees you want the move to be made in. The angle is calculated from the horizontal axis (zero degrees) and the number of degrees is added counterclockwise from the horizontal origin.

Specifying a positive measure for a horizontal move will move selected objects to the right, and a negative measure moves them to the left. Likewise, specifying a positive measure for a vertical move will move the selected objects up, and a negative measure will move the objects down. Negative numbers specified for an angled move will move the objects clockwise from the horizontal origin, rather that counterclockwise.

After you have specified the amount and direction of the move, you can either click the OK button to initiate the move (the double line around this button indicates that it will be selected if you press the Return key); click the Cancel button to abandon the move and return to the active window; or click the Copy button to create and move a duplicate while leaving the original in its place. The check box next to "Move pattern tiles," if checked, will move any pattern associated with the object or objects.

If you have altered the x and y axes in the Constrain angle field in the Preferences dialog box, then movement of the object or objects

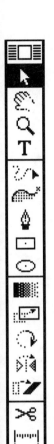

will be relative to the altered x and y axes. For example, if you have rotated the x and y axes by 20 degrees by changing the angle in the Preferences dialog box, any objects that you move will be moved at an additional 20-degree angle: specifying a horizontal move would result in a 20-degree move and specifying a 30-degree move would result in a 50-degree move. If you are moving objects and they seem to be moving in a tilted or exaggerated direction, check the alignment of the x and y axes by looking at the dialog box that appears after you select the Preferences option from the Edit menu (or type Command-K). If there is a number other than zero, the axes are set to an angle. To restore the original x and y axes that are parallel to the sides of the window, set this field to zero.

To move objects in front of or behind other objects, use the Paste In Front and Paste In Back options, or the Bring To Front and Send To Back options, all of which are in the Edit menu. To move an object into the center of the active window, use the Paste option.

Changing Segments and Moving Points

In addition to using the selection tool for moving an entire object without changing it, you can use the tool to change or modify an object by moving one or more of its component parts (i.e., anchor points, direction points, straight line segments, and curve segments). The program gives you a great deal of flexibility to change objects — you can draw shapes roughly with the freehand tool and come back later and fine-tune the drawing with the selection tool.

Adobe Illustrator 88 lets you reshape an object a variety of different ways depending on how the object is selected (see Figures 5-7, 5-8, and 5-9). An object must be selected before it can be manipulated or modified. Only objects in the artwork window can be selected; the template or preview can't be selected.

Normally, if you point within two pixels of an object or several objects (*pixels* are dots on the screen), the topmost object will be selected and all other objects will be deselected. If you point to a location more than two pixels away from any object and click the mouse, all objects will be deselected. If you want the feature that selects anything within two pixels of the arrow to be turned off, select the Snap to Point feature in the Preferences dialog box (described with the Edit menu later in this chapter).

The main techniques used for manipulating objects with the selection tool are moving points or segments. You can move anchor

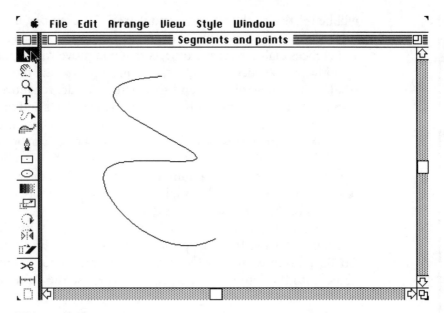

Figure 5-7.
An path consisting of curve segments that is not selected.

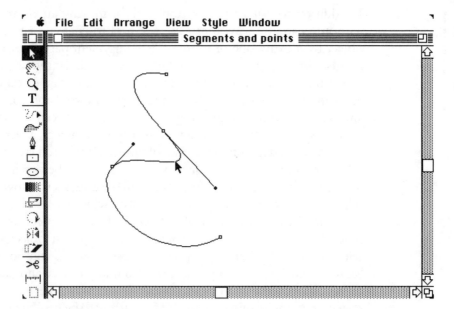

Figure 5-8.
Selecting a curve segment. The program displays endpoints and direction points for manipulating the curve.

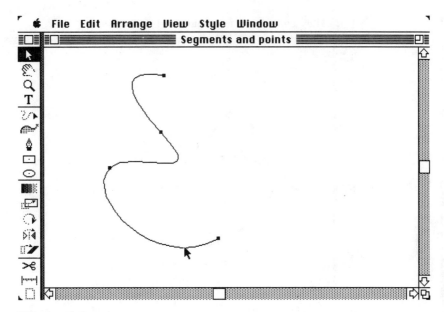

Figure 5-9.
The path selected as a whole by holding down the Option key while clicking on the path. Anchor points, corner points, and endpoints are shown, but not direction points.

points, direction points, corner points, and straight line and curve segments. For making adjustments, the Join and Average commands on the Arrange menu are useful in addition to the selection tool, since these two commands let you move anchor points or endpoints together and join any two of them with a line segment. Join and Average are described later in this chapter with the Arrange menu.

The scissors tool is also helpful — it lets you cut segments in two, and lets you add anchor points to a segment without cutting it. Any segment, or group of segments, can be modified with the scale, rotate, reflect and shear tools. The combination of these tools, commands, and techniques allows excellent control over very precise modifications of the artwork — a luxury not provided with traditional pen and ink.

To move anchor points and endpoints with the selection tool, first select the point or points you want to move, then position the arrow on one of the selected anchor points and drag the point to a new location (Figure 5-10). As you drag the mouse you will notice that any lines or curves attached to any points moved will also change as

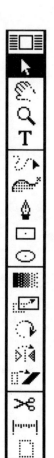

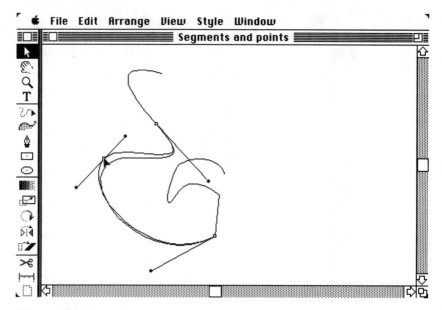

Figure 5-10.
Dragging an anchor point alters the shape of the curve without changing its direction; its original shape remains displayed until you release the mouse button.

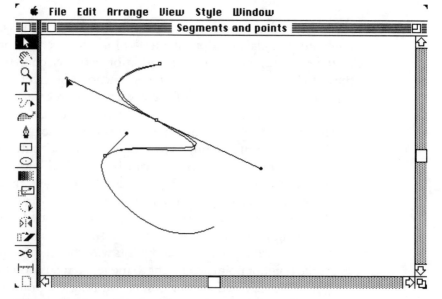

Figure 5-11.
Dragging a direction point alters the shape of the curve without changing its points.

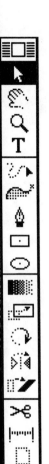

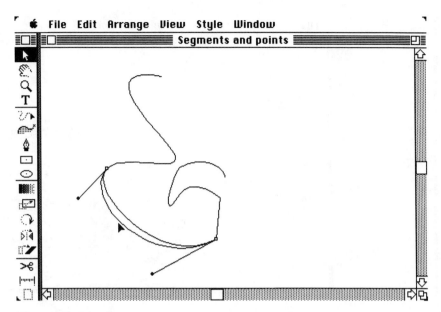

Figure 5-12.
Selecting and moving a curve segment without changing its points.

you move them. The curves will change in a way that will keep the curve directions constant at the anchor points that are being moved.

The previous location and shape of the curve is displayed as well as the new location and shape. To move direction points with the selection tool, first select an anchor point (or an adjacent segment) whose direction point you want to move. Next, point to the direction point that you want to adjust and drag the direction point with the mouse to change the curve of the segment or segments that are connected to the anchor point whose direction point you are moving (Figure 5-11).

To move the line or curve segment itself, select the segment you want to modify, point to an area on the selected segment that is between its anchor points, and drag the segment. As you drag the segment you will notice that any other selected segments also change shape, and the associated direction points move in accordance with the drag, but the selected segments' anchor points remain fixed (see Figure 5-12).

If you select an anchor point by clicking on it, you will also select any segments that are connected to it. If two anchor points are on top of each other, only the topmost anchor point will be selected by clicking on it. To select an anchor point and all the points underneath

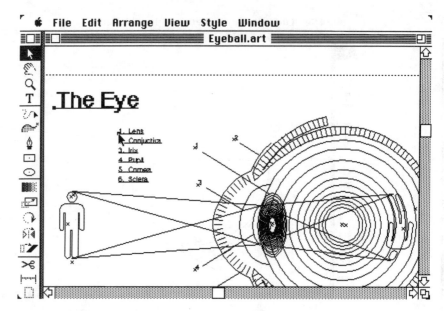

Figure 5-13.
Selecting text by clicking the x mark with the selection tool; holding down Shift lets you select more than one object. Selected text appears with baselines and an alignment point.

it, drag the selection marquee around the points. When an anchor point (or endpoint) is selected, it appears as a solid black square, and all the other anchor points in the object are also displayed. Anchor points that are not selected appear as hollow squares, except for endpoints, which appear as x symbols.

If you select a curved segment, no anchor points will be selected, but the direction points associated with the curved segment will appear as solid black circles (see Figure 5-8). If you select a straight line segment, the direction points will not be displayed since they would be on top of the segment's anchor points.

When you select an entire path by either dragging the selection marquee around it or by pointing to it, holding down the Option key, and clicking the mouse, all the anchor points will be selected, and no direction points will be displayed (see Figure 5-9, a selected path). To select type, point to the "x" symbol in the baseline of the text and click (see Figure 5-13). If several blocks of type are on top of each other, the topmost block of type will be selected. If you use the selection marquee to select type, all the type blocks whose baselines fall even partially within the marquee will be selected.

Selection Tool Summary

(selection tool) + click
Selects the item you are pointing at.

+ Shift key + click
If you hold down the Shift key while you are clicking the mouse or before you start to drag with the mouse, it will extend (or reduce) your selection.

+ Option key + point to path + click
If, while holding down the Option key, you point to a path and click the mouse, the entire path will be selected.

Option key + click (selection tool)
Gets Move dialog box for specifying precise movement.

+ Shift key + drag
If you hold down the Shift key after you have started to drag something with the mouse, it will constrain the motion of the object or objects being dragged to horizontal movement (movement along the x axis), vertical movement (along the y axis), or movement in 45-degree increments (relative to the x and y axes).

+ Option key + drag
Clones (creates duplicates of) all selected objects.

Command Key
Temporarily converts the tool you are using into the selection tool.

Hand Tool

 The hand tool is primarily for scrolling an illustration within an active window. Although you can also scroll the document with the scroll bars on the right and bottom sides of the window, the hand tool gives you more precise control over scrolling.

To use the hand tool, click its icon in the toolbox. The pointer turns into a hand when you move it back into the active window (Figure 5-14). Next, place the hand over the illustration and drag in the direction you want to move it. The artwork doesn't move, but the active window does move to show the object.

Another way to use the hand tool is to press the space bar while using any other tool. Whatever tool you are using changes into the hand tool while you are holding down the space bar, then changes back to the appropriate tool as soon as you release the space bar. This shortcut is handy for moving the window since you don't have to go back to the toolbox and switch tools.

Hand Tool Summary

+ drag
Moves the document around within the active window.

Space bar + drag
Temporarily converts the current tool into the hand tool for moving the document within the active window while using another tool.

Double-click + point to
Displays the entire document in the active window regardless of window size. This is a shortcut for the Fit In Window option in the View menu.

Option key + Double-click + point to
Displays the document at actual size in the active window. This is a shortcut for the Actual Size option in the View menu.

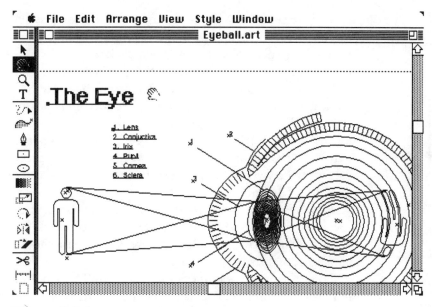

Figure 5-14.
You can move an illustration within the active window with the hand tool.

Zoom Tool

The zoom tool is for zooming into or out from the actual size view of the active window. Zooming in lets you inspect the detail of your artwork; zooming out lets you take a step back and see the big picture.

To zoom into an area of your artwork, click the magnifying glass icon in the toolbox. The pointer changes to a magnifying glass with a plus sign (+) in its center when you move it into the active window. The plus sign indicates that the zoom tool will enlarge your view when you click it anywhere in the active window, showing more detail. This is called zooming in. Be sure to place the magnifying glass on top of an area of the artwork that you want to see. Each click enlarges your view of that area by a factor of two until you reach the largest possible magnification level (1600 percent of the actual size). When you reach that point, the plus sign disappears from the center of the magnifying glass.

To zoom out, hold down the Option key after selecting the zoom tool. The plus sign changes to a minus (-) sign, indicating that the

tool will reduce your view of the artwork and show less detail. As long as you hold down the Option key while clicking, you will reduce rather than enlarge your view. Each click reduces by a factor of two until you reach the smallest reduction (6.75 percent). At the smallest reduction, the minus sign disappears from the center of the magnifying glass indicating that no further reduction is possible.

A document can be viewed at nine different zoom levels as shown in Figures 5-15 through 5-23, ranging from 6.75 percent to 1600 percent. The artwork size is not changed by the zoom tool, only your view of the artwork changes. To change the size of artwork, use the scale tool (described later).

To view the artwork at its actual size, either select Actual Size from the View menu, type Command-H, or double-click the hand tool while holding down the Option key. All three methods change the view to actual size.

To fit the entire document (a 14-inch by 14-inch drawing space) in the active window, you can select the Fit In Window option from the View menu, type Command-M, or double-click the hand tool. Any of these commands also center the drawing space in the window, although your artwork may not be in the center of the drawing space.

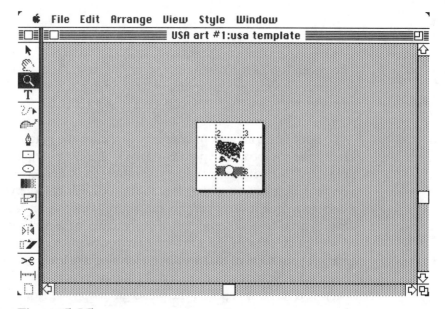

Figure 5-15.
A document viewed at the most reduced zoom level, which is 6.7 percent of the artwork's actual size. Zooming in or out does not change the size of the artwork, only the view.

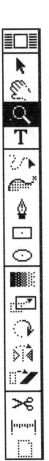

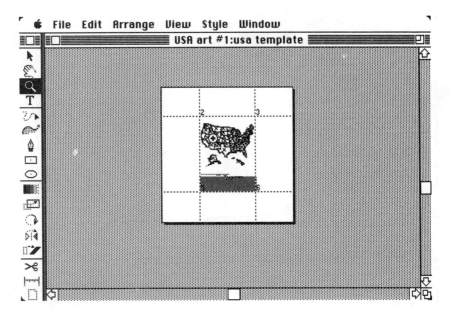

Figure 5-16.
Zooming into the document from the previous figure, now viewed at 12.5 percent of the artwork's actual size.

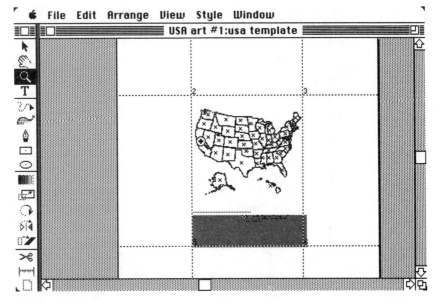

Figure 5-17.
Zooming into the document from the previous figure, now viewed at 25 percent of the artwork's actual size.

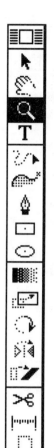

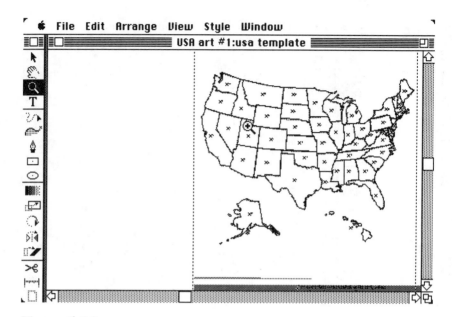

Figure 5-18.
Zooming into the document from the previous figure, now viewed at 50 percent of the artwork's actual size.

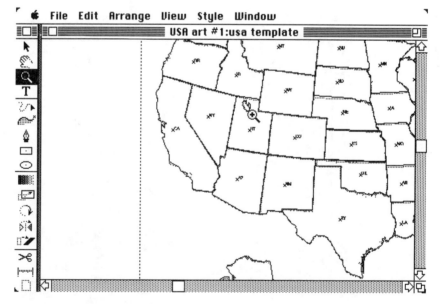

Figure 5-19.
Zooming into the document from the previous figure, now viewed at the artwork's actual size.

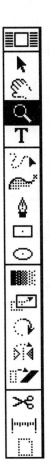

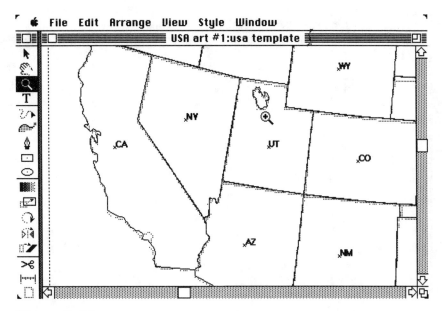

Figure 5-20.
Zooming into the document from the previous figure, now viewed at 200 percent of the artwork's actual size.

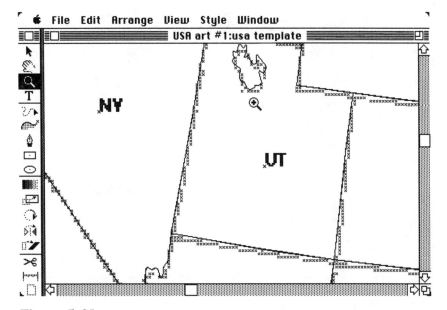

Figure 5-21.
Zooming into the document from the previous figure, now viewed at 400 percent of the artwork's actual size.

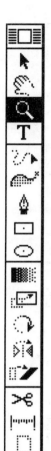

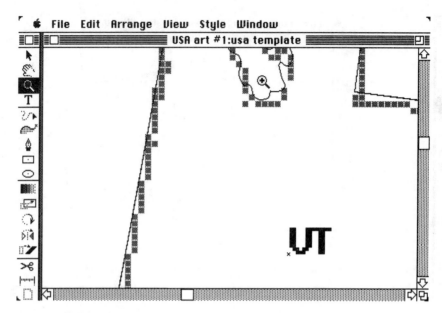

Figure 5-22.
Zooming into the document from the previous figure, now viewed at 800 percent of the artwork's actual size.

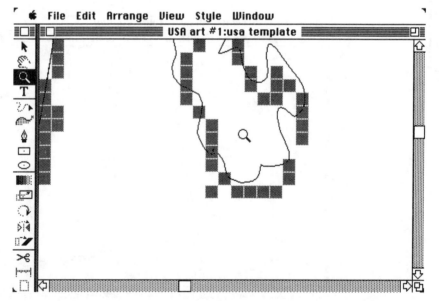

Figure 5-23.
Zooming into the document from the previous figure, now viewed at 1600 percent of the artwork's actual size. Each square is equal to one pixel of a MacPaint document (at 72 pixels per inch).

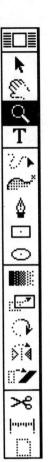

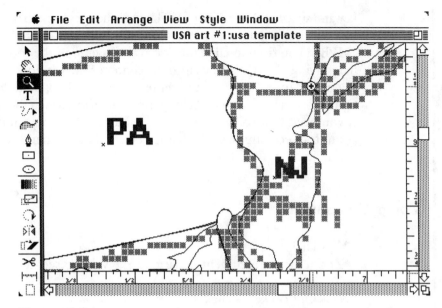

Figure 5-24.
The Show Rulers option in the View menu displays rulers that are calibrated to the measure selected in the Preferences dialog box (by default, inches).

If you open a template but don't see the image in your active window, try the Fit In Window option, then use the zoom tool to zoom into the template image.

The zoom tool also affects the rulers that can be displayed in a window. To display rulers, select the Show Rulers option from the View menu, or type Command-R. Two rulers will appear — one along the bottom of the active window and the other on the right side of the window (Figure 5-24). As you zoom in or out, the ruler tick marks change to provide a more detailed or less detailed ruler. To remove the rulers from view, choose Hide Rulers from the View menu (the Hide Rulers option takes the place of Show Rulers when the rulers are displayed). You can also type Command-R again, which acts as a toggle switch for turning the ruler display on or off.

The program offers a quick way to zoom in or out while you are using another tool (without having to go back to the toolbox to switch tools). Hold down Command key and the space bar simultaneously when using another tool. Whatever tool you are using changes into the zoom tool while you are holding down the Command key and space bar. You can click to zoom in, or use another finger to hold down the Option (key as well as the Command

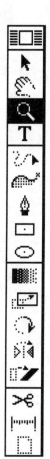

key and space bar) to zoom out. The tool changes back to the original tool as soon as you release the Command key and space bar.

When you double-click the zoom tool's icon in the toolbox (the magnifying glass), it zooms into the center of the window. Similarly, to quickly zoom out from the center of the window, hold down the Option key while double-clicking the zoom tool icon in the toolbox. If you need to scroll and zoom at the same time, you can drag the zoom tool continuously so that it behaves like the hand tool while zooming.

Zoom Tool Summary

+ click
Zoom into a document, enlarging the view to see details.

+ Option key + click
Zoom out from a document, reducing the view to see the big picture.

+ drag
Zoom in and scroll at the same time.

+ Option key + drag
Zoom out and scroll at the same time.

Double-click + point to
Zoom into the center of the window.

Option key + Double-click + point to
Zoom out from the center of the window.

Command key + Space bar + click
Temporarily converts the current tool into the zoom tool for zooming into the document while using another tool.

Command key + Option key + Space bar + click
Temporarily converts the current tool into the zoom tool for zooming out from the document while using another tool.

Command key + Space bar + drag

Temporarily converts the current tool into the zoom tool for zooming into and scrolling the document within the active window while using another tool.

Type Tool

The type tool allows you to incorporate text and typography in your artwork. Any PostScript typeface that is installed on your PostScript printer or typesetting machine will work with the type tool. You use the type tool to add new type and set the type specifications and alignment, and you use the Type option in the Style menu to edit the type and change these specifications.

Adobe Illustrator 88 treats a block of type as a single object that can be manipulated in the same way as any other artwork, except that type can't be blended with the blend tool. (Plate 7, "Swan," and Plate 8, "Violin," use Encapsulated PostScript art from the Adobe Collector's Edition I for the "S" and "V" characters that are blended into a swan and violin, respectively. You can draw characters rather than typing them with the text tool.)

Manipulating type that you create with the type tool is useful for creating such things as typographic design elements, logos, and special headlines. Special text effects can be achieved by rotating, reflecting, scaling, shearing, painting, or stroking type.

The baseline for the text is aligned with the coordinates of Illustrator's current x and y axes, so if you have altered the x and y axes by setting a Constrain angle, the baseline of the text is aligned relative to the new x and y axes. For example, if you have rotated the x and y axes by setting the Constrain angle to 30 degrees (in the Preferences dialog box, available from the Edit menu), any text blocks you create will be drawn at a 30-degree angle.

If your type is not at the angle you want, check the alignment of the x and y axes by looking at the Constrain angle in the dialog box that appears after you select the Preferences command on the Edit menu (Command-K).

Creating Type

To create a block of type, first click the type tool in the toolbox. When you move it into the active window, the pointer changes to the text

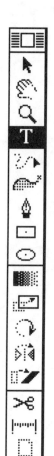

placement cursor, shaped like an I-beam with a small horizontal line slightly above the bottom to represent the baseline of the first line of type that you will create (Figure 5-25). (If your view is set to Preview Illustration, the pointer will remain an arrow, and not change to an I beam, because you can't edit the Preview Illustration view. This tool can be used in the Artwork and Template view, or the Artwork Only view; selected from the View menu.)

Next, place the text placement cursor at the position where you want the first line of type to begin and click. This places the text alignment point in the Illustrator document and brings up the Type dialog box (Figure 5-26). Enter the text you want placed in your Illustrator document into the text entry window in the Type dialog box (see Figure 5-27).

Two important things to keep in mind about entering text in the Type dialog box: you must put Returns at the end of lines, and you are limited to 254 characters of text per text block. Long sections of text must be broken down into smaller blocks of 254 characters or less.

Text can be edited in the Type dialog box using the standard Cut (Command-X), Copy (Command-C), Paste (Command-V), or

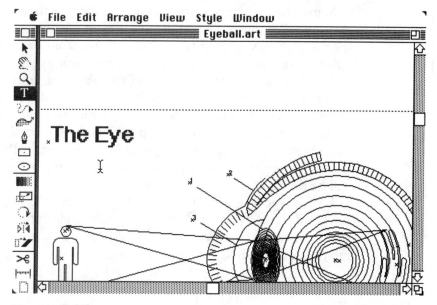

Figure 5-25.
The text placement (I-beam) pointer has a notch to show where the type baseline will appear when you click the text tool.

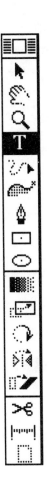

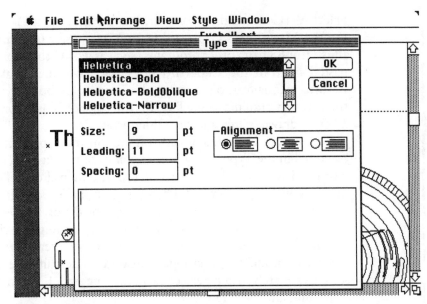

Figure 5-26.
The Type dialog box (after clicking the I-beam pointer), with font, size, spacing, and alignment settings but no text.

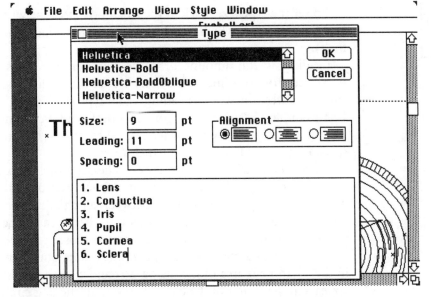

Figure 5-27.
Typing text into the Type dialog box.

Select All (Command-A) commands in the Edit menu. You can also use the Macintosh's Clipboard feature to transfer text into Adobe Illustrator 88 from other programs (such as word processors). If text pasted in from the Clipboard does not have line breaks, insert Returns manually into the text in the Type dialog box. If you don't, the text may run in a single line, off the edge of Illustrator's 14-by-14-inch drawing area and be hidden from view.

Text cannot be edited directly on the Illustrator page, it can only be edited in the Type dialog box. If you want to edit type, select the type block to edit with the selection tool and then choose Type from the Style menu (Command-T) to bring up the Type dialog box.

In addition to typing the text, in the Type dialog box you set the type attributes, such as typeface, type size, leading, spacing, and alignment. Set these attributes either when you create new type or when you modify existing type. Illustrator's default type attribute settings are Helvetica typeface, 12-point type size, 12-point leading, 0 spacing, and left alignment.

To set the typeface of selected text, choose from among the typefaces listed in the scroll box located in the upper left-hand region of the Type dialog box. The scroll bar on the right side of the scroll box lets you scroll through the available typefaces if there are more than will fit into the scroll box.

To set the type size, click in the small box after the word "Size:" and type the size, which is measured in points (one point = 1/72 inch).

Leading is the amount of space between the lines of type, measured from baseline to baseline. To set the leading, click in the small box after the word "Leading:" and type the leading in points. For example, 12-point type on 12-point leading is the default setting, but if you increase the leading to 14 points, the lines will be spaced 2 points (1/36 inch) further apart.

To set the spacing between letters, click the small box after the word "Spacing:" and type the amount of spacing (in points). Spacing determines the measure of space between all characters in the type block; typing a positive number adds space between characters, and typing a negative number brings characters closer together.

To set the alignment of the type, point to one of the small circles in the Alignment area of the dialog box and click; a small black dot appears in the center of the circle. Clicking in the first circle (and its accompanying image of a paragraph) selects left alignment (flush left, ragged right); clicking in the second circle selects center alignment

(each line centered under the next within the text block); and clicking on the third circle selects right alignment (flush right, ragged left).

Type can't be justified (flush left and flush right), but the Spacing control can be used to achieve a justified effect. For example, in Plate 5, the spacing was set to 5 points for the title "ORGANIZATIONAL CHART."

An alignment point appears in the baseline of the type at the left end if the type is left-justified, at the right end if it is right-justified, or in the center if it is centered. This alignment point can be moved by the selection tool (along with the attached baseline) so that you can align the type to an exact point in the artwork.

To modify the attributes of existing type, select one or more blocks of type with the selection tool and then choose Type from the Style menu (Command-T); this will bring up the Type dialog box. If you selected more than one block of text, attributes in common are displayed, but the text is not visible in the text editing block.

Type Tool Summary

You use the type tool to add new type and set the type specifications and alignment, and you use the Type option in the Style menu to edit the type and change these specifications.

Special text effects can be achieved by using the rotate, reflect, scale, and shear tools, and painting and stroking type in the Paint dialog box. If you altered the x and y axes by setting a Constrain angle, the baseline of the text is aligned to the new x and y axes.

When typing text in the Type dialog box, you must put Returns at the end of lines, and you are limited to 254 characters of text per text block. Long sections of text must be broken down into smaller blocks of 254 characters or less.

Command key + K
Activate the Preferences dialog box to check or change the constrain angle that governs the angle of the type baseline.

Command key + T
Activate the Type dialog box to edit a selected block of text and change the type specifications and alignment.

Freehand Tool

The freehand tool is used to draw curves with a free hand, without constraints of any kind. The freehand tool in Adobe Illustrator 88 is similar to the drawing tools found in other graphics programs. You can switch freely among the selection tool, the pen tool, and the freehand tool while drawing an object, making Adobe Illustrator 88 more powerful than most drawing programs.

The freehand tool creates a straight line or curve based on the actual movement of the mouse (or stylus or trackball)— you draw with the mouse as if it were a pencil or paintbrush. Use the Control Panel to adjust the mouse to be less sensitive to variations in your hand movement when sketching, to make it a more natural activity, or use a graphics tablet and stylus.

To draw with the freehand tool, first select the freehand tool by clicking its icon in the toolbox, then position the x marker at the place where you want to start drawing. As you drag this marker, it turns into an arrowhead pointer and leaves behind a dotted line. The faster you drag, the fewer dots are created (Figure 5-28). The tool creates

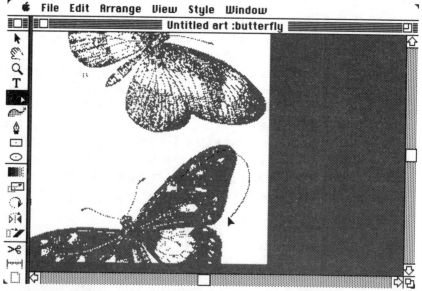

Figure 5-28.
Drawing with the freehand tool around a template. The faster you drag, the less points are created.

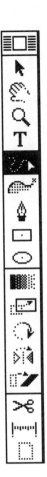

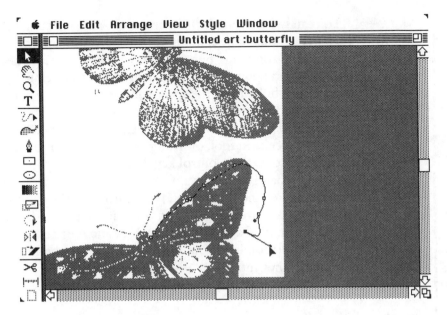

Figure 5-29.
*The freehand tool turns a sketch into a path with points and curve
segments that you can manipulate with the selection tool.*

a normal path with points and curve segments that you can manipulate with the selection tool (Figure 5-29).

The freehand tool responds to shakiness or other slight variations
in your drawing motion, creating bumps. You can set the freehand
tolerance level to reduce (or increase) the number of bumps by
choosing the Preferences option from the Edit menu. The default
setting for the freehand tolerance level is two pixels, which means
that a variation of two pixels will not create a bump.

You can erase any part of the dotted line while you are drawing by
holding down the Command key and dragging back over the line.
However, you can only erase the line if you have not yet released the
mouse button. You can always delete a straight line or curve segment
by selecting it and pressing the Delete or Backspace key.

You can stop drawing freehand at any point, and continue drawing
freehand or use the pen tool to continue the path, by starting at the
endpoint. To create a closed path, keep drawing with the freehand
tool (or establishing points with the pen tool) until you reach the
starting point of the path.

You can switch from the freehand tool to the selection tool to edit the curve segments by holding down the Command key. You can switch to the zoom tool by holding down the Command key and the space bar, and zoom in or hold down Option as well to zoom out. You can also hold down the space bar to switch to the hand tool for scrolling while drawing.

If you are using a Macintosh SE or II, you can switch from the pen tool to the freehand tool, or from the freehand tool to the pen tool, by holding down the Control key. For example, if you are drawing with the freehand tool and want to switch to the pen tool, hold down the Control key and the freehand tool turns into the pen tool. If you are drawing with the pen tool and you want to use the freehand tool for a segment, hold down the Control key and the pen tool turns into the freehand tool. The combination of tools is the most versatile method of drawing.

Freehand Tool Summary

The freehand tool is used to draw curves with a free hand. The freehand tool creates a line or curve based on the actual movement of the mouse — the faster you drag, the fewer dots are created in the path.

✕ + Command key
   Temporarily converts the freehand tool into the selection tool.

✕ + Space bar + drag
   Temporarily converts the freehand tool into the hand tool for moving the document within the active window while drawing.

✕ + Command key + Space bar + click
   Temporarily converts the current tool into the zoom tool for zooming into the document while using another tool.

✕ + Command key + Option key + Space bar + click
   Temporarily converts the current tool into the zoom tool for zooming out from the document while using another tool.

✕ + Control key
   Switch to the pen tool (Macintosh SE and II keyboards only).

Command key + K
Activate the Preferences dialog box to set the freehand tool's tolerance level (default is two pixels).

Command key + drag over previous drawing
To erase any part of the dotted line while you are drawing.

Auto Trace Tool

✕

The auto trace tool automatically traces outlines of shapes in a scanned image used as a template, so that you can start with shapes already drawn.

To make use of a template for tracing, you can first sketch the rough image on paper and use an inexpensive desktop scanner to scan the image into the computer for use as a template. You can also use other painting and drawing programs on your Macintosh (notably MacPaint, MacDraw, or other programs that can create MacPaint

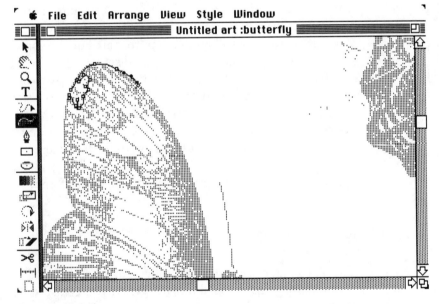

Figure 5-30.
With the auto trace tool selected, you can drag across an area to establish starting and ending points of the automatic trace, rather than tracing the entire shape. The result of dragging across the butterfly's wing tip is a series of curve segments.

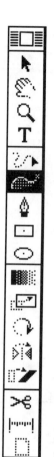

documents) to create or modify a template for use with Adobe Illustrator 88.

Once you have the template image in a MacPaint file (either scanned or painted with a program), you can display the template as a gray-filled background image while the program traces straight lines, curves, and shapes. You can at any time display only what you've drawn, only the template, or both. You can even see a preview of exactly how the artwork will look when printed.

To use the auto tracing feature, first click the auto trace tool icon in the toolbox, then click a starting point near the edge of the scanned shape to be traced. (If your view is set to Preview Illustration, the pointer will remain an arrow, because you can't use the auto scale tool in the Preview Illustration view. This tool is best used in the Artwork and Template view selected from the View menu.)

The program draws an outline around the shape and returns to the starting point. The automatic tracing tool works best with closed shapes, but it may treat a line as a closed shape rather than as a line.

Scanned images and bit-mapped graphics sometimes have gaps that are visible when you enlarge your view with the zoom tool. To control the accuracy with which the auto trace tool creates shapes, you can set the auto trace gap distance in the Preferences dialog box. The auto trace tool will ignore gaps that are equal to or less than the number of pixels you specify for the distance.

The auto trace tool can draw entire paths or parts of a path. To automatically trace a partial path, drag across from the starting point to the desired ending point (Figure 5-30) rather than clicking a starting point. You can also draw a corner with the auto trace tool by clicking on an anchor point of an existing path where you want the corner point to be, and while holding down the Option key, dragging to the area where you want the path to end.

Auto Trace Tool Summary

The auto trace tool automatically traces outlines of shapes in a scanned image used as a template. When you click a starting point, the program draws an outline around the shape and returns to the starting point. When you drag across an area to establish starting and ending points, the program draws a partial outline.

X + click anchor point + Option key + drag

Automatically draw a corner with the auto trace tool, establishing a corner point at the anchor point.

Command key + K

Activate the Preferences dialog box to set the auto trace gap distance(default is zero pixels).

Pen Tool

X   You use the pen tool to create points, curves, and lines. Although the freehand tool also creates points, straight lines, and curve segments, and is similar to the drawing tools found in other graphics programs, the pen tool is not the same. The pen tool does not draw lines — you use it to establish points for the program to precisely draw the straight line or curve segment to connect the points.

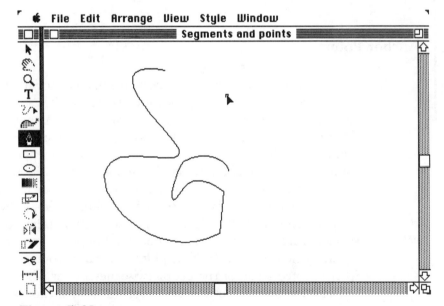

Figure 5-31.
After clicking the pen tool, the pointer turns into an x. Click an end-point to start the line segment, and the pointer turns into an arrowhead briefly, then into a plus (+) sign to indicate that a path is being created.

The process of drawing with the pen tool is more like a connect-the-dots puzzle. Rather than drawing freehand so that the lines and curves reflect the actual mouse movement while drawing (as with the freehand tool), you click points and the program draws the lines and curves accurately between the points. To control the directions and shapes of curves, you drag with the pen tool while establishing points, and you can later select points or curve segments with the selection tool. You can switch from the pen tool to the selection tool in order to move the points, lines, and direction pointers to change the shape of a curve, then switch back to the pen and continue establishing more points.

You can build an entire illustration by establishing the points along a path with the pen tool, linking those points with straight lines (by clicking without dragging) or curves (by dragging). Since the pen tool does not literally translate your mouse movements into lines and curves in a freehand style (which may produce a lot of bumps if you have an unsteady hand), you can use the pen tool to make accurate lines and curves without any drawing skill.

Anchor Points

The pen tool is mostly used to place points that link together straight line and curve segments or define the ends of paths. These points that the pen tool can establish are called anchor points. An anchor point determines the starting and ending point of any straight line or curve segment. Anchor points are invisible unless any segment of the path formed by the segments is selected. A single anchor point that has no line or curve segment attached to it appears as an x when not selected.

Endpoints are a special case of anchor points, defining the beginning and end of a path, which can consist of straight line and curve segments linked by regular anchor points. Endpoints appear as black squares when selected (anchor points appear as round black dots when selected as part of a path, otherwise they appear as hollow dots).

Direction points, which seem to sprout from anchor points that define an end of a curve segment, control the direction that a curve segment is going from the anchor point. Each anchor point has two direction points associated with it, although if the anchor point links a straight line to a curve, one of those points is not visible (it is behind the straight line). When you select a curve segment, a direction point at each end becomes visible (as shown in Figure 5-8, in the

description of the selection tool). When you select the next curve, the other direction point associated with the common anchor point is displayed (see Figure 5-12, also in the section on the selection tool). The shape of the curve can be changed by moving those direction points with the selection tool.

A smooth point is an anchor point that connects two curve segments whose direction points point in the same direction (there is no sharp turn in direction). A corner point, on the other hand, is an anchor point that connects two curve segments, two straight line segments, or a curve and a line segment in such a way that the direction points point in different directions, forming a sharp turn.

Lines, Curves, and Paths

There are two types of segments in Adobe Illustrator 88: straight lines and Bézier curves. All artwork is fashioned from these segments. Ovals and circles are actually drawn with curve segments and can be ungrouped into individual segments. Segments start and end with anchor points.

Unless the segment is a straight line, the segment's curvature is determined by two direction points connected to the anchor points by tangent lines. Direction points and associated tangent lines are invisible when not selected (they also do not print).

A path is either a solitary anchor point, a solitary segment, or a group of connected segments. A path is open if it starts at a distinct endpoint and ends at another distinct endpoint. A path is closed if the starting and ending point are the same point. The difference between a closed and an open path is important when painting paths; you can get white streaks in an object if the path is not properly closed because the program draws an imaginary line from the two endpoints of an open path in order to paint the path.

Drawing With the Pen Tool

To begin drawing a segment, click the pen tool icon in the toolbox. The pointer turns into an x when you move it into the active window. Next, click an endpoint in your drawing space to start the segment (Figure 5-31). The pointer changes to a plus (+) sign indicating that a path is under construction. (If your view is set in the View menu to

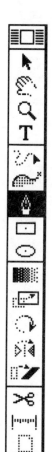

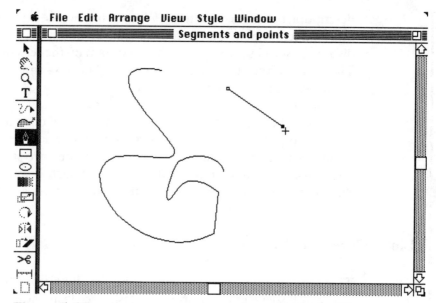

Figure 5-32.
After clicking the second point (an anchor point), the program draws a straight line between the two points. You can continue to add line segments to the path by clicking more anchor points.

Preview Illustration, the pointer will remain an arrow, and not change to a plus sign, because you can't edit the Preview Illustration view. This tool can be used in the Artwork and Template view, or the Artwork Only view; selected from the View menu.)

To draw a straight line, click another point where you want this line segment to end. The program automatically draws a straight line (Figure 5-32), and the pointer remains a plus (+) sign. You can click another point and draw another straight line, which is added to the path. Each point is an anchor point, and you have one endpoint on the path.

If you drag rather than click a point, the program draws a curve. As you begin dragging the mouse, the program creates an anchor point, the pointer changes to an arrowhead, and direction points appear in the direction of your dragging (Figure 5-33). The curve changes shape as you drag the direction points (Figure 5-34).

When you release the mouse, the pointer changes back to the plus (+) sign to indicate that you can add more segments to the path. You can continue to add curve segments to the path by dragging new points; each time you drag an anchor point, a curve is drawn with

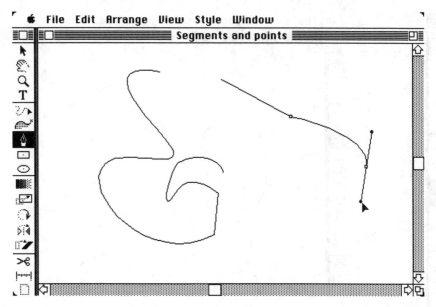

Figure 5-33.
*As you drag, a curve is drawn to link that point with the previous
anchor point, the pointer changes to an arrowhead, and direction points
appear in the direction of your dragging.*

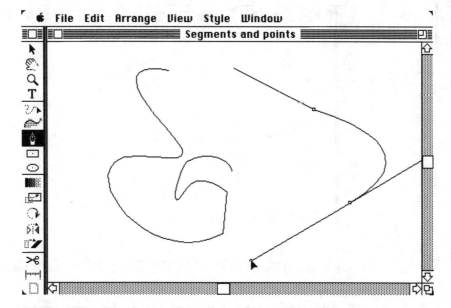

Figure 5-34.
The curve changes shape as you drag the direction points.

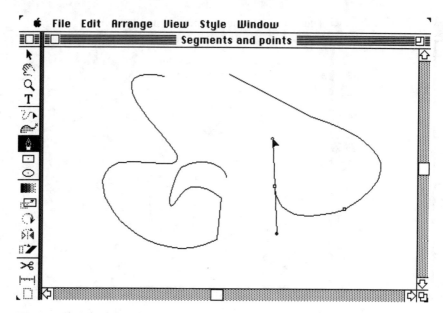

Figure 5-35.
Extending the path with another curve segment by dragging to establish another anchor point. The anchor points in this path are smooth.

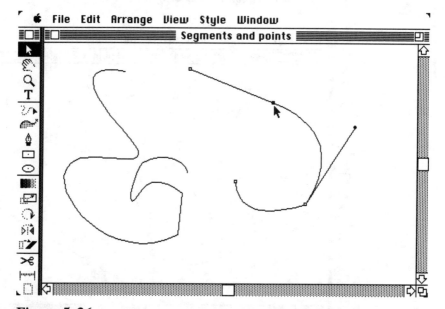

Figure 5-36.
The anchor point between the straight line and curve segments does not have a direction point because it is a special form of a corner point, dedicated to the direction of the straight line.

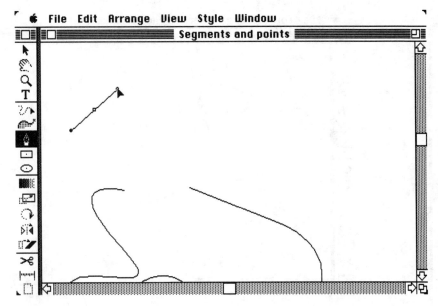

Figure 5-37.
To start a path with a curve going in a particular direction, drag the
first endpoint in that direction to establish the direction point for the
endpoint.

direction points attached to the anchor points (Figure 5-35). Each
anchor point is a smooth point.

Note, however, that the anchor point between the straight line
and curve segments does not have a direction point (Figure 5-36).
This is because that point is a special form of a corner point, dedicated
to the direction established by the straight line. To start drawing a
curved path, you should start by dragging the first endpoint (Figure
5-37), so that the first point also has direction points (Figure 5-38).

You need to create corner points to make an angled or sharp turn
of direction between curves or to join a straight line to a curve. To
add a corner point and change the direction sharply for the next
curve, hold down the Option key and either drag (to create another
curve segment) or click (to create a straight line segment) to start the
segment from that anchor point (Figure 5-39). When you release the
mouse and Option key, the anchor point turns into a corner point.
If you drag the next anchor point (Figure 5-40), the curve is shaped
by the corner point's direction point. Hold down the Option key
while clicking or dragging an anchor point if you want the point to
act as a corner point.

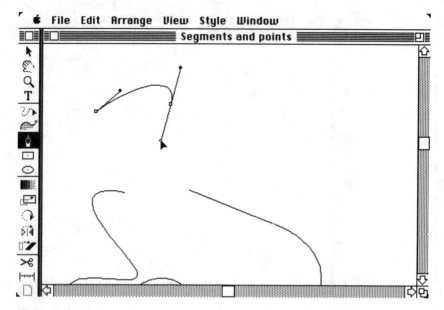

Figure 5-38.
Drag the next anchor point in the same general direction, moving the direction point to alter the shape of the curve. You can continue to add curve segments by dragging more anchor points.

To close a path and make it a solid object, click or drag the last anchor point of the path in the same location as the first endpoint, completing a loop. The pointer changes to an x to show that a path has been completed and the tool is ready to create another path.

To stop drawing an open path, simply click the pen tool or any other tool in the toolbox, and the pointer will change. If you click the pen tool, the pointer changes to an x so that you can start drawing a new path.

To extend an existing open path, click (to extend with a straight line) or drag (to extend with a curve) an endpoint of the path, holding down the Option key if you want the point to act as a corner point, or without Option to have the point act as a smooth point. The pointer should turn into a plus (+) sign. Then click or drag another anchor point to make a new segment. The new segment and further segments connected to it become part of the path.

When drawing straight lines with the pen tool, if you hold down the Shift key when clicking the anchor point it will constrain the line being drawn horizontally, vertically, or in increments of 45 degrees. If you change the Constrain angle in the Preferences dialog box, the

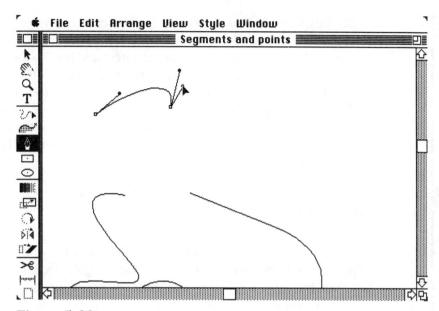

Figure 5-39.
To establish a corner point, hold down the Option key and drag from the anchor point in a new direction.

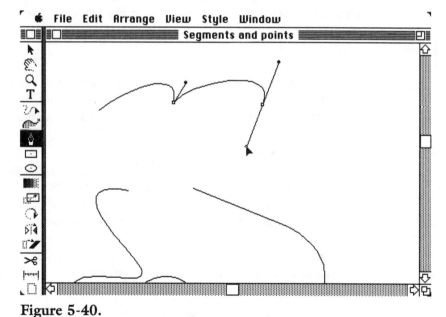

Figure 5-40.
The next curve is shaped by the direction point attached to the corner point as well as the direction point of the new anchor point.

degree of constraining is relative to the new x and y axes.

If you are using a Macintosh SE or II, you can switch from the pen tool to the freehand tool, or from the freehand tool to the pen tool, by holding down the Control key. For example, if you are drawing with the freehand tool and want to switch to the pen tool, hold down the Control key and the freehand tool turns into the pen tool. If you are drawing with the pen tool and you want to use the freehand tool for a segment, hold down the Control key and the pen tool turns into the freehand tool.

Pen Tool Summary

The pen tool puts down anchor points (including endpoints, corner points, and smooth points) for linking segments, and direction points for curve segments. The program draws the straight line or curve segments.

✕ + click

Creates the first anchor point for a straight line if starting a new path or extending a path; or creates a second anchor point and a straight line segment in the new path or in an extension to an existing path.

✕ + drag

Creates the first anchor point for a curve if starting a new path or extending a path; or creates a second anchor point and a curve segment in the new path or in an extension to an existing path.

✕ + Shift key + drag

If you hold down the Shift key while drawing with the pen, it will constrain the line being drawn horizontally (i.e., along the x axis), vertically (along the y axis), or in increments of 45 degrees (relative to the x and y axes set in the Preferences dialog box).

✕ + Option key + drag

Creates a corner point and establishes a new direction for the next segment, thereby changing the direction of the path you are drawing.

✕ + Control key

Switch to the freehand tool (Macintosh SE and II keyboards only).

Rectangle Tool

The rectangle tool is used to create rectangles and squares. Although it is certainly possible to construct rectangles and squares by using the pen tool to draw a path consisting of four straight lines, the rectangle tool is much faster and easier to use for this task, because it also creates a center point for the rectangle or square, and groups it all together as a single object. You can delete the center point if you don't need it, but you must first select the object and use the Ungroup command in the Arrange menu (Command-U).

To begin drawing a rectangle, click the rectangle tool in the toolbox. The arrow pointer will change into a plus sign (+) when you move it into the active window, signifying that you are about to begin drawing an entire path rather than placing an endpoint. (If your view is set to Preview Illustration, the pointer will remain an arrow, and not change to a plus sign, because you can't edit the Preview Illustration view. This tool can be used in the Artwork and Template view, or the Artwork Only view; selected from the View menu.)

Position the (+) pointer where you want one of the corners of the rectangle to be placed. Drag left, right, up, down and diagonally,

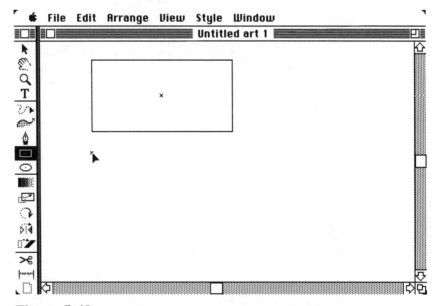

Figure 5-41.
The starting point of a rectangle as it is drawn with the rectangle tool.

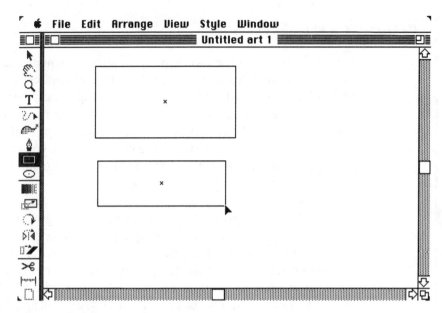

Figure 5-42.
Dragging the rectangle to the size and shape desired.

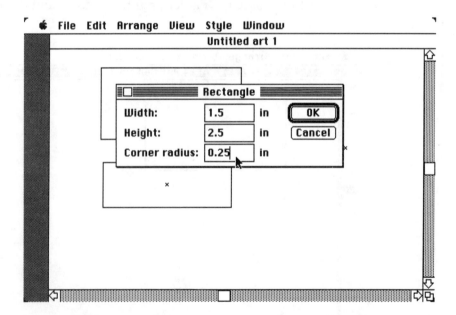

Figure 5-43.
Clicking the center point with the rectangle tool and the Option key to bring up the Rectangle dialog box, which lets you specify dimensions and the corner radius.

until the rectangle is the size and shape you desire. The program changes the (+) pointer into an arrowhead; the point indicates the starting corner of the rectangle (Figure 5-41), and the rectangle forms starting at the point where you began dragging. The pointer moves with the corner diagonally opposite from the original corner (Figure 5-42).

Although the program usually creates a rectangle from corner to corner, you can hold down the Option key as you drag to draw a rectangle from the center point to a corner. The point where you start dragging becomes the center point, and the point where you release the mouse button becomes a corner point.

If you click instead of drag, a center point is placed where you clicked, and the Rectangle dialog box appears so that you can specify dimensions for height and width, and a corner radius (Figure 5-43). If you specify a corner radius, that radius is applied to all new squares or rectangles you draw, until you change it again in the Rectangle dialog box (or change it in the Preferences dialog box). Always specify the corner radius before drawing the rectangle, because you can't apply a new corner radius to an existing rectangle.

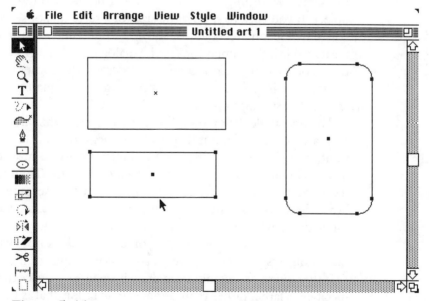

Figure 5-44.
The specified corner dimensions in the Rectangle dialog box draw a round-cornered rectangle. Both the round-cornered rectangle and a 0 corner rectangle are selected, showing corner points and center points.

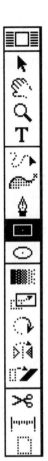

Rectangles created with the rectangle tool are actually two grouped paths. One path consists of the four straight lines that are connected by the four corner points (this is a closed path), and the other path is the center point. The center point is created by the program as a reference point for aligning or manipulating a rectangle. The center point looks like an x when it is not selected, and like a regular small square anchor point when it is selected (Figure 5-44).

Since the center point and the four lines are a group, selecting the center point will also select the lines and vice-versa. You can ungroup the two paths if you want to remove the center point; to do this, select both paths and choose Ungroup from the Arrange menu (or type Command-U).

You create a square the same way that you create a rectangle except that you hold down the Shift key (to constrain the rectangle into a square) while dragging. To construct a square from center to corner, hold down both the Shift and Option keys while dragging.

If you have created a rectangle or square and want to clone it, no matter whether you dragged or clicked to create the first object, you can click where you want the duplicate object's center to be, then press the Return key or click OK when the dialog box appears, and the same size settings you last used will be used to draw the new object. If you click to specify the size for a rectangle or square, then you draw a second rectangle or square by dragging, and then click to create a third, the dimensions in the dialog box represent the size of the second rectangle, not the first. However, the corner radius you set remains in effect for all new rectangles or squares, until you change the setting again in the dialog box.

The Rectangle dialog box allows you to specify the dimensions of a square or rectangle, but if the unit of measure is not the one you want, click Cancel and first use the Preferences option in the Edit menu (Command-K) to change the unit of measure. Then select the rectangle tool and click a center point to get the Rectangle dialog box, where you can specify height and width, and a corner radius, using the newly specified unit of measure. (Changing the unit of measure only affects new objects you draw. It does not change the size of objects previously drawn using another unit of measure.)

If the square or rectangle you draw is small, and the corner radius specified is large, rather than using a circle radius that is too big for the object, the program substitutes the largest circle that can fit inside the square. This effect produces an oval for certain sizes, until the

square or rectangle reaches a large enough size to use the specified corner radius. From that point, no matter how large a square or rectangle you draw, only the specified corner radius is used.

The four sides of any rectangle or square that you draw are aligned with the angle of the current constraining x and y axes, set in the Preferences dialog box. If the Constrain angle setting in the Preferences dialog box in the Edit menu (Command-K) is not 0, the diagonal dragging of the mouse (and therefore the construction of the square or rectangle) is relative to the new x and y axes.

When you change the Constrain angle, the new angle only applies to new objects you draw. For example, if you have rotated the x and y axes by 30 degrees (in the Preferences dialog box, setting the Constrain angle to 30°), then all rectangles and squares will be drawn at a 30-degree angle. If you can't get right angles on your parallelograms, check the alignment of the x and y axes by looking at the Constrain angle setting in the Preferences dialog box (the default setting is zero).

Neither the size nor the angle of constraint for a rectangle or square can be changed after it's drawn. Set the desired angle of constraint before drawing, and don't stop dragging until the size is right.

Or, after drawing it, you can select the object and use the rotate tool to change the angle of rotation, or use the scale tool to change the size of the object. While the object is still selected, you can also fill or stroke (outline) it with black and colors, using the Paint command in the Style menu (Command-I).

Rectangle Tool Summary

+ + drag
   Draws a rectangle from corner to corner as you drag.

+ + Option key + drag
   Draws the rectangle from its center to its corner as you drag, instead of drawing the rectangle from corner to corner.

+ + Shift key + drag
   Draws a square by constraining a rectangle to equal dimensions for height and width as you drag from corner to corner.

+ + Option key + Shift key + drag

Draws a square from center to corner as you drag instead of drawing the square from corner to corner.

+ + click

Establishes a center point and displays a dialog box where you specify precise dimensions for height, width, and corner radius. Use the same number for height and width to create a square. Dimensions remain the same for the next rectangle unless you drag to draw a different-sized rectangle or change the settings in the dialog box.

Oval Tool

+

The oval tool is used to create ovals and circles. Although you can construct ovals and circles by using the pen tool to create a series of connected curves, the oval tool is much faster and easier to use, because it also creates a center point for the oval or circle, and groups it all together as a single object. You can delete the center point if you don't need it, but you must first select the object and use the Ungroup command in the Arrange menu (Command-U).

To draw an oval, click the oval tool in the toolbox. The arrow pointer will change into a plus sign (+) when you move it into the active window, signifying that you are about to begin drawing an entire path rather than placing an endpoint. (However, if your view is set to Preview Illustration, the pointer will remain an arrow, and not change to a plus sign, because you can't edit the Preview Illustration view. This tool can be used in the Artwork and Template view, or the Artwork Only view; selected from the View menu.)

Position the (+) pointer where you want one side of the oval to begin. Drag left, right, up, down and diagonally, until the oval is the size and shape you desire. The program changes the (+) pointer into an arrowhead; the point indicates the starting edge (Figure 5-45), and the oval forms starting at the point where dragging began. The pointer moves as you drag across to the edge on the opposite side; thus the width or height of the oval is the distance between where you began dragging and the current pointer position (Figure 5-46).

Although the way that the oval tool usually creates an oval is from the edge to edge of the perimeter, you can also draw an oval from the center point to an edge. Select the oval tool and hold down the

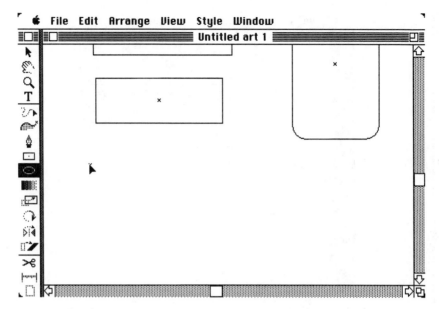

Figure 5-45.
Starting to draw an oval from edge to edge with the oval tool. Hold down the Option key to draw an oval from center to edge.

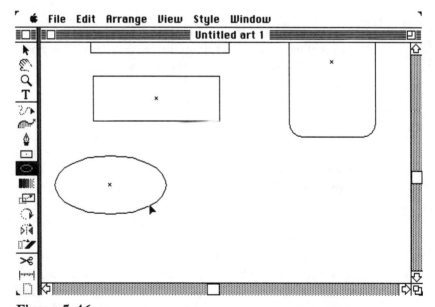

Figure 5-46.
Dragging the edge of the oval (to make a perfect circle, hold down the Shift key while dragging).

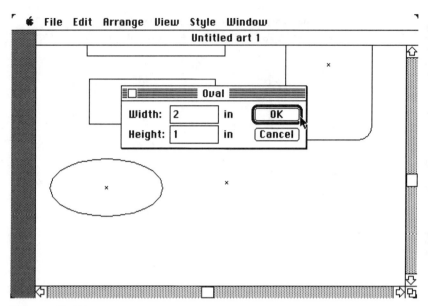

Figure 5-47.
The Oval dialog box lets you specify the dimensions of an oval or circle in width and height. Use the same number for both entries to specify the diameter of a circle.

Option key while dragging to draw an oval from center to edge. The point at which you start dragging becomes the center point, and the point at which you release the mouse button becomes an anchor point at the edge of the oval.

If you click a center point instead of dragging an oval, a center point is placed where you clicked, and the Oval dialog box appears (Figure 5-47) that lets you specify dimensions for height and width of the oval or circle. If the unit of measure is not the one you want, Cancel, and change it in the Preferences dialog box available from the Edit menu (Command-K) to points/picas, inches, or centimeters. (Changing the unit of measure only affects new objects you draw. It does not change the size of objects previously drawn using another Ruler unit setting.)

Ovals or circles created with the oval tool are technically two grouped paths. One path consists of the four curved segments connected by four anchor points (this is a closed path), and the other path is the center point. The center point looks like an x when it is not selected, and like a regular small square anchor point when it is selected. The center point is created by the program as a reference

point for aligning or manipulating an oval.

Since the center point and the four lines are a group, selecting the center point will also select the lines and vice-versa. You can ungroup the paths if you want to cut the oval with the scissors — select the oval and either choose Ungroup from the Arrange menu or type Command-U.

You create a circle the same way you create an oval except that you hold down the Shift key (to constrain the oval into a circle) while dragging up, down, left, right or diagonally, to form a circle from edge to edge. If you hold down both the Option key and the Shift key as you drag, the circle will be constructed from center to edge. To create a circle with the Oval dialog box (activated by clicking rather than dragging with the oval tool), specify the same numbers for both height and width.

As a shortcut, no matter whether you click or drag to draw an oval or circle, if you want to clone it, click at the center point desired for positioning the duplicate object, and then press the Return key or click the OK button when the dialog box appears, and the size settings you last used will be used again to draw the new object. If you click to specify the size for a circle or oval, draw a second circle or oval by dragging, and then click to create a third, the dimensions in the dialog box represent the size of the second object, and not the first.

The four sides of any oval or circle that you draw are aligned with the coordinates of the program's current x and y axes. However, if you have altered the x and y axes by changing the Constrain angle setting in the Preferences dialog box (select the Preferences command from the Edit menu, or use Command-K), the circle or oval is drawn aligned to the new angle of constraint of the x and y axes. If you have altered the x and y axes, the diagonal dragging of the mouse (and therefore the construction of the oval or circle) is relative to the new x and y axes.

When you change the Constrain angle setting, the new angle only applies to new objects you draw. This means that if you have rotated the x and y axes by 30 degrees, any ovals and circles you then create with the oval tool will be drawn at a 30-degree angle.Ovals, circles, rectangles, squares, and type are placed at whatever angle of constraint is specified. If you aren't getting circles when you hold down the Shift key, check the alignment of the x and y axes by looking at the Constrain angle setting in the dialog box that appears after you select the Preferences option in the Edit menu (Command-K). The default setting is zero.

Neither the size nor the angle of constraint for an oval or circle can be changed after it's drawn. Set the desired angle of constraint before drawing, and don't stop dragging until the size is right. Or, after drawing it, you can select the object and use the rotate tool to change the angle of rotation, or use the scale tool to change the size of the object. While the object is still selected, you can also fill or stroke (outline) it with black and colors, using the Paint command in the Style menu (Command-I).

Oval Tool Summary

+ drag
Draws an oval from edge to edge as you drag.

+ Option key + drag
Draws an oval from its center to its edge as you drag instead of drawing it from edge to edge.

+ Shift key + drag
Draws a circle from edge to edge by constraining an oval.

+ Shift key + Option key + drag
Draws a circle from its center to its edge as you drag instead of drawing it from edge to edge.

+ click
Establishes a center point and displays a dialog box where you specify precise dimensions for height and width. Use the same number for height and width to create a circle.

Blend Tool

Adobe Illustrator 88 offers the unique blend tool that can automatically blend one shape into another and one color, gray shade, or tint into another. The blend tool can create a blend of intermediate steps between any two paths or objects, but can't blend typed text. You can use the blend tool to blend one color into another to achieve an airbrush effect (see Plates 7 and 8, "Swan" and "Violin").

To perform a blend operation, first select the two objects or paths

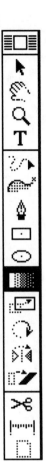
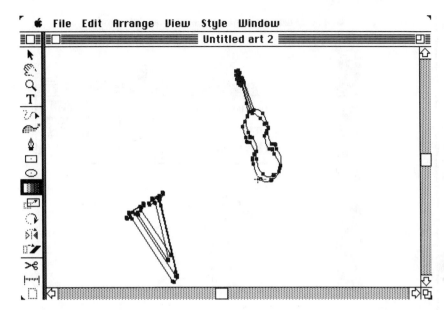

Figure 5-48.
After selecting the two paths and the blend tool, click one point on the starting path and one point on the ending path.

that define the starting and ending shapes, and after selecting the blend tool, you click one point of the starting object or path and a corresponding point of the ending object or path (Figure 5-48). The program displays a dialog box asking for the number of steps, or specific shapes, that the program should create between the starting and ending shapes (Figure 5-49). The program then creates all these shapes automatically (Figure 5-50).

The blend tool works best if both objects use the same pattern (if any), but you can use different colors, gray scales, and stroke widths. The blend tool can blend process colors, gray scales, and stroke widths to achieve special effects such as an airbrush effect or a contour with different line weights. The number of steps you specify in the Blend dialog box determines the color and tint blending percentages. You can also change the percentages of the first and last intermediate steps in order to fine-tune the blending or produce special effects.

The program interpolates shapes between the two points you clicked with the blend tool, and calculates percentages of color and black for the steps. The program calculates the blend based on the selected points in both paths. Before using the blend tool, you can

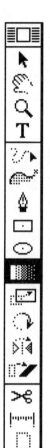

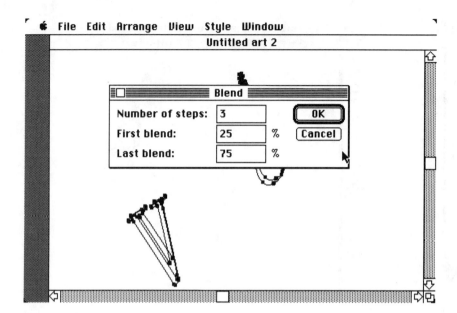

Figure 5-49.
The Blend dialog box appears after you select the click the second point.
You can specify the number of intermediate steps and the percentages for
the first and last intermediate steps.

select more than two points with the selection tool (such as two entire paths) to have more control over the results.

Paths must be ungrouped first before blending. To blend between open paths, select an endpoint on each path. You can create up to 1008 steps; the more steps you specify, the finer the gradation will be between the starting and ending shapes. Blending can occur between two open or two closed paths, but not between an open and a closed path.

Blending works between two objects painted with process colors or custom colors, and between a PANTONE or custom color and a process color. Process colors are used for all intermediate shapes between any two colors. Tints are blended by percentage in the same color, whether it is a process, custom, or PANTONE color.

You can't use the blend tool with typed characters — a set of drawn characters are provided in the *Adobe Collector's Edition I* available from Adobe Systems. Also, you can't use a blend as a masking object (although each intermediate step could be a masking object for a set of masked objects).

You can blend two objects that have the same pattern, but not objects with different patterns unless one of the patterns is defined

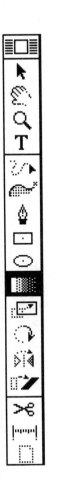

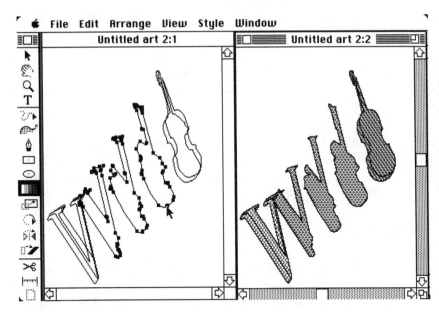

Figure 5-50.
The results of the blend operation shown in the Preview Illustration window (the objects are from the illustration in Plate 8, "Violin").

with artwork that is a transformation of the other pattern (the blend produces intermediate shapes with intermediate transformations of the pattern).

Blend Tool Summary

The blend tool creates intermediate shapes that are blends between two open or closed paths. Blending also calculates percentages of color, gray scale, or tint and assigns them to the intermediate steps. You select both paths (more points selected offers more control), and click a point on each path with the blend tool, then specify the number of steps in the Blend dialog box (including the percentages for the first and last steps).

-¦- + Command key
   Temporarily converts the blend tool into the selection tool.

-¦- + Space bar + drag
   Temporarily converts the blend tool into the hand tool for moving

the document within the active window while selecting paths for blending.

-∤- + Command key + Space bar + click
Temporarily converts the current tool into the zoom tool for zooming into the document while using the blend tool.

-∤- + Command key + Option key + Space bar + click
Temporarily converts the current tool into the zoom tool for zooming out from the document while using the blend tool.

Scale Tool

-∤-   The scale tool is used for stretching or shrinking objects. You can scale objects horizontally (i.e., along the x axis), vertically (along the y axis), or a varying amount of both. The scale tool can also be used as a built-in "stat camera" that allows you to enlarge or reduce your artwork to fit into an allotted space in a page layout or to fit in with some other graphic design element. Using Adobe Illustrator 88 as a substitute for a stat camera involves stretching or shrinking objects in equal amounts both vertically and horizontally; this is best accomplished through use of the Scale dialog box, which offers a Uniform scaling option.

Objects are scaled relative to a focal point you specify, so that you can scale an object from different vantage points to produce different effects. Scaling a path or other object is the only way to alter its size; zooming in and out with the zoom tool, or setting the enlargement or reduction options in the Page Setup dialog box in the Print menu does not affect the actual size of paths or objects. Since your drawing area is limited to 14-inches by 14-inches, the scale tool can also be handy for shrinking the size of your artwork to fit in the work area or to fit on a single page.

Before you use the scale tool you must first select the path or object you want to scale (you can select multiple segments and paths). To select a grouped object to scale, simply click on the object; alternatively, you can hold down the Command key to temporarily change the scale tool to the selection tool, and drag a selection marquee around any object or objects you wish to select.

To select an entire path for scaling, first position the arrow pointer anywhere on the path, hold down the Option key, and click. To select more than one object to scale, either drag a selection marquee

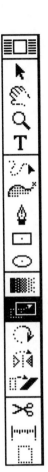

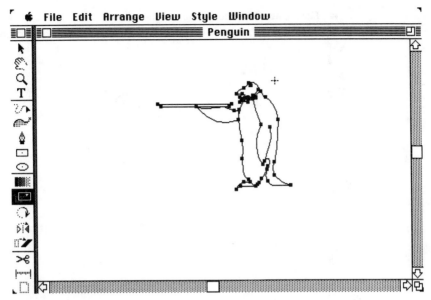

Figure 5-51.
The scale tool displays a plus (+) sign for the pointer. You select a focal point for the scale, which is the point of origin from which a transformation begins.

around the objects, or select one object first, then hold down the Shift key and continue to select the remaining objects. (If you click a selected object with the Shift key depressed, it will become deselected, until you click it again to select it.) To quickly select the entire piece of artwork for scaling, choose Select All from the Edit menu (or Command-A).

Once the item that you wish to scale is selected, you can either use the mouse to scale the selected object by dragging, or you can click to request the Scale dialog box and specify precise amounts of enlargement or reduction, including whether to scale or preserve line weights for uniform scaling, and other scaling options, such as the Copy option. And, if you don't get the result you expected, you can immediately use the Undo command at the top of the Edit menu, then try again.

If you want to drag to stretch or shrink the selected object, first click the scale tool in the toolbox. The pointer will turn into a plus sign (+) when you move it into the active window (Figure 5-51). (The window's view must be set to either Artwork and Template or Artwork Only).

Click at the spot you want to use as a focal point for the scaling

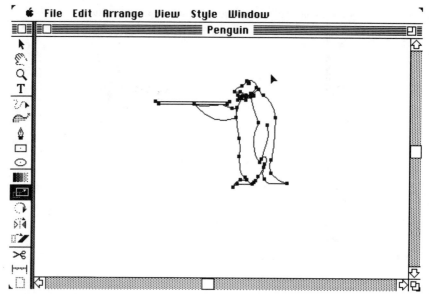

Figure 5-52.
The pointer changes to an arrowhead after clicking the focal point.

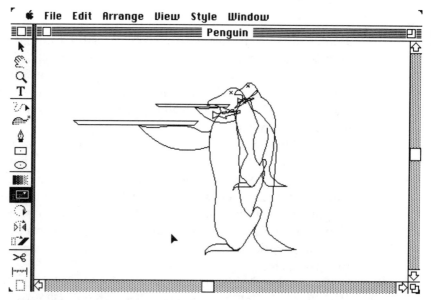

Figure 5-53.
Dragging from the second point in the direction to be scaled; both the original object outline and the scaled object are shown while dragging.

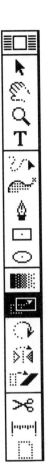

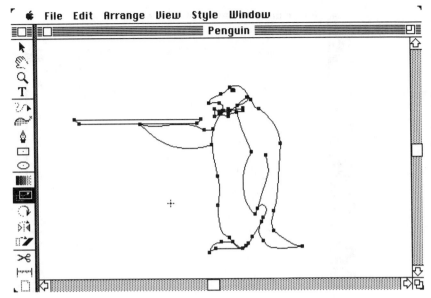

Figure 5-54.
The result of scaling the object.

operation, and the plus sign pointer changes to an arrowhead to indicate that the focal point, or *point of origin*, has been established (see Figure 5-52). The focal point or point of origin is the point where the transformation starts; the direction you drag in from that point determines the size and shape of the object.

Next, drag from the focal point in the direction that you want the selected object to be scaled in (Figure 5-53). While dragging, both the original object you selected and the scaled counterpart are visible on the screen as the counterpart changes size and shape.

If you want to stretch the object, move the mouse away from the focal point; if you want to shrink the object, move the mouse towards the focal point. The direction in which you drag the mouse also affects the dimension in which the selected object is scaled; if you move the mouse horizontally, the object will be stretched (or shrunk) horizontally; if you move the mouse vertically, the object will be stretched (or shrunk) vertically; and if you move the mouse diagonally, the object will be stretched (or shrunk) both vertically and horizontally (useful for creating perspective views).

For example, to create a rectangle of half the size, and to the right of a selected rectangle, click the scale tool and then click a focal point

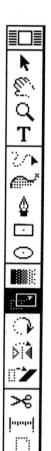

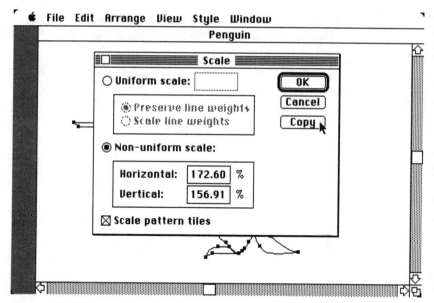

Figure 5-55.
Activate the Scale dialog box by holding down the Option key while clicking a focal point. The scale is set up for a vertical stretch and to scale pattern tiles with the object. You can click the Copy button to scale a duplicate without changing the original.

to the right of the selected rectangle. If you drag away from the focal point, the shape will be scaled up; drag toward the focal point and the shape is scaled down.

The closer your second point is to the focal point, the less mouse movement is required to alter the size and shape of the selected object. In order to get better control of the scaling process, it's a good idea to select a second spot that is as far away from the focal point as practical. You can select a second spot at the far edge of the active window if you are shrinking the selected object. However, when stretching an object by dragging from a second point that is far away from the first (perhaps at the edge of the active window), your view of the object may scroll about as you stretch the object, and the scrolling can be quite distracting.

You may notice that while scaling you can also create a reflection of the object by dragging to the left of or above the focal point. However, it is easier to use the reflect tool to create reflections.

When you have finished stretching or shrinking the selected object, release the mouse button and the original object will be

erased, leaving only the scaled object (see Figure 5-54). However, if you hold down the Option key while dragging, a scaled duplicate will be created while leaving the original in its place.

Scaling objects by dragging is good for quick stretching or shrinking, but it can be hard to control. For better control over scaling, hold down the Shift key while dragging; this constrains the direction in which the selected object is scaled. If the Shift key is held down while you stretch or shrink something, dragging horizontally will only scale the object along the current x axis; dragging vertically will only scale the object along the y axis; and dragging diagonally will scale equally along both the x and y axes.

For precise control over scaling of both objects and line weights, use the Scale dialog box. Line weights cannot be scaled by dragging; you must use the Scale dialog box for this task. After clicking the scale tool in the toolbox, the pointer turns into a plus sign (+) when you move it into the active window. Position the plus sign on the spot that you want to become the focal point of the scaling operation. Hold down the Option key while clicking the point. When you depress the Option key, the (+) pointer changes into a (+-) pointer, indicating that the Scale dialog box is ready to be requested; as soon as you click the mouse button, the Scale dialog box appears (Figure 5-55).

The Scale dialog box lets you choose between uniform scaling and non-uniform scaling, and between preserving the line weights or scaling the line weights if you choose uniform scaling.

When the dialog box appears, it contains the settings from the previous scaling operation; if this is the first use of the Scale Tool since you started up the program, the values will be set to "Uniform Scale" at 100 percent and "Preserve line weights." If you want uniform scaling, i.e. scaling performed equally along the x and y axes, make sure that the radio button in front of "Uniform scale:" is checked (i.e., has a small black spot inside the circle). Then point to the small box after the "Uniform Scale:" heading, click the mouse, and enter the scaling factor number as a percentage (Figure 5-56). Numbers greater than 100 will enlarge the object and numbers less than 100 will reduce the object.

If uniform scaling is selected, you can also specify whether or not you want the lines weights of the selected object scaled or preserved (when you scale by dragging, line weights are always preserved, or kept the same amount). Simply click the radio button preceding the line weight scaling option or the preserve line weight option. One of the features of Adobe Illustrator 88 that makes it especially valuable

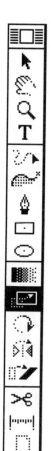

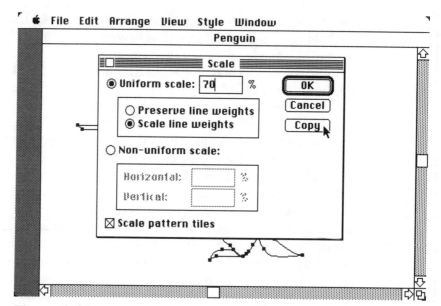

Figure 5-56.
When you switch to uniform scaling, you have the option to scale or preserve the line weights.

to graphic artists is the ability to preserve line weights while scaling, which is why that is the default setting. Preserving the line weights of a drawing while enlarging or reducing it is useful when you are creating a publication where consistent line weights for illustrations are desired throughout the publication. Normal enlargement or reduction methods such as using a stat camera always scale line weights.

When you want line weights scaled, you must select the "Scale line weights" option in the Scale dialog box after selecting uniform scaling. However, if you want to scale both a drawing and its line weights to be a great deal smaller than the original size, be careful that no line weights are scaled so thin that the press can't print them properly. Adobe Illustrator 88 offers more precision than some printing methods you can use to reproduce your drawing, so ask your printing press representative how thin a line can be preserved by the printing method you will use.

If you choose the "Non-uniform scale:" option by clicking in the radio button preceding it, you will not be able to scale line weights, but you will be able to type different scaling factors for the horizontal and vertical axes. To enter the horizontal scale factor, click in the box

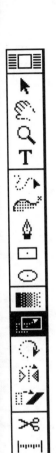

after the word "Horizontal:", and type the scaling factor number. Likewise, to enter the vertical scale factor, click in the box after the word "Vertical:", and type the desired value. You enter the scale factor as a percentage of the original size.

You can also type negative numbers to reflect and scale the drawing at the same time, which is equivalent to dragging to the left (or above) the focal point when scaling by dragging. As with scaling by dragging, you can therefore use the Scaling dialog box to create a reflection of the selected object along an imaginary line that passes through the focal point you established for the scaling operation.

To see how this technique can be used for reflecting, try specifying -100 percent horizontal scaling and 100 percent vertical scaling; the result will be a reflection of the image across a vertical line that passes through the focal point. If the man in the "Organizational Chart" (Plate 5) was selected, and the scale tool was clicked while holding down the Option key at the top of his head to establish a focal point, the Scale dialog box would appear, and using the numbers above and clicking the Copy button would result in two men, with the duplicate man upside down, connected to the original one head to head. You can use percentages other than 100 percent to accomplish scaling and reflecting simultaneously. However, for better control over reflecting, use the reflect tool.

When you are finished specifying the scaling options, click the OK button in the dialog box to perform the scaling operation; click the Cancel button to abandon your specifications and return to the unaltered active window; or click Copy to create a scaled copy while leaving the original in its place. The double line surrounding the OK button indicates that pressing the Return key can be used as a shortcut for selecting the OK option. After you have finished scaling, you can repeat the procedure as often as you want by selecting Transform Again from the Arrange menu or by pressing Command-D as a shortcut.

However, if you have altered the x and y axes using the Constrain angle setting in the Preferences dialog box in the Edit menu (Command-K), the scaling of the selected object is relative to the altered x and y axes. For example, if you have rotated the x and y axes by 30 degrees using the Constrain angle setting (Command-K), any objects you scale with the scale tool will be drawn at a 30-degree angle. If you are unsure about the alignment of the x and y axes, you can check their settings by looking at the Constrain angle setting in the dialog box that appears after you select the Preferences command

on the Edit menu (or type Command-K as a shortcut for requesting the dialog box).

Scale Tool Summary

-¦- + drag
Stretches or shrinks any selected objects relative to a focal point that you first specify by clicking.

-¦-+ Shift key + drag
Constrains the object being scaled along the x axis, the y axis, or both axes.

-¦- + Option key + click
Displays the Scale dialog box for specifying precise scaling amounts, with the options of scaling or preserving line weights for a uniform scale, and another option to copy the object (create a duplicate object with the specified settings for size and position).

-¦-+ Option key + drag
Creates a scaled duplicate while leaving the original object in its place; useful for creating different sized copies of an object.
If you use the Scale dialog box instead of dragging, you can create duplicates with precision, and repeat the same settings for subsequent scaling operations.

Command-D
Repeat the previous transformation, which may be a scaling operation, or a combination of scaling and cloning and movement.

Rotate Tool

-¦- The rotate tool is used for rotating objects around a focal point that you specify. The rotate tool is useful for rotating objects around a common point such as spokes on a wheel or petals on a flower, for rotating objects for positioning, or for creating special effects.
Before you use the rotate tool you must first select the path or any other object that you want to rotate (you can select multiple

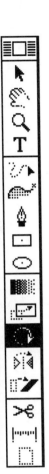

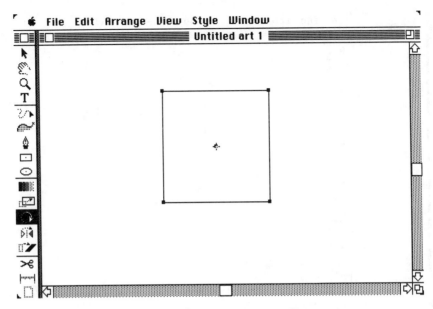

Figure 5-57.
To rotate the square, position the pointer over the axis of rotation (in this case, through the center) and click to establish the rotation focal point.

segments and paths). To select a path to rotate, first position the pointer anywhere on the path, hold down the Option key, and press the mouse button. To select a grouped object to rotate, simply point at the object and click the mouse; alternatively, you can use the selection tool to drag a selection marquee around the object you wish to select. To select more than one object to rotate, either drag a selection marquee around the objects or select one object first by clicking it, and then hold down the Shift key as you click to select each remaining object. (Clicking the selected object a second time will deselect it; click a third time to select it again.) To select the entire piece of artwork for rotating, either choose Select All from the Edit menu or use Command-A as a shortcut.

Once you have selected the object that you wish to rotate, you can either rotate the selected object by dragging, or you can request the Rotate dialog box for specifying precise amounts of rotation.

If you want to rotate the selected object by dragging, first click the rotate tool in the toolbox. The pointer will turn into a plus sign (+) when you move it into the active window. However, if the view is set to Preview Illustration, you must first select another view from the

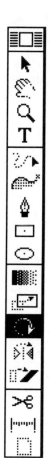

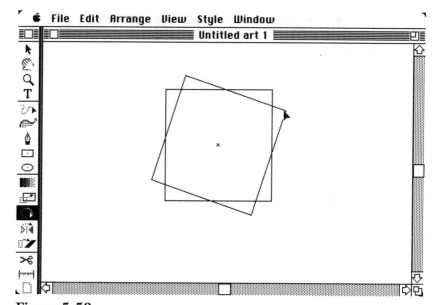

Figure 5-58.
You can rotate the object freely with the mouse after clicking the focal point; holding down the Option key rotates a duplicate and leaves the original in place.

View menu to use the rotate tool; either Artwork and Template (Command-E), or Artwork Only (Command-W).

Next, click at the point you wish to establish as the point of rotation; the axis around which the selected object will be rotated. Clicking establishes the center of rotation (see Figure 5-57).

The pointer changes from a plus sign to an arrowhead to indicate that the center point has been established. When you hold down the mouse button and drag the mouse in a circular motion around the center point; the selected objects will rotate around the center point (see Figure 5-58).

While dragging, you will see both the original object you selected and the rotating counterpart. When you have finished rotating the selected object, release the mouse button and the original object will be erased, leaving only the rotated object. However, if you hold down the Option key while dragging, a duplicate will be created and rotated, leaving the original in its place (Figure 5-59). (You will notice that while rotating you can also create a reflection of the object; however, it is easier to use the reflect tool to create reflections.)

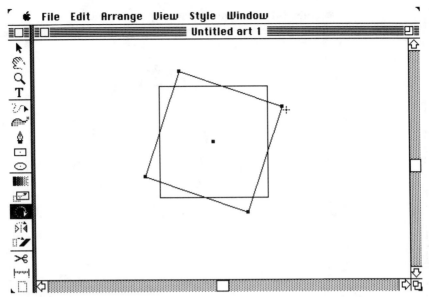

Figure 5-59.
Holding down the Option key while dragging with the rotate tool.

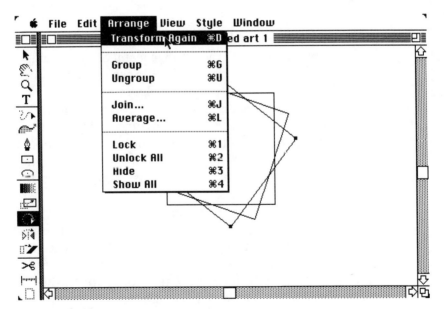

Figure 5-60.
Using the Transform Again option to repeat the transformation (in this case, a rotation). You can repeat the transformation over and over with this option, or with the Command-D shortcut.

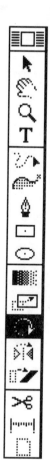

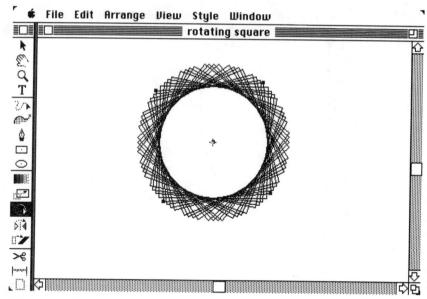

Figure 5-61.
The result of many Transform Again commands to continually rotate and duplicate the square.

You can repeat the rotation as often as you want by selecting Transform Again from the Arrange menu or by pressing Command-D as a shortcut (Figure 5-60). You can achieve special effects by using Transform Again over and over (Figure 5-61).

Even if rulers are displayed (Show Rulers command in the View menu, or Command-R) rotating objects by dragging a precise amount can be difficult. For better control over rotation, hold down the Shift key while dragging; this constrains the rotation angle to multiples of 45 degrees. For precise control over the angle of rotation, use the Rotate dialog box.

To use the Rotate dialog box for rotating objects by a precise amount, first click the rotate tool in the toolbox. The arrow pointer will turn into a plus sign (+) whenever you move it into the active window. (If you don't get the plus sign pointer, use the View menu to change views. You can't use the Rotate tool if the view is set to Preview Illustration or Template Only.)

Next, position the pointer over the spot that you want to become the axis around which the selected object will be rotated, hold down the Option key, and click once to establish the center of rotation. As soon as you hold down the Option key, the (+) pointer changes into

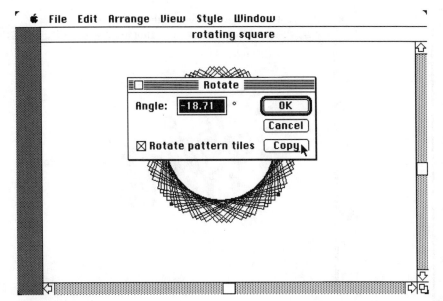

Figure 5-62.
Hold down Option when clicking the focal point with the rotate tool to activate the Rotate dialog box. You have the option to rotate pattern tiles if the object is painted or stroked with a pattern. You can rotate a clone (and leave the original in place) by clicking the Copy button.

a (+-) pointer, indicating that the Rotate dialog box is ready to be requested; when you click the mouse, the Rotate dialog box will appear (Figure 5-62).

The Rotate dialog box retains the settings from the previous rotation. If this is the first use of the rotate tool since you started up the program, the rotation angle is set to zero.

Specify the desired angle of rotation in degrees. The angle of rotation that you specify is applied relative to the x axis, and objects are rotated around the center point (which is the intersection of the x and y axes). You can specify angles from 360 degrees to -360 degrees. Positive numbers will rotate the selected object counterclockwise and negative numbers will rotate the object clockwise. By specifying a 180-degree rotation, the item will be reflected across the x axis; however, for better control over reflecting, use the reflect tool (described next).

Once you have specified the angle of rotation, you can either click the OK button in the dialog box to perform the rotation; click the Cancel button to abandon your specifications and return to the

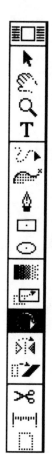
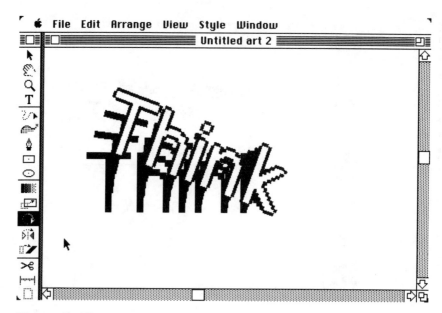

Figure 5-63.
Rotating text that was selected, and using Transform Again to create an effect.

unaltered active window; or click Copy to create a rotated copy while leaving the original in its place. (The double line surrounding the OK button indicates that pressing the Return key can be used as a shortcut for selecting the OK button.)

You can also rotate type that has already been defined with the text tool. Simply select the text, click the focal point with the rotate tool and drag, or Option-click to get the Rotate dialog box. With the Transform Again command you can produce special effects with text (Figure 5-63).

If you aren't getting the results you expect, check the Constrain angle setting in the Preferences dialog box in the Edit menu. The rotation of the selected object is relative to the current x and y axes. For example, if you had set the Constrain angle for the x and y axes to 30 degrees using the Preferences command in the Edit menu (Command-K), when you select objects to rotate with the rotate tool, they will be rotated at the angle you specify, plus the additional 30-degree constraint angle. If you are unsure about the alignment of the x and y axes, you can check their settings by looking at the Constrain angle setting in the dialog box that appears after you select the Preferences command on the Edit menu (or type Command-K as a shortcut for requesting the Preferences dialog box).

Rotate Tool Summary

-╎- + click on axis + drag
   Rotates any selected objects around a focal point that you specify.

-╎- + click on axis + Shift key + drag
   Constrains the rotation angle of the selected object to increments of 45 degrees (relative to the x and y axes).

-╎- + click on axis + Option key + click
   Displays the Rotate dialog box for specifying precise amounts of rotation.

-╎- + click on axis + Option key + drag
   Creates a rotated duplicate while leaving the original object in place.

Reflect Tool

-╎-   The reflect tool is used to create mirror images of objects. Before you use the reflect tool, you must first select the path or other objects you want to reflect.

   To select a grouped object to reflect, simply click the selection tool (hold down the Command key to temporarily change any tool to the selection tool), or drag a selection marquee around any object or objects you wish to select.

   To select an entire path for reflecting, first position the arrow pointer anywhere on the path, hold down the Option key, and click. To select more than one object to reflect, either drag a selection marquee around the objects, or select one object first, then hold down the Shift key and continue to click to select the remaining objects. (If you click a selected object with the Shift key depressed, it will become deselected, until you click it again to select it.) To quickly select the entire piece of artwork for reflecting, choose Select All from the Edit menu (or Command-A).

   Once you have selected the object that you wish to reflect, you can either reflect the selected object by dragging, or you can request the Reflect dialog box for specifying precise amounts of reflection.

   If you want to reflect the selected object by dragging, first select the reflect tool by clicking it in the toolbox. The arrow pointer will turn into a plus sign (+) when you move it into the active window,

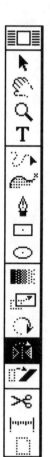

provided the view is set to Artwork & Template (Command-E) or Artwork Only (Command-W) in the View menu.

Point to the spot that you want to become the first point of the axis around which the selected object will be reflected and click the mouse button. The pointer will change to an arrowhead to indicate that the first axis point has been established. Then, select a second point that along with the first point will define the imaginary line that the program will use for the axis of reflection. To reflect the object across this imaginary line, simply click the mouse button. On the other hand, if you want to adjust the axis of reflection, do not click. Instead, drag the arrowhead pointer around the original focal point; the axis of reflection will change as you drag.

While dragging, both the original object you selected and the reflected counterpart are visible on the screen. When you release the mouse button, the original object is erased, leaving only the reflected object. If you hold down the Option key while dragging, a reflected duplicate will be created while the original remains unchanged in its place. Even if rulers are displayed (Show Rulers command in the View menu or Command-R), reflecting objects by dragging a precise amount can be difficult.

You can better control certain angles of reflection by applying constraint as you reflect the object. Hold the Shift key down while dragging to constrain the reflection axis to multiples of 45 degrees. For precise control over the angle of reflection, use the Reflect dialog box described below.

If you want to use the Reflect dialog box for reflecting items by a precise amount, first click the reflect tool in the toolbox. Next, hold down the Option key, and click at the spot along an imaginary line that you want to become the fixed point that defines the axis around which the selected object will be reflected. As soon as you hold down the Option key, the (+) pointer changes into a (+-) pointer, indicating that the Reflect dialog box is ready to be requested; the Reflect dialog box will appear at the next click.

The dialog box contains the settings from the previous reflection. If this is the first use of the reflect tool since you started up the program, the reflection option will be set to reflect items across the horizontal axis. Specify whether you want the selected object reflected across a horizontal axis running through the fixed point, a vertical axis through the point, or across an angled axis by clicking in the circle preceding the desired option. If you select the option for reflecting items across an angled axis, you must then enter a number

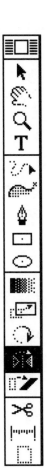

in the box that represents the angle of rotation (in degrees) of the reflection axis about the focal point relative to the x and y axes.

When you are finished specifying the reflection options, you can either click the OK button in the dialog box to perform the reflection; click the Cancel button to abandon your specifications and return to the unaltered active window; or click Copy to create a reflected copy while leaving the original in its place. The double line surrounding the OK button indicates that pressing the Return key can be used as a shortcut for selecting the OK option. After you have finished reflecting, you can repeat the procedure as often as you want by selecting Transform Again from the Arrange menu or by pressing Command-D as a shortcut.

If you have altered the Constrain angle with the Preferences command on the Edit menu, the reflection of the selected object is aligned to the constraint angle of the x and y axes. This means that if you have rotated the x and y axes by 40 degrees using the Constrain angle setting in the Preferences dialog box (Command-K), any items you reflect with the reflect tool will be rotated at an additional 40-degree angle. If you are unsure about the alignment of the x and y axes, you can check their settings by looking at the Constrain angle setting in the dialog box that appears when you select the Preferences command on the Edit menu (or type Command-K as a shortcut for requesting the dialog box).

Reflect Tool Summary

-¦- + click first point on axis + click to establish next point
Reflects a mirror-image of any selected object across an imaginary reflection line defined by your points.

-¦- + click first point on axis + drag to next point
Reflects a mirror-image of any selected object across a rotating reflection line defined by your dragging away from the reflection line defined by the first and second points.

-¦- + click + Shift key + drag
Constrains the reflection of the selected object to horizontal (reflected across the x axis), vertical (reflected across the y axis), and increments of 45 degrees (relative to the x and y axes).

-┼- + Option key + click
Displays the Reflect dialog box for specifying precise amounts of reflection.

-┼- + click first point on axis + Option key + drag to next point
Creates a reflected clone while leaving the original object in its place.

Shear Tool

-┼-

The Shear Tool is used to put a uniform slant on an object. The shear tool uniformly shears the selected object or objects along a horizontal, vertical, or angled axis.

Before you use the Shear Tool, you must first use the selection tool to select the path or other objects that you want to shear. To select a path to shear, first position the selection pointer anywhere on the path, hold down the Option key, and click. To select a grouped object to shear, simply point at the object and click; alternatively, you can drag a selection marquee around the object you wish to select. You can switch from the shear tool to the selection tool by holding down the Command key.

To select more than one object to shear, either drag a selection marquee around the objects or select one object first by clicking it, and then hold down the Shift key and select the remaining objects by clicking them. To select the entire piece of artwork for shearing, either choose Select All from the Edit menu or press Command-A as a shortcut.

Once you have selected the item that you wish to shear, you can either use the mouse to shear the selected object by dragging, or you can request the Shear dialog box for specifying precise amounts of shearing.

If you want to use the mouse to shear the selected object by dragging, first select the shear tool by clicking its icon in the toolbox. The pointer will turn into a plus sign (+) when you move it into the active window, provided the view is set to Artwork & Template (Command-E) or Artwork Only (Command-W) in the View menu.

Click a point to define the axis along which the selected object will be sheared (Figure 5-64). Then start dragging from another point

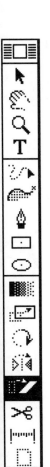

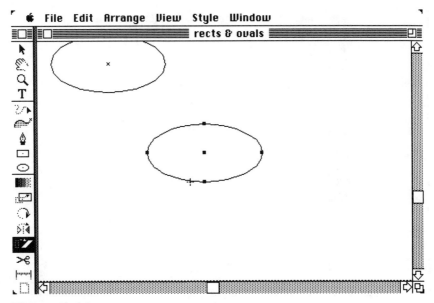

Figure 5-64.
*Click to establish the axis for shearing the selected object; the axis points
do not move. The axis passes through this point horizontally or vertically
for shearing by dragging.*

away from the axis in the direction of the shear. All points along the
shear axis will remain fixed. The pointer will change to an arrowhead
to indicate that the shear axis has been established. The object
changes shape as you drag; release the mouse button when you have
the shear that you want (Figure 5-65). The further away from the axis
point that you start your dragging, the greater control you will have
over the shearing. Drag horizontally to shear the selected object
along the x axis, drag vertically to shear along the y axis, or drag
diagonally to shear along both the x and y axes.

While dragging, both the original object you selected and the
sheared counterpart are displayed. When you have finished shearing
the selected object, release the mouse button and the original object
will be erased, leaving only the sheared object. If you hold down the
Option key while dragging, a sheared clone will be created while
leaving the original in its place.

Shearing objects by dragging, even with rulers displayed (Command-R) is difficult to do precisely. To get better control over
shearing, hold the Shift key down while dragging; this constrains

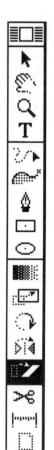

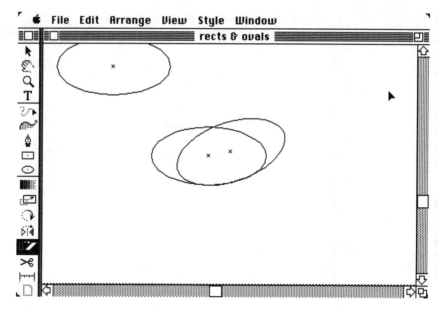

Figure 5-65.
Start dragging from another point in the direction of the shear; if you start dragging from a point far away from the axis, you have more control.

shearing to an angle that is a multiple of 45 degrees (relative to the x and y axes).

For precise control over shearing at any angle, use the Shear dialog box. First click the shear tool icon in the toolbox. The pointer will turn into a plus sign (+) when you move it into the active window. Next, hold down the Option key, and click a point to define the axis along which the selected object will be sheared. As soon as you hold down the Option key, the (+) pointer changes into a (+-) pointer, indicating that the Shear dialog box is ready to be requested; as soon as you click, the Shear dialog box appears (Figure 5-66).

When the dialog box appears it contains the settings from the previous shearing; if this is the first use of the shear tool since you started up the program, the shear angle will be set to zero and horizontal shearing will be selected.

Specify the desired angle of shearing in degrees by clicking in the box located after the word "Angle:". The degree of shearing that you specify corresponds to the amount of slant you want to put on the selected object, relative to an axis that is perpendicular to the axis point you clicked. A positive angle performs a clockwise shear and a

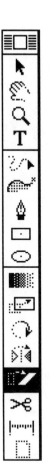

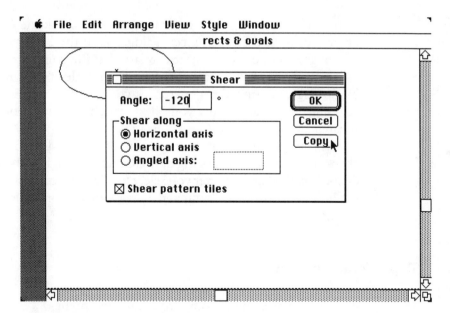

Figure 5-66.
Hold down the Option key when clicking the shear tool's axis point to get this dialog box for accurate shearing. You can shear pattern tiles along with the object, and use the Copy button to shear a clone and leave the original object unchanged.

negative angle performs a counterclockwise shear (this is in contrast to rotation angles, where a positive angle performs a counterclockwise rotation and a negative angle performs a clockwise rotation).

Next, click either a horizontal shear, vertical shear, or angled shear by clicking the appropriate radio button. If you select an angled shear you must also click in the box after the words "Angled axis:" and then specify the angle (in degrees) of the shear axis around the fixed point that you established, relative to the x and y axes.

When you are finished specifying the shear options, you can click the OK button in the dialog box to perform the shear; click the Cancel button to abandon your specifications and return to the unaltered active window; or click Copy to create a sheared copy while leaving the original in its place. The double line surrounding the OK button indicates that pressing the Return key can be used as a shortcut for selecting the OK option. After you have finished shearing, you can repeat the procedure as often as you want by selecting Transform Again from the Arrange menu or by pressing Command-D as a shortcut.

If you aren't getting the results you expect, check the Constrain angle setting in the Preferences dialog box in the Edit menu. The shearing of the selected object is relative to the x and y axes. This means that if you have rotated the Constrain angle of the x and y axes by 60 degrees using the Preferences command in the Edit menu (Command-K), any items you shear with the shear tool will be sheared at an additional 60-degree angle.

If you are unsure about the alignment of the x and y axes, you can check their settings by looking at the Constrain angle setting in the dialog box that appears after you select the Preferences command on the Edit menu (or type Command-K as a shortcut for requesting the dialog box).

Shear Tool Summary

-¦- + click an axis point + drag from a second point
Shears any selected object uniformly along an imaginary axis line that runs through the two points; the axis point, and the second point (where you start dragging) defines the shear axis.

-¦- + click an axis point + Shift key + drag from a second point
Constrains the shearing of the selected object to horizontal (sheared along the x axis), vertical (sheared along the y axis), and shearing in increments of 45 degrees (relative to the x and y axes).

-¦- + Option key + click
Displays the Shear dialog box for specifying a precise angle of shearing, with options for shearing pattern tiles, and a Copy button to create a sheared clone, leaving original in place.

-¦- + click an axis point + Option key + drag from a second point
Creates a sheared duplicate, leaving the original object in place.

Scissors Tool

+ The scissors tool is used to cut a segment into two segments, cut an open path into two open paths, break a closed path into one open path, split an anchor point into two endpoints, and add anchor points to a segment. The scissors tool cannot be used to split endpoints of

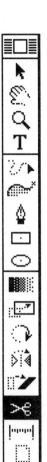

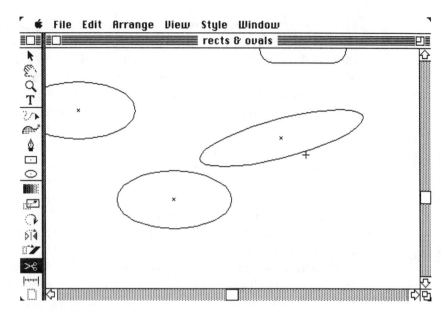

Figure 5-67.
Before clicking the scissors tool on an ungrouped path.

an open path, nor will it work on any grouped objects. If you want to use the scissors tool on a grouped object you must first select the object and ungroup it by selecting Ungroup from the Arrange menu (or by typing Command-U as a shortcut).

To use the scissors tool, first click the scissors icon in the toolbox. The pointer turns into a plus sign (+) when you move it into the active window (Figure 5-67).

To cut a segment into two segments, position the (+) pointer where you wish to cut the segment and then click the mouse button. The segment is split into two segments where you clicked (Figure 5-68). Two new endpoints appear, although it appears that there is only one anchor point because the two new endpoints are directly on top of each other, and they are both selected. Since you can't tell from looking at the screen that there are actually two endpoints on top of each other, it's a good idea to move the endpoints apart right after you make the cut (Figure 5-69).

To move the two new endpoints apart, first replace the scissors with the selection tool (arrow), either by clicking the selection tool in the toolbox, or by holding down the Command key. (The Command key temporarily changes any tool into the selection tool.)

Then point to the endpoints, hold down the Shift key, and click to deselect the endpoint on top while leaving the one beneath it selected. You can then move the bottom endpoint by positioning the arrow over it and dragging the endpoint to a new location.

The procedure for cutting an open path into two new open paths is quite similar. The only difference is that you can either cut a path in the middle of a segment to create two new endpoints, or you can cut a path on an anchor point to turn the existing anchor point into an endpoint and create a new endpoint on top of it.

Since you'll be faced with the same problem of having two endpoints on top of each other, you'll either want to move an endpoint as described above, or you may want to move one of the new paths. In order to move a path, first switch to the selection tool by clicking its icon in the toolbox (or hold down the Command key). Then point somewhere in the active window (but away from any artwork) and click to deselect all the objects in the artwork. Next, hold down the Option key, and click on the path that you want to move. Move the path to the new location by dragging it there.

Breaking a closed path into an open path is much like the previous procedure except that you wind up with only one path instead of two. Whether you cut the closed point in the middle of a segment or at an anchor point, it's a good idea to move the two endpoints away from each other right after you cut them, since the screen shows them overlaying each other, and it is impossible to see that there are two, not just one, endpoints at that location.

You can also use the scissors tool to add new anchor points to any line segment in a path without cutting or breaking the path. Since adding anchor points does not add any new endpoints or break any paths, a single open path remains a single path, and a closed path stays closed. However, adding new anchor points gives you a greater degree of control over the shape of a path or object, since you can change the shape of the line segments where the new anchor points are added. This technique is very useful for fine-tuning small details in a complex piece of artwork, and for adding or deleting anchor points in an object that was traced with the auto trace tool.

To add new anchor points to an existing line segment, first click the scissors tool in the toolbox. Next, position the (+) pointer where you want the new anchor point to be located, hold down the Option key, and click. A new anchor point will appear, and it will be the only selected point.

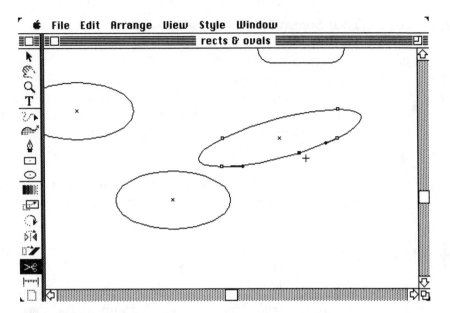

Figure 5-68.
After clicking the scissors tool, the segment is divided into two segments joined by a new anchor point.

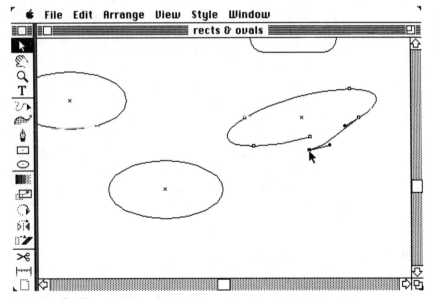

Figure 5-69.
Separating the new endpoints created by clicking the scissors tool.

Scissors Tool Summary

+ + click
Cuts a segment into two segments, cuts an open path into two open paths, breaks a closed path into one open path, splits an anchor point into two endpoints, leaving the new points selected. Objects must be ungrouped before using the scissors tool on them.

+ + Option key + click
Adds a new anchor point to a line segment, creating two segments but not cutting or breaking the original segment.

Measure Tool

The measure tool measures the distance between any two points or two areas in your drawing space, and displays the amount in the measure selected in the Preferences dialog box in the Edit menu (the default Ruler units are in inches, or click to select picas/points, or centimeters to use for the Riuler units).

To measure distance, click the measure tool icon in the toolbox, then click the first point (Figure 5-70) and the second point (Figure 5-71). The Measure dialog box appears with information about the distance between the two points, the angle of an imaginary line connecting the two points, and the distance along the horizontal and vertical axes between the two points (the dimensions of a triangle).

You can use the measure tool in any window view, including the Preview Illustration view. You can constrain the measurement by holding down the Shift key when clicking the second point. If the second click is on an anchor point, the Shift key does not constrain the measure. If the second click is at a 45-degree angle, then measurement is constrained to where the path intersects the imaginary 45-degree axis running through the second point.

Measure Tool Summary

-¦- + click first point + click second point
Displays the Measure dialog box with the following information: the distance between two points or areas of the drawing space, the angle of an imaginary line passing through both points, and the

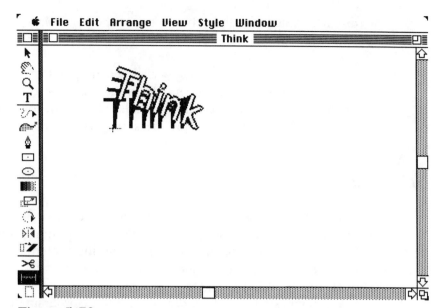

Figure 5-70.
Clicking the first point in the artwork (in a Preview Illustration window) with the measure tool.

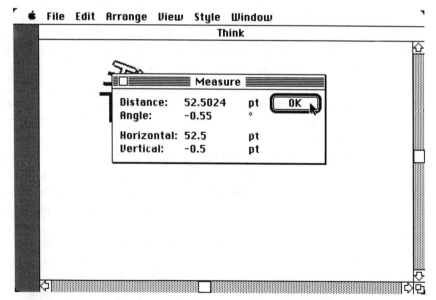

Figure 5-71.
The Measure dialog box with distance and angle information. The angle describes the line between the two points clicked, and the distance along the horizontal and vertical axes.

distance along the x and y axes between the two points, describing a triangle.

-¦-+ click first point + Shift key + click second point
   Constrains the measurement to the x and y axes, or to a 45-degree offset from the x and y axes, displaying the Measure dialog box. If the second point is an anchor point, measuring will not be constrained.

The Page Tool

-¦-   The page tool is used to control how Adobe Illustrator 88 divides its 14-inch by 14-inch drawing space into pages for printing. Since very few PostScript printers are capable of printing the entire drawing space on a single piece of paper, the program divides the space into smaller sections for printing.

When you start up Adobe Illustrator 88, the program divides the work area into nine regions, with only one full-sized page region that is located in the center of the work area (page 5). These regions are related to the printable area of the page size specified in the Page Setup dialog box. The printable area is the region within the page that your PostScript printer is capable of actually printing.

In order to let you know where the page breaks will occur, the program marks the 14-inch by 14-inch drawing space with a page grid made of dotted lines that represents the printable area of each page. The dotted lines of the page grid are visible in all views of the active document (e.g. if you have another view of the same piece of artwork in another window, the page grid will be transferred to that view as well).

The program measures the height and width of your artwork to create an imaginary rectangle of page boundaries around your artwork. It then numbers the actual pages it will print from left to right, top to bottom, starting in the upper left-hand corner of the imaginary rectangle of page boundaries.

Depending on the shape of your artwork and positioning of the page boundaries, one or more blank pages may be printed — this is not a bug in the program but merely a result of the method that the program uses to divvy up the work area for printing. This page numbering system is only used internally by the program and the numbers are not printed on the pages, although they are displayed in the Print dialog box as you are printing the document as a way to

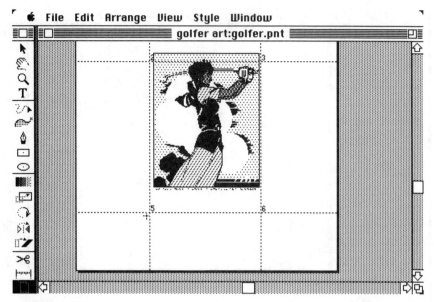

Figure 5-72.
After selecting the page tool to adjust the page boundaries, click the lower left corner of page 5 to drag that page over the artwork. You can use the page tool in any view including the Preview Illustration view.

gauge the progress of the print job.

The size and shape of the printable page region is automatically changed if you change the page size specifications by choosing Page Setup from the File menu and altering the specifications in the Page Setup dialog box. It's important to remember that the Page Setup dialog box is not always the same; since the page setup capabilities are different from printer to printer, the information displayed in the Page Setup dialog box is supplied by the printer icon in the system file for the printer that is actively in use (the Chooser in the Desk Accessory menu allows you to inspect and/or change the active printer). However, the way that Adobe Illustrator 88 automatically breaks up the work area into regions may not be well suited to your particular piece of artwork. In order to correct this, you can use the page tool to control how Adobe Illustrator 88 divides the 14-inch by 14-inch drawing space into printable page areas.

If your artwork is large enough to fit on a single page but the program's preset page breaks cause your artwork to be split into two or more pages, the page tool can be used to position the artwork entirely within one page region. If your artwork is too large to fit on

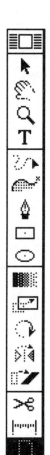

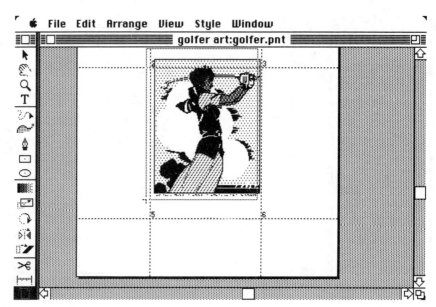

Figure 5-73.
Dragging the boundaries of page 5 to center the artwork for printing.

a single page, the page tool can be used to place the page breaks on the best places to divide your artwork. Placing the page breaks creatively can make it easier to reassemble large pieces of artwork from their component printouts.

Before you use the page tool you will probably want to use either the zoom tool to zoom out to a view that will allow you to see the entire 14-inch by 14-inch drawing space within the active window, or choose Fit In Window from the View menu (or press Command-M or double-click on the hand tool as shortcuts). You can use the page tool in the Preview Illustration view as well as with other views.

To use the page tool, click it in the toolbox. The pointer will turn into a plus sign (+) when you move it into the active window.

In order to move the page grid, first place the pointer over your artwork and hold down the mouse button; as soon as you depress the button, the program displays a dotted rectangle that corresponds to the printable area of a page (as currently defined in the Page Setup dialog box). The pointer (+) will be positioned at the lower left-hand corner of the dotted rectangle (Figure 5-72).

While holding down the mouse button, drag the rectangle (Figure 5-73) to the desired position over your artwork and release the

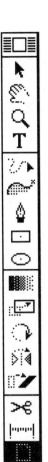

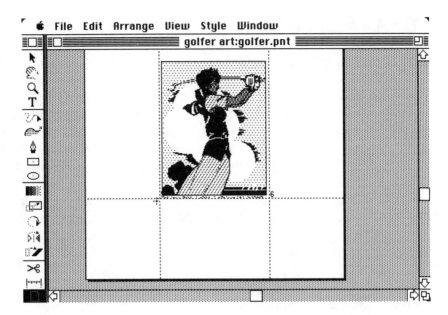

Figure 5-74.
The program draws the page boundaries according to the adjustment made by dragging the dotted lines.

button. The program will then draw the page grid according to your placement of the dotted rectangle (Figure 5-74).

If the artwork doesn't quite fit onto a single page you can experiment with reducing the image that will be printed on the page by choosing Page Setup from the File menu and altering the reduction specifications in the Page Setup dialog box. This will squeeze more artwork on the page and will also enlarge the size of the printable page area on the page grid of the active document. If your artwork is short and wide rather than tall and narrow, you can also use the Page Setup dialog box to change the orientation of the page from normal (the image in the dialog box is vertical) to landscape (the image in the dialog box is on its side). For more detailed information on the Page Setup dialog box see the section about the Print command on the File menu.

Keep in mind that reducing or enlarging the image using the Reduce or Enlarge options in the Page Setup dialog box only affects printing and has no effect on the size of the artwork in your Illustrator document; the only way to alter the size of your artwork is with the scale tool.

The Apple Menu

About Adobe Illustrator 88™...

Alarm Clock
Art Grabber+™
Calculator+
Calendar 1.7
Camera
CheapPaint™
Chooser
Control Panel
DiskTop
Find File
Guidance
Key Caps
MockWrite
SmartScrap™
Stars1.8

The Apple menu is located to the far left of the menu bars and appears as a small Apple Computer logo. It contains the About Illustrator command, the Help command, and the Macintosh's desk accessories that are always available to you while you are using most Macintosh applications. The exact number and type of desk accessories that appear on this menu depends on what desk accessories have been installed in your Macintosh startup disk's system file with the Font/Desk Accessory Mover or other program. See your Macintosh owner's manual for more information about the Font/Desk Accessory Mover and the Macintosh's supplied desk accessories. See your local user group and computer store for additional desk accessories you can install.

About Adobe Illustrator 88

The About Adobe Illustrator 88 option under the Apple menu brings up the Adobe Illustrator 88 information box (Figure 5-75). Useful information found in this box includes the version number of

Figure 5-75.
The Adobe Illustrator 88 startup and information box.

the program and the amount of free memory available when you started the program without any open documents (expressed both in terms of bytes and as a percentage of free memory).

Help

The Help command is used for accessing help screens that explain how commands and tools work. Selecting Help in the Apple menu brings up an open file dialog box. Open the folder containing the Adobe Illustrator 88 Help file, select the file, and click the Open button. To use the program's Help facility you must have the help folder on the same disk as the Adobe Illustrator 88 program.

The Alarm Clock

Selecting the Alarm Clock desk accessory in the Apple menu brings up a box containing the date and time. When first displayed, the clock only displays the time; clicking on the small lever at the right-hand side of the desk accessory expands the clock to allow you to see or set the date and alarm or set the time. Set the time by clicking on the image of the clock face (bottom left). Change the date by clicking on the calendar (bottom center). Set the alarm by clicking on the alarm clock (bottom right). When the clock is displayed, you can use the Copy and Paste commands in the Edit menu to copy the displayed time and paste it into any Macintosh document. You may have a different version of clock, or the clock could be elsewhere in your Apple menu (for example, in the Control panel).

Calculator

Selecting the Calculator desk accessory in the Apple menu displays a small calculator, useful for calculations, such as determining the percentage reduction or enlargement needed to scale your artwork to fit into a particular page layout. Calculator supports standard Cut (Command-X), Copy (Command-C), and Paste (Command-V) commands; copy a number from a document and paste it into the calculator for use in a calculation, or, you can copy the result of the calculation and paste it into any Macintosh document.

To remove the Calculator desk accessory from view until you select it in the Apple menu again, click the small close box in the upper left-hand corner of the Calculator desk accessory. You may have a different version of calculator, or a calculator could be elsewhere in your Apple menu (it could be from another supplier, and have a different name).

Chooser

Selecting the Chooser desk accessory in the Apple menu brings up the Chooser dialog box that is used for selecting printers, file servers, imagesetters, modems, and other remote devices that can be attached to your Macintosh.

See your computer manual for more information about the version of the Chooser accessory for your computer.

Control Panel

Selecting the Control Panel desk accessory in the Apple menu brings up the Control Panel dialog box that is used for selecting options related to the mouse, keyboard, monitor or other system peripherals currently being used by your Macintosh.

See your computer manual for more information about the version of the Chooser accessory for your computer.

Key Caps

Selecting the Key Caps desk accessory in the Apple menu brings up an image of the keyboard that appears in the middle of the screen, and a special Key Caps menu that appears as the last item on the menu bar. The Key Caps menu allows you to choose one of the typefaces (fonts) available in the system file of the startup disk for displaying on the Key Caps keyboard. The Key Caps keyboard lets you see what the different typefaces installed in your Macintosh's system file look like. When you choose a typeface from the Key Caps menu, you will see its lowercase character set on the Key Caps keyboard. If you want to see the uppercase characters, simply press the Shift key. Likewise, pressing the Caps Lock, Shift, Command, or Option keys, or any combination, will display the characters that will be generated if you were to type the same combination of keys in that particular typeface while using any Macintosh application. This provides a handy way to find out how to generate special characters and symbols in a particular typeface.

You can type on your actual keyboard, or you can type a key on the Key Caps keyboard by clicking it. Anything you type while the Key Caps desk accessory is active is displayed in the text window at the top of the Key Caps keyboard; this text can be cut, copied, or pasted into any other desk accessory or Macintosh document. To remove the Key Caps desk accessory from view until you select it in the Apple menu again, click the small close box in the upper left-hand corner of the desk accessory.

Note Pad

Selecting the Note Pad desk accessory in the Apple menu brings up an image of a small 8-page note pad that can be used for storing text only. Text can be cut (Command-X), copied (Command-C), and pasted (Command-V) to and from a Macintosh document using these Edit menu commands. Text in the Note Pad can also be cut and pasted into the Type dialog box in sections up to 254 characters in length. Text in the Note Pad is automatically saved when you close the Note Pad. To close the Note Pad, click the small close box in the upper left-hand corner of the desk accessory.

Scrapbook

Selecting the Scrapbook desk accessory in the Apple menu brings up the Scrapbook. The Scrapbook can hold many items, either text or graphics. To place something in the Scrapbook, first select it, then move it to the Clipboard by cutting it (Command-X) or copying it (Command-C). Next, open up the Scrapbook by selecting it from the Apple menu and paste the cut or copied object into the Scrapbook by using the Paste command in the Edit menu (Command-V). To copy something from the Scrapbook, first select Scrapbook from the Apple menu and then issue the copy command by either selecting Copy from the Edit menu or by pressing Command-C.

The Scrapbook displays items in a window. This window often doesn't let you see the entire item, but it is good enough for most identification purposes. Below the window is a scroll bar that scrolls the various items that are stored in the Scrapbook past the window. You can move forward or backward through the items in the Scrapbook by clicking in front of or behind the box in the scroll bar; alternatively you can click the small arrow on the right end of the scroll bar to go forward or the small arrow on the left end to go backward. Beneath the left end of the scroll bar are a pair of numbers separated by a slash, indicating the number of items and the currently selected item in the Scrapbook.

Items stored in the PICT and MacPaint formats in the Scrapbook cannot be pasted into template documents with Adobe Illustrator 88. You must paste them into template documents with the MacPaint program or another painting or drawing program that is compatible with MacPaint or PICT files. However, pieces of Adobe Illustrator 88 artwork such as paths or other objects can be pasted into the Scrapbook as Illustrator objects and stored for later use.

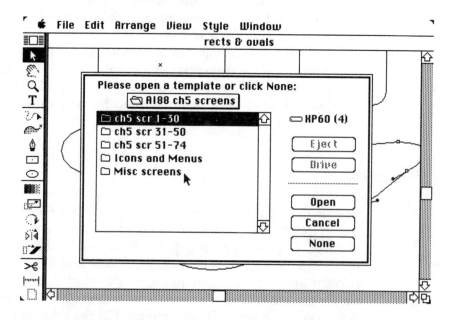

Figure 5-76.
The "open a template" dialog box activated by the New command in the File menu so that you can select a template for the new artwork (you can also click None for no template).

Also, Adobe Illustrator 88 includes the Drawover program to convert PICT files to Illustrator artwork files.

To close the Scrapbook, click to the small close box in the upper left-hand corner of the desk accessory. You can save different scrapbooks by renaming the Scrapbook File icon in the system folder (usually named "System Folder") and saving it in a different folder. The Macintosh operating system will only use the Scrapbook named "Scrapbook File" that is located in the same folder as the System and Finder icons; renaming a Scrapbook or moving it to another folder or disk prevents it from being used. If the system does not find a Scrapbook named "Scrapbook File" in the same folder with the System and Finder icons, the system will automatically create a new empty Scrapbook in that same folder as soon as you select Scrapbook in the Apple menu.

If you use SmartScrap (Solutions, Inc), ArtGrabber+ (MacroMind, Inc.) and other Scrapbook desk accessories, they provide more functionality and utilities than the Scrapbook desk accessory described in your computer manuals.

File Menu

File	
New...	⌘N
Open...	⌘O
Place...	
Close	
Save	⌘S
Save As...	
Page Setup...	
Print...	⌘P
Quit	⌘Q

The File menu is used for working with Illustrator artwork and template documents. The commands in the File menu let you create new Illustrator documents, open existing Illustrator documents, open a template document while creating a new Illustrator document, close and save Illustrator documents, set up pages for printing, print Illustrator documents, and quit the Illustrator program to return to the Macintosh's Finder. The File menu gives you access to the Macintosh's operating system from within the Illustrator program.

New...

The New command creates a new Illustrator document. Select New in the File menu (or press Command-N as a shortcut), and it automatically brings up the Get File dialog box asking you to "open a template or none" (Figure 5-76).

You can then use the scroll box to select either a MacPaint file or PICT file to use as a template for tracing with Illustrator, or you can click on the button labeled "None" to create a new Illustrator document without a template.

New documents are automatically given the name "Untitled art" followed by a colon (:) and the name of the template, if a template was used. To name a new Illustrator document, you must save the document using either the Save, Save As or Quit options in the File menu. The Adobe Illustrator 88 program will not let you quit without first naming any unnamed documents.

Open...

The Open command opens an existing Illustrator document and an associated template (if any), or opens a template document with a new untitled Illustrator document. You can issue the Open command by either selecting Open in the File menu or by pressing Command-O as a shortcut.

Use the Open command when you want to work on an existing Illustrator document, or as an alternative to the New command when you want to create a new Illustrator document from an existing template.

After you select Open, the Get File dialog box appears and prompts you to select either an Illustrator document or a template (MacPaint or PICT file) from the scroll box. If you select an Illustrator document, the Illustrator program will attempt to locate the template that was used to create the Illustrator document (if there was a template). When the active window appears, it will highlight the name of the Illustrator document in the window's title bar; if there is a template associated with the Illustrator document, the name of the Illustrator document will be followed by a colon (:) and then the name of the template document.

If you want to force the Illustrator program to prompt you to select a template when you open an existing Illustrator document (instead of automatically trying to retrieve a template), you can hold down the Option key while selecting Open in the File menu (or while pressing Command-O as a shortcut). Forcing Illustrator to prompt you for another template is useful when you are creating a piece of artwork that is based on more than one template.

If you select a template document from the scroll box, the program will assume that you want to create a new Illustrator document based on that template. When the new active window appears, the name of the Illustrator document will appear as "Untitled Art" followed by a colon (:) and then the name of the template document.

After you open the template and/or Illustrator document, you may not be able to see all of (or any of) the image in the active window. To bring the image into view, you should first try scrolling the image using either the scroll bars or the hand tool. If the image is too large to fit into the active window, you can use the zoom tool to zoom out from the image step by step until it fits in the window. Alternatively, you can select Fit In Window from the View menu or double-click on the hand tool to fit the entire 14-inch by 14-inch drawing space in the window and then use the zoom tool to zoom in on the image.

Place

The Place command can place a complete Encapsulated PostScript file into an Adobe Illustrator 88 document. Encapsulated PostScript (EPS) is a standard format for transferring PostScript graphics to and from PostScript drawing and page makeup programs, and from scanner programs and clip art libraries.

The contents of the EPS file occupy a box in your drawing space, and an image may also appear in the box that represents the graphics. You can move, scale, rotate, reflect, or shear the box just as any other piece of artwork. However, you can't adjust any of the anchor points, segments, or paths of the EPS graphics, nor can you apply paint or stroke colors or gray shades. The box always appears as a parallelogram even after transformations, but the graphics are transformed.

When you use the Preview Illustration command, you will see either a gray box or an image of the EPS graphics, depending on the type of EPS file saved by the other application. Adobe Illustrator 88 also lets you save Illustrator artwork as EPS files with the Save As command.

Close

The Close command is used to close the current Illustrator document and template (if any) without quitting the program. Use the Close command when you have finished working with one document and want to work on another.

Selecting Close in the File menu is equivalent to clicking inside the small close box located in the upper left-hand corner of the window's title bar. When you issue the Close command, the file is closed and removed from the Illustrator desktop, if no changes have been made to the document since the last time it was saved. If changes have been made since the last save, a dialog box will ask if you want the changes to be saved. Click the Yes button if you want to save the changes; click No to close the document without saving the changes; or click Cancel to return to the Illustrator file and cancel the Close command. The bold double line surrounding the Yes button indicates that if you simply press the Return key, that button will be activated to save your changes.

If it is a new untitled document, the program will bring up the Save File dialog box and request that you give the document a name to save it with.

Save

The Save command is used to save and name a new untitled Illustrator document or to periodically save an existing document. You should remember to save your documents frequently while you are working on them as a preventative measure against a problem with the document, a system crash, or a power failure. You can issue the Save command by either selecting Save in the File menu or by pressing Command-S.

The Save command does not affect the template document since the template cannot be altered by the program. If you are saving a new untitled document for the first time, you will be presented with the Save As dialog box, which will prompt you for the name that you want to use for saving the document. For more information about the Save As dialog box see the section on the Save As command below.

If you have already saved the document (i.e., if it already has a name other than "Untitled Art"), then issuing the Save command will not bring up the Save As dialog box. Instead, the document will be saved under the current name, on the same volume (folder, disk drive, or other storage device) that it was opened from, and the saved document will replace the previous version of the document.

Save As...

The Save As command is used to either save the active Illustrator document under a different name, on a different volume (a volume can be a folder, disk drive, or other storage device), or in the Encapsulated PostScript (EPS) file format with a preview bit map for IBM or Macintosh programs. To issue the Save As command, you must select Save As in the File menu; this command brings up the Save As dialog box that lets you specify how you want the Illustrator document in the active window to be saved.

If you want to save the document under a different name, you simply type in the new name in the box that appears below the words "Save illustration as:" in the dialog box (Figure 5-77). You can then either save the file in the current folder that is displayed at the top of the dialog box, or you can select a different file folder and/or disk drive. To select a different folder, point to the folder name and scroll down the list of folders (if any) that will appear under the current folder (Figure 5-78). If the file is stored on the disk without being placed in a folder, the icon and name of the disk will appear where the folder appears at the top of the dialog box.

If you want to save the file on a different disk drive, point to the Drive button and click the mouse button; each click will display a different disk drive until all the drives connected to the system (including AppleShare and other network drives) have been displayed; after that the list recycles with each new click. If only one drive is connected, the Drive button will be grayed-out and cannot be used. If a drive with removable disks is selected, the Eject button appears normal and pressing it would eject the disk from its drive so that another disk could be inserted.

Adobe Illustrator 88 normally saves Illustrator documents as PostScript-only files for use with Adobe Illustrator 88. However, you can use Illustrator-created artwork with a variety of page layout and presentation programs on the Macintosh and on IBM-compatible PCs and PS/2 computers, as long as you save a copy of the artwork in an Encapsulated PostScript (EPS) file. The Save As command offers both the Macintosh and IBM versions of Encapsulated Post-Script.

Some page makeup and presentation programs, and many graphics programs, are not capable of reading Encapsulated PostScript

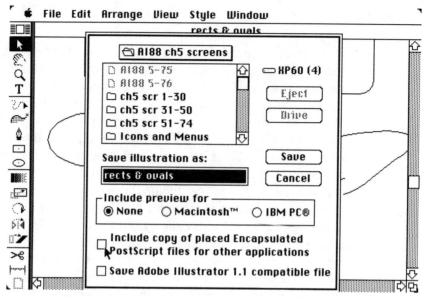

Figure 5-77.
The Save As dialog box lets you save an illustration in another folder, on another disk, or in a different format such as Encapsulated PostScript for the Macintosh or PC, or Illustrator 1.1 format for the older version of Adobe Illustrator.

files. Check your application program to verify that it will work with Encapsulated PostScript files before you decide to use that program with Illustrator-created artwork. Adobe Illustrator 88 clip art provided in EPS format for use and modification is sold by Adobe Systems, T/Maker Company, and other vendors.

To select one of the two Encapsulated PostScript formats, click the radio button next to either the Macintosh or IBM PC preview options. Adobe Illustrator 88 uses special icons to represent Encapsulated PostScript files which, unlike regular PostScript files, cannot be viewed and edited with most word processing programs. The Macintosh Encapsulated PostScript files contain a QuickDraw PICT format image of the preview artwork for use as a guide in placing it in a page layout or other program.

Another alternative is available if your application has a PostScript Place function (i.e., the ability to incorporate PostScript commands directly into a document). The disadvantages here are that the application will not be able to display a screen representation of the PostScript artwork and you may need to know where the importing

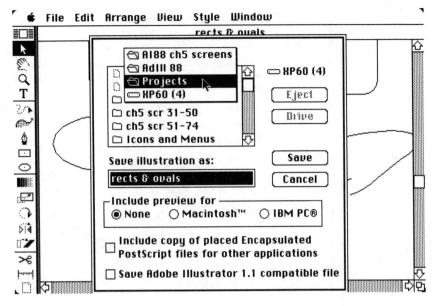

Figure 5-78.
Dragging down from the current folder to switch folders on the same disk.

application expects the origin (0,0 point) to be, and other details specific to PostScript (see Chapter 6). To use this method, you should save your Illustrator file as "PostScript only" (rather than Encapsulated PostScript) — click the None option for preview in the Save As dialog box. Since "PostScript only" is simply a text file of PostScript commands, it should be possible to incorporate these commands into any application that has a PostScript Place capability.

When you have finished selecting the Save As options you desire, click the Save button. If you want to return to the Adobe Illustrator 88 program without saving your work, press the Cancel button to send the dialog box away and return to the program.

Page Setup...

The Page Setup command is used to select the page-oriented (as opposed to printer-oriented) options that affect how the page will be printed. Selecting the Page Setup command in the File menu brings up the Page Setup dialog box (Figure 5-79), allowing you to specify

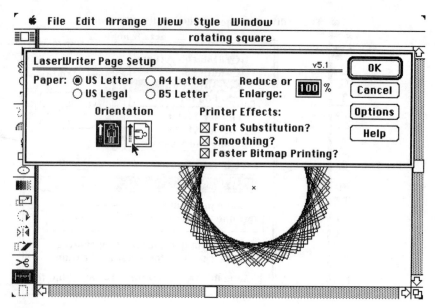

Figure 5-79.
The Page Setup dialog box for the Apple LaserWriter laser printer.

the paper size, either vertical (portrait) or horizontal (landscape) page orientation, a percentage of reduction or enlargement, and other printer options available for the selected printer.

Unlike most of the other dialog boxes in the Adobe Illustrator 88 program, the Page Setup dialog box and the related Print dialog box are provided by the Macintosh's operating system, not the program. Although the Page Setup dialog boxes for different printers appear similar, there are some important differences, described here in greater detail. For more information about printing, see the section on the Print command.

The options you specify in the Page Setup dialog box are only applied to the Illustrator document displayed in the window that was active when you selected the Page Setup command. Any options you specify will be saved with the Illustrator document. Since the options you select only affect the document in the active window, you will need to select Page Setup and specify the options for other documents separately, after you have activated each of the windows that display those documents.

Because the Page Setup options are saved with the document, and the options and dialog boxes vary for different printers, Adobe Illustrator 88 will not automatically change all the Page Setup

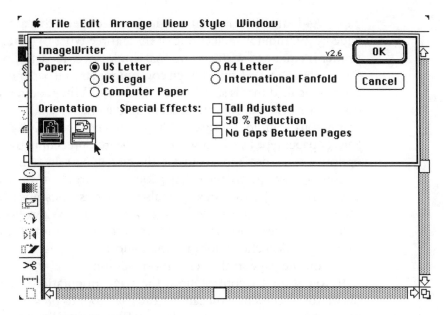

Figure 5-80.
The Page Setup dialog box for the Apple ImageWriter dot matrix printer.

options if you change printers. If you use a different printer than the one you specified in the Page Setup dialog box, Adobe Illustrator 88 will use the default options provided by the new printer's system resource file instead of the options that were saved with the document. Therefore, if you change printers with the Chooser, check the Page Setup dialog box to make sure that the options you desire are selected.

ImageWriter Page Setup

You can use the Apple ImageWriter for printing. If you select the ImageWriter with the Chooser desk accessory, you get the ImageWriter Page Setup dialog box when you choose the Page Setup command (Figure 5-80). The ImageWriter's Page Setup dialog box is revised from time to time by Apple, and the current version number is displayed on the top right of the dialog box near the OK button.

You can specify the exact size of the paper you are using with the ImageWriter. US Letter means single sheets of standard 8 1/2-by-11-inch paper. US Legal refers to single sheets of 8 1/2-by-14-inch paper. A4 Letter describes international-sized sheets that are 210mm wide by 297mm tall. Select one of these three types of paper if your printer is equipped with an optional single-sheet feeder. Computer Paper refers to 8 1/2-by-11-inch continuous fanfold paper used with the tractor-feed that is standard on the ImageWriter and most other dot-matrix printers. International fanfold is the A4-sized sheets in a continuous fanfold for use with tractor-feed equipped printers. Select a paper type by clicking in the small circle preceding the desired option; a small dot appears inside the circle you selected.

You can also specify the orientation of the printout: vertical (also known as portrait), or horizontal (also known as landscape). Vertical (portrait) is the standard way pages are printed. When horizontal (landscape) orientation is selected, the artwork is printed sideways, which is an ideal choice for printing a short, wide image that would not fit on the page in the vertical orientation.

If you want to control how the page orientation affects the Illustrator document, you can use the page tool to preview how the page will be set up and change the way Illustrator splits up the pages for printing. Changes made in the Page Setup dialog box will be reflected in the grid controlled by the page tool. You can select either the vertical orientation icon or the horizontal orientation icon by simply pointing to it and clicking the mouse button. The selected icon will appear black.

The "Special Effects" options in the ImageWriter's Page Setup dialog box relate to special effects to select to modify the printing process. The first of these effects is called "Tall Adjusted"; it adjusts the ImageWriter's printing to compensate for the fact that, unlike the LaserWriter, there are a different number of dots per inch vertically than there are horizontally. Because Adobe Illustrator 88 is designed for a PostScript printer with the same number of dots both horizontally and vertically, you should always select the Tall Adjusted option when printing Illustrator documents on the ImageWriter to prevent the artwork from being distorted. To select the Tall Adjusted option, click in the small box preceding the option; a small x will appear inside the box to signify that the option has been selected.

The next option is called "50% Reduction"; it allows you to specify whether or not you want your artwork reduced by 50 percent (i.e., shrunk down to half its size) before it is printed. You select this option by clicking in the box preceding it.

The last option is "No Gaps Between Pages;" this option is not relevant to Illustrator and should not be selected.

LaserWriter Page Setup

If you are using the LaserWriter for printing, you will see a Page Setup dialog box (see Figure 5-79) that resembles the ImageWriter's dialog box. The LaserWriter's Page Setup dialog box is revised from time to time by Apple, and the current version number is displayed on the top right of the dialog box near the OK button.

The first set of options are grouped together to the right of the word "Paper." These options allow you to specify the exact size of the paper that you are using with the printer. US Letter means sheets of the standard 8 1/2-by-11-inch paper. US Legal refers to sheets of 8 1/2-by-14-inch paper. Although the LaserWriter can handle legal-sized sheets of paper, it will only print on the top section of the paper in an area equivalent to that of a regular 8 1/2-by-11-inch page. However, there are other PostScript printers that can print on the entire legal-sized page or even larger pages. A4 Letter refers to international-sized sheets of paper that are 210mm wide by 297mm tall. B5 Letter refers to a smaller international-size sheet of paper, 176mm wide by 250mm tall. Select the type of paper you are using by clicking in the small circle preceding the desired option. A small dot appears inside the circle for your selection.

To the right of the "Paper" option is the "Reduce or Enlarge:" option that lets you specify a percentage to enlarge or reduce the Illustrator document for printing. After the words "Reduce or Enlarge:" is a small box followed by a percent sign(%). If you want to reduce or enlarge your document prior to printing, you can click this box, and enter a percentage that represents the final size you desire. Selecting a 70 percent reduction will print the page 30 percent smaller, and selecting 140 percent will print the page 40 percent larger. Each PostScript printer has a different range of enlargements or reductions that it can perform; the Apple LaserWriter Plus allows a maximum 400 percent enlargement (four times as large as the original) and a minimum 25 percent reduction (four times as small). Therefore, with the LaserWriter Plus you can enter any percentage between 25 percent and 400 percent. Reducing the image can be handy for getting it to fit on a single page; enlarging is great for inspecting details.

However, reducing or enlarging documents with the Page Setup dialog box does not affect the size of the actual document or the artwork in the document. The only way to actually change the size of the artwork in a document is to use the scale tool.

You can also specify the orientation of the printout: vertical (also known as portrait), or horizontal (also known as landscape). Vertical (portrait) is the standard way pages are printed. When horizontal (landscape) orientation is selected, the artwork is printed sideways, which is an ideal choice for printing a short, wide image that would not fit on the page in the vertical orientation.

If you want to control how the page orientation affects the Illustrator document, you can use the page tool to preview how the page will be set up and change the way Illustrator splits up the pages for printing. Changes made in the Page Setup dialog box will be reflected in the page-division grid controlled by the page tool. You select either the vertical orientation icon or the horizontal orientation icon by simply clicking it. The icon that is selected will turn black.

The last of the LaserWriter's Page Setup options is titled "Printer Effects." This set of options is not relevant to the Illustrator program. Smoothing is used to smooth out the step-ladder effect of bit-mapped images such as a MacPaint document; since Illustrator stores artwork as vector graphics as opposed to bit-mapped graphics, the Smoothing option is ignored by Illustrator. Although the Font Substitution option also has no effect on the printout, turning it off wastes computer memory and can slow down printing. Therefore, you should be sure that the Font Substitution option is selected (i.e., be sure that there is a small x in the box preceding the words "Font Substitution?"). If the Font Substitution option is not selected, select it by clicking in the small box preceding the option. A small x will appear inside the box to signify that the option has been selected.

Print...

The Print command is used to select the printer-oriented (as opposed to page-oriented) options that affect how the page will be printed. Before printing you should familiarize yourself with the Page Setup options described above and make sure that the proper options are selected in the Page Setup dialog box. Selecting the Print command in the File menu (or pressing Command-P as a shortcut) brings up the Print dialog box. If you want to print without bringing up the Print dialog box (because you have already set the printer options the way you want), hold down the Option key while issuing the Print command.

The Print dialog box allows you to specify the number of copies to be printed, the range of pages to be printed, how the paper is handled by the printer, and other options that may be available for a particular printer. Unlike most of the other dialog boxes in the Adobe Illustrator 88 program, the Print dialog box and the related Page Setup dialog box are provided by the Macintosh's operating system, not the program. Although the Print dialog boxes for different printers look similar, there are some important differences. The exact dialog box that will be presented depends on what printer is currently installed in the system and selected for use, and which version of the system software is used.

To select a printer (if there is more than one installed in your system and connected to your Macintosh), use the Chooser desk accessory. It's usually a good idea to check the Chooser before printing to make sure the correct printer has been chosen. Also, if you have changed printers, you should check the Page Setup settings before printing, using the Page Setup command in the File menu.

Keep in mind that Adobe Illustrator 88 is designed to work with PostScript printers. If you are using an ImageWriter or other dot-matrix or laser printer that uses the Macintosh's native QuickDraw graphics language instead of PostScript, the results will not be as good as they would be with a PostScript printer. Be sure to check your printer's documentation to find out if it uses PostScript. Some printers provide for PostScript as an option; if so, check to find out if that option is installed in your printer. Although the ImageWriter and other QuickDraw printers do not produce the best results, they are still useful for getting a rough idea of how the final PostScript printout will look. If you don't own a PostScript printer, you can make drafts on your ImageWriter (or similar printer) and take your Illustrator document to a service bureau or other location that has a PostScript printer connected to a Macintosh for getting the final printout.

ImageWriter Printing

If you are using the ImageWriter printer (and it is properly attached, chosen, and set up), issuing the Print command will bring up an ImageWriter Print dialog box (Figure 5-81). The Print dialog box is revised periodically, and the current version number is displayed at the top right of the dialog box near the OK button.

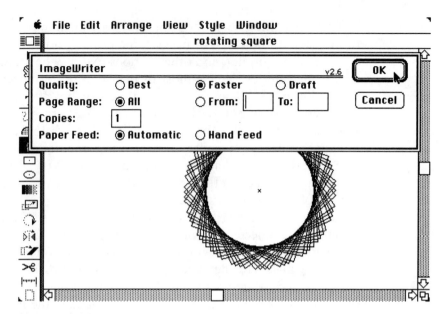

Figure 5-81.
The Print dialog box for the Apple ImageWriter dot matrix printer.

The first set of options is labeled "Quality:." The print quality options let you select from two different densities of dots, "Best" and "Faster," and a high-speed text-only printing mode called "Draft." Illustrator artwork can only be printed in the Best or Faster modes. Illustrator text files can be printed in any mode using a word-processing program. Since the Adobe Illustrator 88 program only prints the artwork, choose either Best or Faster; as implied in the choice, the Best mode takes considerably longer to print. If the ImageWriter is only used for printing rough drafts, printing documents in the Faster mode saves time and wear on the printer and ribbon.

Below the "Quality:" options are the "Page Range:" options. Usually you will want to select all pages to be printed. "All" is the default setting, so it will probably be selected already. You can tell if it is selected by the dot inside the radio button that precedes the word "All." If it is not selected, you can select it by clicking in the radio button.

You might have to print a specified range of pages if you are printing a piece of artwork that will not fit on one page and you do not want to print the entire 14-inch by 14-inch document. In order to determine (or control) how the Adobe Illustrator 88 program divides the Illustrator document into pages for printing, you should familiarize yourself with the page tool. If you know how the program will number the pages (described in the section about the page tool), you can specify the range by clicking inside the circle preceding the word "From:" and then entering the two range numbers in their respective boxes. Before you can type a number in one of the range boxes, you must select the box by clicking in it.

Below the "Page Range:" option is the "Copies:" option that lets you specify how many copies of the document you would like to be printed. The default value is one copy. If you want to print two or more copies, click in the box after the word "Copies:," and enter the number of copies you want printed.

At the bottom of the ImageWriter's Print dialog box are the "Paper Feed:" options. Select the "Automatic" option by clicking on it (if it's not already selected) if you are using a tractor-feed or automatic sheet-feeder on your ImageWriter. Select the "Hand Feed" option if you are going to hand feed each sheet into the printer.

When you have selected the Print options that you want, you can initiate the printing process by clicking the OK button. If you don't want to print, click on the Cancel button to return to the Adobe Illustrator 88 program. The double line around the OK button indicates that the button will be pushed if you press the Return key. After you click the OK button, a dialog box will be displayed, indicating that the connection to the printer is being established. Once the printing process has started, another dialog box is displayed, indicating which page is currently being sent to the printer.

If you want to stop the printing process while either of the two above dialog boxes are displayed, hold down the Command key while typing a period(.); this will cancel the printing. The printer may not stop right away due to the fact that the ImageWriter contains a small memory buffer that must be depleted before the Cancel command actually takes effect.

LaserWriter Printing

If you are using the LaserWriter printer (and it is properly attached, chosen, and set-up), issuing the Print command will bring up a Laser-Writer Print dialog box (Figure 5-82). The LaserWriter Print utility (and dialog box) is revised periodically by the printer manufacturer,

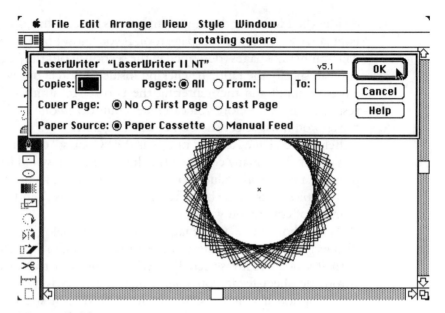

Figure 5-82.
The Print dialog box for the Apple LaserWriter II NT.

and the current version number is displayed at the top right of the dialog box near the OK button.

The first of the LaserWriter print options is the "Copies:" option that lets you specify how many copies of the document you would like printed. The default value is one copy. If you want to print two or more copies, click in the box after the word "Copies:," and enter the number of copies you want printed.

Next to the "Copies:" option is the "Pages:" option that lets you specify the range of pages you want printed. Usually you will want to select all pages to be printed, and "All" is the default setting that will probably be selected when the dialog box appears. You can tell if it is selected by a small spot inside the radio button that precedes the word "All." If there is no spot inside the circle, it is not selected; you can select it by clicking in the circle (or anywhere on the word "All"). You will need to print only a specified range of pages if you are printing a piece of artwork that will not fit on one page and you do not want to print the entire piece of art. In order to determine (or control) how the Adobe Illustrator 88 program divides the Illustrator document into pages for printing, you should familiarize yourself with the page tool.

If you know how the program will number the pages (described in the section about the page tool), you can specify the range by clicking inside the circle preceding the word "From:" and then entering the two range numbers in their respective boxes. Before you can type a number in one of the range boxes, you must select the box by clicking it.

The next set of options is the "Cover Page:" options. Cover pages are not usually used, so the "No" selection is the default setting and will probably be selected when you bring up the dialog box. If you do want a cover page, select "First Page" by clicking on it to print the cover page before your artwork, or select "Last Page" by clicking on it to print the cover page after your artwork.

At the bottom of the LaserWriter's Print dialog box are the "Paper Source:" options. Select the "Paper Cassette" option by clicking on it (if it's not already selected) if you are using the normal paper tray in your LaserWriter. Select the "Manual Feed" option if you are going to hand feed each sheet into the printer.

When you have selected the Print options that you want, you can initiate the printing process by clicking the OK button. If you don't want to print, click on the Cancel button to return to the Adobe Illustrator 88 program. The double line around the OK button indicates that the button will be pushed if you press the Return key. After you press the Return key or click the OK button, a dialog box will be displayed, indicating that the connection to the printer is being established and, if necessary, that the Macintosh is initializing the printer. Once the printing process has started, another dialog box is displayed, indicating which page is currently being printed.

If you want to stop the printing process while either of the two above dialog boxes are displayed, hold down the Command key while typing a period(.); this will cancel the printing. The printer may not stop right away due to the fact that the LaserWriter contains a memory buffer that must be depleted before the Cancel command actually takes effect; using a print spooler can further prolong the time it takes to stop printing.

Quit

The Quit command ends your current session with Adobe Illustrator 88 and returns you to the Macintosh desktop. You can issue the Quit command by either selecting Quit in the File menu or by pressing Command-Q as a shortcut.

If you have not made any changes to the Illustrator document since the last time you saved it (changing the Page Setup options would count as a change), the program will end your session, close any documents, and automatically return you to the Macintosh desktop.

However, if you have made any changes to the Illustrator document, the program will ask whether or not you would like to save any changes you've made. If you click the "Yes" button, Adobe Illustrator 88 will save any open documents and then close them before returning to the Macintosh desktop. The double lines around the Yes button indicate that it will be selected if you press the Return key.

If there are any new Illustrator documents (i.e. any that are named "Untitled Art"), the Save As dialog box will be displayed so that you can name each untitled document before quitting. If you select the "No" button by clicking on it, that document will be closed without any changes being saved.

If you select the Cancel button, the Quit command will be canceled and you will return to the Adobe Illustrator 88 program.

Edit Menu

Edit	
Undo Copy	⌘Z
Cut	⌘X
Copy	⌘C
Paste	⌘U
Clear	
Select All	⌘A
Paste In Front	⌘F
Paste In Back	⌘B
Bring To Front	⌘=
Send To Back	⌘-
Preferences...	⌘K

The Edit menu is used for selecting various commands used to edit your Adobe Illustrator 88 documents. The commands on the Edit menu allow you to undo the last action made by you or the computer; redo actions that were undone; cut, copy, and paste objects to and from the clipboard; clear (delete) artwork objects from the document; select all the objects in a document, paste objects in front of or behind other objects, move object in front or behind other objects, and invoke the Preferences dialog box in which you can change many settings, such as units of measurement, freehand tolerance, auto trace gap distance, and the angle of constraint.

Undo

The Undo command can be used to immediately undo the last operation, but only if it's used right away, before doing anything else.

To choose the Undo command, select Undo in the Edit menu or press Command-Z as a shortcut. After you select Undo, that menu slot is occupied by the Redo command so that you can redo the last operation that was undone.

The Undo command is not always available. If the Undo command is not available, it will appear grayed-out. If the Undo command is available, it will be listed in the menu followed by the action that will be undone if the command is chosen.

Redo

The Redo command can be used to undo the last Undo command. To choose the Redo command, select Redo in the Edit menu (it is in the same place as the Undo command) or press Command-Z as a shortcut.

The Redo command is only available after the Undo command has been chosen. If the Redo command is not available, it will appear grayed-out. If the Redo command is available, it will be listed in the menu followed by the action that will be redone if the command is chosen. To undo the Redo command, see Undo above.

Cut

The Cut command removes all the selected objects from the document and places them in the Clipboard for temporary storage, ready for a Paste command. The objects are stored in the Clipboard until something else is copied or cut to the Clipboard with the Copy or Cut command.

You can choose the Cut command by either choosing Cut in the Edit menu or by pressing Command-X as a shortcut. Issuing the Cut command replaces whatever else was contained in the Clipboard with the selected objects. After you choose the Cut command, you can check the contents of the Clipboard by issuing the Show Clipboard command in the Window menu.

In order to permanently store objects that are temporarily placed in the Clipboard, you must either paste them to an Adobe Illustrator 88 document using the Paste, Paste In Front, or Paste In Back commands, or transfer them to the Scrapbook by selecting the

Scrapbook from the Apple menu and selecting the Paste command (Command-V).

If you want to undo a cut that you have made, select Undo Cut from the Edit menu or press Command-Z as a shortcut. In order to retrieve an object that was cut and placed in the Clipboard, click inside the window where you want the object to go and then choose one of the Paste commands (Paste, Paste In Front, or Paste In Back); the object will be pasted into the document according to the chosen Paste command.

Copy

The Copy command is similar to the Cut command described above except that it places a copy of the selected objects in the Clipboard without removing them. To choose the Copy command, either choose Copy in the Edit menu or press Command-C as a shortcut.

Issuing the Copy command copies all the selected objects in the active window and places them in the Clipboard for temporary storage (this replaces whatever else was contained in the Clipboard). You can then Paste the objects to the Scrapbook if you want to store them there.

To retrieve an object that was copied or cut and placed in the Clipboard, click inside the window where you want the object to go and then choose one of the Paste commands described below (Paste, Paste In Front, or Paste In Back); the object will be pasted into the document.

The Copy command can also be used to generate a PICT-format image of the Preview Illustration view of the artwork. To create a PICT preview of the artwork, hold down the Option key while issuing the Copy command.

Paste

The Paste command retrieves objects that are temporarily stored in the Clipboard and places them in the document. You can choose the Paste command by either selecting Paste in the Edit menu or by pressing Command-V as a shortcut.

Only Adobe Illustrator 88 artwork objects that were cut or copied can be pasted directly into an Adobe Illustrator 88 document, with the exception of type into a type block.

When you choose the Paste command, any objects that are in the Clipboard will be pasted into the center of the active window and will be placed on top of all the other objects in the document. Even though pasting places all the objects in the Clipboard on top of everything else in the document, the relative painting order of the objects being pasted stays the same. If you want to place the pasted object in back of all or some of the objects, or if you want the objects pasted at the same locations they were cut or copied from, use one of the other Paste commands (either Paste In Front or Paste In Back).

When you paste objects from the Clipboard into an Adobe Illustrator 88 document using the Paste command, the objects that are pasted will be selected and all the other objects will be deselected. Since the Paste command does not remove the contents of the Clipboard, you can continue to Paste the same objects into the document or into other documents.

Clear

The Clear command deletes any objects that are selected. You can choose the Clear command by selecting Clear in the Edit menu or by pressing either the Delete key (Backspace key on the Macintosh Plus) or the Clear key as shortcuts. For more information on how to select the objects that you want to delete, refer to the section about the selection tool.

To delete all of the objects in an Adobe Illustrator 88 document, first click in the document's window, then choose Select All in the Edit menu (or press Command-A as a shortcut), and then choose Clear in the Edit menu (or press the Delete/Backspace key or Clear key as a shortcut). This action will delete everything in the document, and all the objects in the window will disappear.

Select All

The Select All command selects all of the objects (points, lines, curves, etc.) that are contained in the document that is displayed in the active window. You can choose the Select All command by either choosing Select All in the Edit menu or by pressing Command-A as a shortcut.

After selecting all objects, if you now want to deselect all the objects, simply click in any blank area in the document. If you want to deselect one of the selected objects, point to the object you want to deselect and hold down the Shift key while clicking the mouse button; alternatively you can hold down the Shift key and drag the selection marquee around the object to deselect it (be careful not to accidentally include another object in the marquee). If you want to deselect more than one of the selected objects, you can continue the deselection process by holding down the Shift key while pointing to the next object you want to deselect and either click on the object or drag the selection marquee around it.

Be sure that the objects you want deselected are actually selected in the first place; if you try deselecting an object that is not already selected, it will be added to the group of already selected objects instead. Also keep in mind that selecting or deselecting objects has no effect on the order in which they are painted by the program. Use the Paste in Front, Paste in Back, Send to Front or Send to Back commands to change the order.

Paste In Front

The Paste In Front command is used for pasting objects stored in the Clipboard in front of the objects that are selected in an Adobe Illustrator 88 document. You can choose the Paste In Front command by either selecting Paste In Front in the Edit menu or by pressing Command-F as a shortcut. Only Adobe Illustrator 88 artwork objects that were cut or copied onto the Clipboard can be pasted directly into an Adobe Illustrator 88 document.

When you choose the Paste In Front command, any objects that are in the Clipboard will be pasted in front of all the selected objects in the document, and behind the objects in the document that are not selected. Even though pasting the group of objects in the Clipboard changes the order in which that group is painted by the program, the relative painting order of the objects being pasted stays the same. If you want to place the pasted object in back of all or some of the objects, use the Paste In Back command described next.

When you paste objects from the Clipboard into an Adobe Illustrator 88 document using the Paste In Front command, the objects that are pasted will be selected and all the other objects will be deselected. It will also paste in front of everything if nothing is selected. Issuing the Paste In Front command does not remove the contents of the Clipboard.

The Paste In Front command is handy for placing duplicate objects on top of each other for special effects, such as placing an object that was outlined over an object that was filled with a shade of gray or color. Since pasting does not remove the contents of the Clipboard, all you need to do to create a duplicate of an object is to select it, copy it to the Clipboard, and choose the Paste In Front command.

Paste In Back

The Paste In Back command is used for pasting objects stored in the Clipboard behind the objects that are selected in an Adobe Illustrator 88 document. You can choose the Paste In Back command by either selecting Paste In Back in the Edit menu or by pressing Command-B as a shortcut. Only Adobe Illustrator 88 artwork objects that were cut or copied onto the Clipboard can be pasted directly into an Adobe Illustrator 88 document.

When you choose the Paste In Back command, any objects that are in the Clipboard will be pasted in back of all the selected objects that are in the document, and in front of the objects in the document that are not selected. Even though pasting the group of objects in the Clipboard changes the order in which that group is painted by the program, the relative painting order of the objects being pasted stays the same. If you want to place the pasted object in front of all or some of the objects, use the Paste In Front command described above.

When you paste objects from the Clipboard into an Adobe Illustrator 88 document using the Paste In Back command, the objects that are pasted will be selected and all the other objects will be deselected. It will also paste in back of everything if nothing is selected. Issuing the Paste In Back command does not remove the contents of the Clipboard.

Bring To Front

The Bring To Front command is used for placing objects in the frontmost position in an Adobe Illustrator 88 document. You can choose the Bring To Front command by either selecting Bring To

Front in the Edit menu or by pressing the Command key and the equal (=) sign key as a shortcut. When you choose the Bring To Front command, any objects that are selected are placed in front of all other objects in the document.

Send To Back

The Send To Back command is used for placing objects behind all other objects in an Adobe Illustrator 88 document. You can choose the Send To Back command by either selecting Send To Back in the Edit menu or by pressing the Command key and the dash (-) key as a shortcut. When you choose the Send To Back command, any objects that are selected are placed in back of all other objects in the document.

Preferences...

You can select the Preferences command from the Edit menu, or press Command-K. The Preferences command displays a dialog box (Figure 5-83) that contains all of the preferences settings for your session with Adobe Illustrator 88. You can set the snap-to point, preview and print patterns, the ability to transform pattern tiles, the constrain angle, the corner radius for rectangles, the cursor key distance, the freehand tolerance level, the auto trace gap distance, ruler units, and color settings for your display.

The Snap to point setting determines whether an object should snap to an anchor point whenever the pointer is within two pixels of that anchor point. The Snap to point feature makes it possible to place one point on top of another without having to zoom into the drawing to see much more detail..

The Preview and print patterns option determines whether the program should print patterns and display them with the Preview Illustration command.

The Transform pattern tiles option determines whether pattern tiles will be transformed or moved along with an object that is undergoing a transformation or a move. This option is automatically turned on if you choose to transform pattern files in any of the transformation or move dialog boxes. Ordinarily patterns are not moved or transformed with an object.

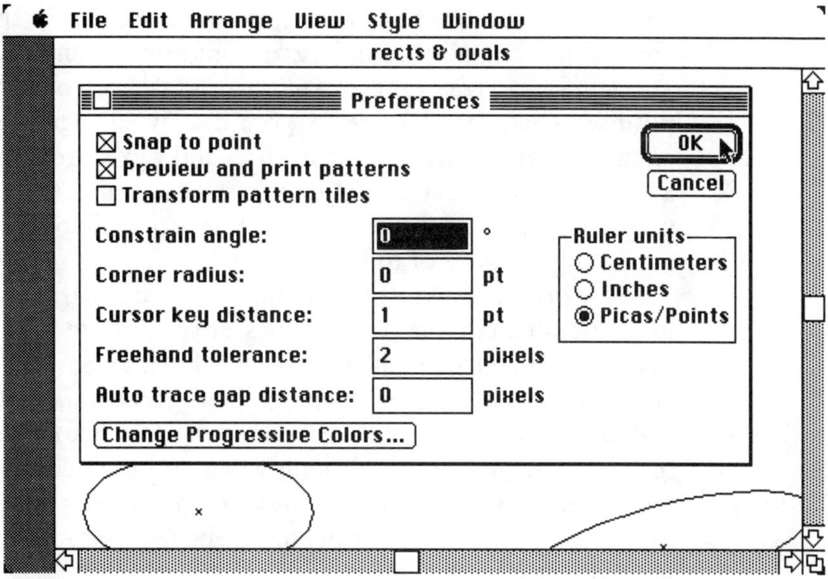

Figure 5-83.
The Preferences dialog box for changing the snap-to point, preview and print patterns, the ability to transform pattern tiles, the constrain angle, the corner radius for rectangles, the cursor key distance, the freehand tolerance level, the auto trace gap distance, ruler units, and color settings for your display.

The Constrain angle lets you rotate the x and y axes of the document. Each time you start the Adobe Illustrator 88 program, the x and y axes are set parallel to the sides of your display, vertically and horizontally. When you draw, move, or transform an object while holding down the Shift key, the drawing, movement, or transformation occurs relative to the x and y axes at 45-degree increments. You can set the Constrain angle to change the x and y axes relative to its original position as vertical and horizontal, and the new axes will affect transformations and movements in any other documents you open or create during that session (until you quit the program). The new axes are rotated counterclockwise from the horizontal origin if you specify a positive angle, or clockwise if you specify a negative angle.

The new constrain angle does not affect freehand drawing, blending, or automatic tracing. It affects all transformations and constrained movements, drawing with the rectangle and oval tools, and constrained drawing with the pen tool. Always specify the constrain angle before drawing, because you can't apply a new constraint to an existing object without transforming the object.

If you want to reset the axes to the original horizontal and vertical position parallel to the sides of your display, change the Constrain angle to zero. Changes made to the x and y axes are not saved with a document; the next time you open the document (during another program session) the axes will be reset to their original position parallel to the sides of the document.

The Corner radius setting specifies the radius of the circles used to form rounded corners of rectangles. If you specify a corner radius, that radius is applied to all new squares or rectangles you draw, until you change it again in the Rectangle dialog box or in the Preferences dialog box. Always specify the corner radius before drawing the rectangle, because you can't apply a new corner radius to an existing rectangle. You specify the amount of movement in the current measurement used for the ruler units (inches, centimeters, or picas/points).

If the radius you specify is too large for the rectangle (more than one-half the size of either the height or width, whichever is smaller), then the program uses the radius for the largest oval that can fit in the corner of the rectangle. Specify a radius of zero for ordinary square-cornered rectangles.

The Cursor key distance describes the distance a selected object will move when you press one of the cursor control keys. You can press the cursor keys as many times as you want to move selected objects, and change direction at will. You specify the amount of movement in the current measurement used for the ruler units (inches, centimeters, or picas/points).

The Freehand tolerance setting determines how sensitive the freehand tool will be to sudden quirks and changes in your hand movement. The freehand tool responds to shakiness or other slight variations in your drawing motion, creating bumps. You can set the freehand tolerance level to reduce (or increase) the number of bumps. The default setting for the freehand tolerance level is two pixels, which means that a variation of two pixels will not create a bump. The larger the number of pixels, the more bumps the program will ignore, providing for smoother lines.

The Auto trace gap distance is also measured in pixels, and determines the largest gap that the auto trace tool will jump across in an effort to continue tracing a shape. Scanned images and bit-mapped graphics sometimes have gaps that are visible when you enlarge your view with the zoom tool. The auto trace tool will ignore gaps that are equal to or less than the number of pixels you specify for the distance.

The Ruler units can be set to centimeters, inches, or picas and points. These units are used in the rulers, which change along with the zoom tool to show greater or lesser magnification. They are also used in dialog boxes.

Preferences: Change Progressive Colors

Adobe Illustrator 88 provides a way to adjust the display of your Macintosh II so that colors more closely match the printed colors. You make these adjustments by referring to a sample progressive color bar from your printer (see Plate 1). Progressive color bars are printed on color separations on the right edge by the Adobe Separator program. The printer prints color bars on the press. Color bars and other marks are trimmed off before a print job is finished. It is helpful to get a color sample with color bar printed on the paper stock, from same printer that will be printing the color artwork or publication, so that you can match a specific paper's ink coverage.

A progressive color bar shows cyan, yellow, magenta, and the following combinations: magenta and yellow, cyan and yellow, cyan and magenta, and then all three colors, followed by black.

Although Adobe Illustrator 88 can display colors on a monitor set in the Control Panel to 16 colors, you get best results in matching the printed version by using a monitor set to 256 or more colors.

After running the monitor for about 20 minutes (so that it warms up), choose Preferences from the Edit menu and click the Change Progressive Colors button, which displays the Progressive Colors dialog box showing the four process colors, white, and the same combinations found on the color bar (Figure 5-84). You can hold your printer's color bar up to the display and compare it to the colors in this dialog box. See page 2 of the *Adobe Illustrator 88 Color Guide* for the sequence of progressive colors used in the dialog box.

If one or more colors in the dialog box do not match the printed colors closely enough, click on the color in the Progressive Colors

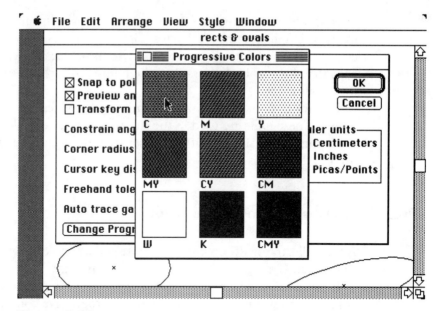

Figure 5-84.

The Change Progressive Colors dialog box, shown here with patterns for a black and white Macintosh SE, displays the progressive colors. You can hold your printer's color bar up to the display and compare it to these colors, then click any color that does not match, and change it on the color wheel.

dialog box to change it. The program displays the standard Macintosh color wheel for selecting a color from the more than 16.7 million colors available. You can move the tiny white dot across the color wheel to change the hue and saturation, and scroll through brightness levels, to get the right color. Or you can specify a color exactly by typing its hue, saturation, and brightness values or its red, green, and blue values.

Since ambient light and general room conditions can vary over the course of a day, you may need to adjust the monitor a few times in order to get a close match to the printed version. However, the monitor can never be as close in matching the final printed version as a PostScript color printer can be, since a color printer also uses ink and paper. You may be able to cut down on the costs of consumables in the proofing process, but you still need the best possible proof to be sure of quality. The best possible proof is an on-press proof using the actual printing press that will do the final job.

Arrange Menu

Arrange	
Transform Again	⌘D
Group	⌘G
Ungroup	⌘U
Join...	⌘J
Average...	⌘L
Lock	⌘1
Unlock All	⌘2
Hide	⌘3
Show All	⌘4

The Arrange menu is used for manipulating, modifying, and arranging artwork objects. The commands on the Arrange menu allow you to repeat the transformation (scaling, rotating, reflecting, shearing, or moving) of an object or group of objects, combine objects into a unified group, join two endpoints, average two or more endpoints, lock objects so that they can't be selected, unlock all objects, hide selected objects, and show all objects.

Transform Again

The Transform Again command repeats the last transformation of an object or group of objects. You can choose the Transform Again command by either selecting Transform Again in the Arrange menu or by pressing Command-D as a shortcut.

A transformation refers to the action of scaling, rotating, reflecting, shearing, or moving. If your last transformation created a transformed duplicate (because you held down the Option key while performing the transformation), the Transform Again command will both transform and create a duplicate for the object again each time that you choose the command.

Repeating transformations a number of times can be used to create special effects. For example, objects can be rotated around a central point (e.g. spokes on a wheel, petals on a daisy, etc.) by using the rotate tool and Rotate dialog box to specify a precise amount of rotation for an object, clicking on the Copy button in the dialog box, and issuing the Transform Again command to repeat the rotation and duplication. The Transform Again command can be chosen repeatedly (to create any number of transformed duplicate objects) until you ultimately run out of memory in your computer.

Group

The Group command consolidates a number of artwork objects into a single object. To choose the Group command, either select Group in the Arrange menu or press Command-G as a shortcut. Issuing the Group command converts all the objects that are selected in the

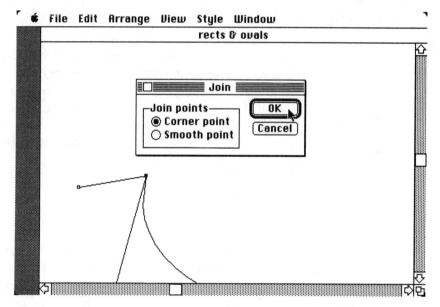

Figure 5-85.

After selecting two endpoints in which one is on top of the other, use the Join command to join them into an anchor point that can be either a corner point or a smooth point.

document into a single composite object.

To select the objects that you want to group together you can either: 1) drag the selection marquee around the objects; 2) select the objects one-by-one by first clicking on an object and then holding down the Shift key while you click on the other objects you want included in the group; 3) select all the objects in the document for grouping by issuing the Select All command found in the Edit menu; or 4) choose the Select All command and then deselect the objects that you don't want in the group.

Keep in mind that only complete paths can be grouped; therefore if any of the objects you have selected for grouping includes a partially selected path, the entire path will become part of the group. After you have selected the objects that you want grouped together you can choose the Group command to combine all the selected objects into a single grouped object.

Once a number of objects are grouped together with the Group command, they can be selected, deleted, moved, scaled, rotated, reflected, sheared, cut, copied, pasted, or painted as a single unit.

Combining objects into a group does not change the relative painting order of the objects in the group, but it does change the painting order of the group as a whole. When objects are grouped together, the program paints them starting with the top object in the group. If you want to change the painting order of objects within a group, you must first ungroup the objects using the Ungroup command described below, and then use the Paste In Front and Paste In Back, or Bring To Front and Send To Back commands (in the Edit menu) to change the order in which the component objects are painted.

Grouped objects can be combined with other groups and/or objects to create a larger grouped object. Grouped objects cannot be changed with the pen tool unless they are ungrouped with the Ungroup command. Because grouped objects are more resistant to changes than ungrouped objects, grouping objects is a convenient way to "freeze" a path or object once you are finished drawing it, to prevent accidental changes. You can also lock an object so that it can't be selected — see the Lock command.

Ungroup

The Ungroup command breaks a grouped object down into its original component parts. You can choose the Ungroup command by either selecting Ungroup in the Arrange menu or by pressing Command-U.

If any of the original components were also grouped objects, the Ungroup command will leave the component groups intact. If you want to break any of these component groups down into their original parts, you must repeat the Ungroup command after selecting the component group.

Issuing the Ungroup command has no effect on which objects are selected or on what order the program paints the objects that were contained in the group.

Join...

The Join command is used to connect two endpoints in order to close a open path or to connect the endpoints of two open paths. The Join command either connects two endpoints that are apart from each other with a straight line or it combines two endpoints that are directly on top of one another into a single anchor point.

You can select Join from the Arrange menu or press Command-

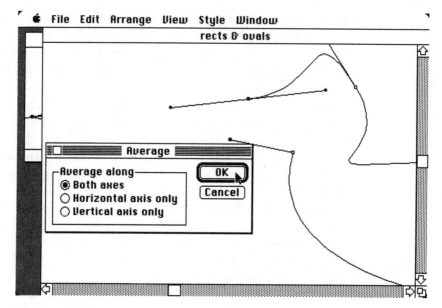

Figure 5-86.
*The Average dialog box lets you specify which axis or both axes for
performing the average operation. Two endpoints are selected for
averaging.*

J as a shortcut. Two endpoints must already be selected. To select
two endpoints that are on top of each other, drag the selection
marquee over the points. The two endpoints can't belong to a
grouped object; you must ungroup the object with the Ungroup
command before joining the two endpoints.

When you select two endpoints on top of each other, the Join
command displays a dialog box to let you specify the point to be a
corner point or a smooth point (Figure 5-85). The program replaces
the points with a single anchor point.

The Join command draws a straight line segment between two
endpoints that are apart from one another, leaving both the line and
the two endpoints selected. If you selected the two endpoints of an
open path when you selected the Join command, the path will be
closed with a straight line. If you selected the endpoints of two
different paths when you selected the Join command, the two paths
will be connected (either with a straight line or by combining the two
points) and will become one longer path. Joining points that are on
top of each other is handy for connecting objects that were cut apart
with the scissors tool.

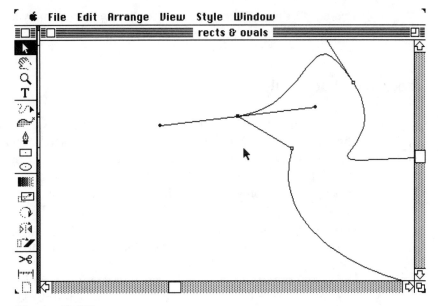

Figure 5-87.
The results of averaging on both axes the two endpoints in the previous figure.

Average...

The Average command moves two or more anchor points to the average location of the points, and you can specify along one or both of the x and y axes. You can choose the Average command by either selecting Average in the Arrange menu or by pressing Command-L as a shortcut. You can only choose the Average command if there are two or more anchor points selected.

If you have chosen the Average command with two or more anchor points selected, a dialog box appears (Figure 5-86) for choosing which axis, or both axes, should be used to constrain the averaging.

By averaging with both axes, the selected anchor points move to the average location along both axes (Figure 5-87). The paths and shapes connected to the points change shape, as they always do when any of their anchor points are moved.

The Average command only moves anchor points on top of each other; it does not connect them, merge them, or join them. If you want to connect anchor points, you have to use the Join command described above to connect them (two anchor points can be connected at a time). Averaging anchor points is used mainly for moving points, paths, or other objects next to each other.

Lock and Unlock All

Objects can be locked so that they can no longer be selected unless they are unlocked. First select the object or objects to be locked, then choose the Lock command from the Arrange menu or press Command-1. If you hold down the Option key, all unselected objects are locked, leaving only selected objects unlocked.

When objects overlap each other, it is useful to be able to lock certain objects so that they no longer get in the way of selecting other objects. You can lock only entire paths; if you select only a segment, the entire path is locked anyway.

Locked objects are saved with the document in their locked state. To unlock, use the Unlock All command, which unlocks all locked objects at once. You can choose the Unlock command from the Arrange menu or press Command-2.

Hide and Show All

Objects can be hidden from view with the Hide command. After selecting the object or objects to hide from view, you choose the Hide command from the Arrange menu or press Command-3.

Hiding objects can be useful if objects are too close together or overlapping, and you need to work on other objects that are partially or fully obscured. You can hide only paths; if you select only a segment, the entire path is hidden anyway. A hidden object can't be selected and it doesn't appear in print or in the Preview Illustration view.

Hiding is not saved with the document; therefore, all objects are shown when you open a document. You can also show all objects by choosing the Show All Command from the Arrange menu, or press Control-4. Neither Hide nor Show All can be undone by the Undo command.

View Menu

View
Preview Illustration ⌘Y
Artwork & Template ⌘E
✓Artwork Only ⌘W
Template Only
Actual Size ⌘H
Fit In Window ⌘M
Show Rulers ⌘R

The View menu contains various commands that allow you to alter your view of the Adobe Illustrator 88 document in the active window. The View commands let you see a preview of the printed artwork, the artwork and the template together for tracing the template, the Adobe Illustrator 88 artwork only, or the template document only. You can control the size at which the document is viewed, and control whether or not the toolbox and rulers are displayed, in the active window.

Preview Illustration

The Preview Illustration command creates an approximate view of what Adobe Illustrator 88 artwork will look like when it is printed. Select Preview Illustration from the View menu (Command-Y), and the program changes its view of the document and uses the current Paint and Type settings to display an approximation of what your artwork would look like if it were printed. You can't modify the image of the artwork directly in the Preview Illustration view.

The only operations you can perform on a Preview image are those that alter your view of the image such as the scroll bars, hand tool, zoom tool, and page tool. However, if you have open windows that represent more than one view of a document (created with the New Window command in the Window menu), the windows that contain previews of the artwork will be updated automatically when changes are made in other views of the document that do allow alterations of the artwork.

Previews of gray-scales and color shades are not accurate, and only serve as a very rough approximation of the final output. Preview is very useful for checking the order in which objects are painted by the program.

To change the colors used in the Preview Illustration view, use the Preferences command in the Edit menu to display the Preferences dialog box, then click the Change Progressive Colors button to show the cyan, yellow, magenta, and black combinations for comparison to printed color bars. See Preferences: Change Progressive Colors for more information.

Artwork & Template

The Artwork & Template command displays both the Adobe Illustrator 88 document and the template beneath it (if any) in the active window. The Artwork & Template view is what is displayed when you first open a document, and it is the view that you will probably use most of the time for creating and working on your artwork. Select it from the View menu, or as a shortcut use Command-E.

Artwork Only

The Artwork Only command displays only the Adobe Illustrator 88 document in the active window, and hides the template document from view. The Artwork Only view is handy for working on the artwork when the template is distracting you from the fine details. Select it from the View menu, or as a shortcut use Command-W.

Template Only

The Template Only command displays only the template document in the active window, and hides the Adobe Illustrator 88 document from view. The Template Only view is useful for inspecting the original scanned image without it being obscured by the artwork. Although the template is usually grayed in the Artwork & Template view, in Template Only view the template is fully black as it would look in MacPaint or a similar painting program.

Actual Size

The Actual Size command displays the document in the active window at the actual size of the Adobe Illustrator 88 document. At this size one screen pixel is equivalent to one point (1/72 of an inch).

You can choose the Actual Size command by either selecting Actual Size in the View menu, pressing Command-H, or holding down the Option key while double-clicking the hand tool. Issuing the Actual Size command also centers the document (and accompanying template, if any) in the active window.

Fit In Window

The Fit In Window command displays the entire 14-inch by 14-inch drawing space containing the document in the active window. Select Fit In Window in the View menu, press Command-M, or double-click on the hand tool. The Fit In Window command also centers the document (and accompanying template, if any) in the active window.

Show Rulers

The Show Rulers command displays two rulers, one along the right-hand side and one along the bottom of the active window. Show Rulers only appears as a menu option if the rulers are not currently displayed in the active window; if the rulers are already displayed, the Hide Rulers command occupies this position in the menu instead.

The rulers are useful for precision work where measurements or sizes are important. Every window can have its own set of rulers. When you first create a document or first start the program and open an existing document, the rulers will not be displayed. To display the rulers, select Show Rulers in the View menu (Command-R).

The rulers use one of three different units of measurement: centimeters, inches, or picas and points (one point = 1/72 of an inch, one pica = 12 points or 1/6th of an inch). In Figure 5-88 the rulers are numbered in picas at actual size, with tick marks corresponding to 4-point intervals and numbered subdivisions at 4-pica intervals. As the magnification or reduction of the view changes, the numbering system on the ruler also changes (Figure 5-89).

When the rulers are displayed you will notice that as you move the mouse, the pointer's position is indicated by a dotted line on each of the rulers. The ruler origin point for the rulers (i.e., the zero point for each ruler) is tied to the document, not the window, so if you

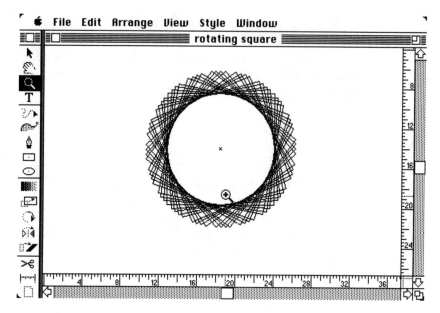

Figure 5-88.
The rulers are displayed by the Show Rulers (Command-R) command.
This view is actual size.

scroll, move, or zoom around in the document, the numbers on the
rulers will change to reflect the document's ruler origin.

When the document is created, the ruler origin for the rulers is the
lower left-hand corner. If you want to change the ruler origin, move
the arrow cursor over the lower right-hand corner of the active
window, where the rulers intersect, and a set of dotted cross-hairs
appears (Figure 5-90). Hold down the mouse button and the pointer
changes into a plus sign(+) when you move it into the active window.
Drag the cross-hairs over the point that you want to become the new
origin for the rulers and release the mouse button.

For color separation purposes, you should be aware that this point
also becomes the PostScript origin point for the measurements of the
bounding box. The bounding box describes the smallest rectangle
that defines the outside dimensions of the entire illustration, and
controls where trim marks and registration targets appear in the color
separation produced by the Adobe Separator program. You may
want to reset the ruler origin point before saving the illustration
document for producing color separations. The lower-left corner of
page five is the logical ruler origin for specifying the bounding box
in the Adobe Separator program.

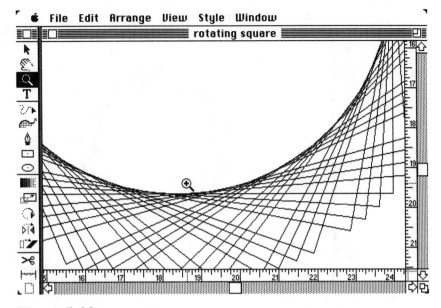

Figure 5-89.
The ruler unit marks change as you zoom into or out from a document to provide precise measuring.

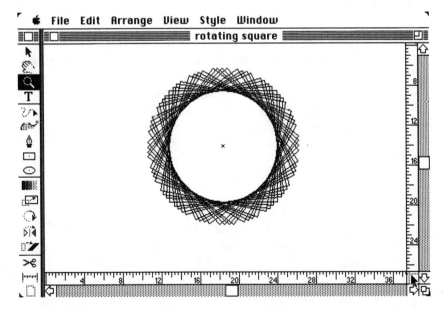

Figure 5-90.
Clicking the intersection point that defines the ruler origin (where zero appears on each ruler).

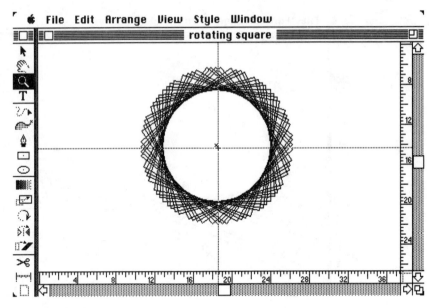

Figure 5-91.
Dragging the ruler origin to be in the center of the circle.

Hide Rulers

If you want to remove the rulers from view, you can do so by either
choosing Hide Rulers in the View menu or by pressing Command-
R as a shortcut. The Hide Rulers command only appears as a menu
option if the rulers are currently displayed in the active window; if the
rulers are not displayed, the Show Rulers command will occupy this
position in the menu instead.

Style Menu

The Style menu contains two commands, Paint and Type, that allow
you to specify attributes that determine how the artwork will be
painted and how the type will be displayed. There are two kinds of
color you can assign to artwork: a mix of the process colors (cyan,
yellow, and magenta), or premixed PANTONE colors. Learning to
use these commands is critical to creating Adobe Illustrator 88
artwork. In addition, Adobe Illustrator 88 offers the ability to make

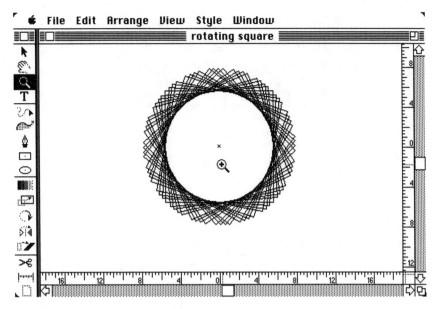

Figure 5-92.
The ruler's zero points now define the center of the circle.

custom patterns and mix custom colors (or rename PANTONE colors) from the Style menu.

Paint...

The Paint command lets you control how regions are filled and how paths are stroked. You can specify no fill and no stroke, or white, 100 percent black, a percentage of black (for gray), percentages of process colors (cyan, yellow, and magenta), or a PANTONE or custom color, for both fill and stroke. If you have created custom patterns, you can also assign them to paths in the Paint dialog box.

In addition, for strokes you can specify either solid or dashed lines, the pattern for dashed lines, the line weight, the type of line cap and join, and the miter limit on miter joins. You can also attach text notes to use as descriptions of objects in the document (the text notes become PostScript comments in the file and are useful for PostScript programming, which is described in Chapter 6).

To choose the Paint command, you can either select Paint in the Style menu or press Command-I as a shortcut. Choosing the Paint

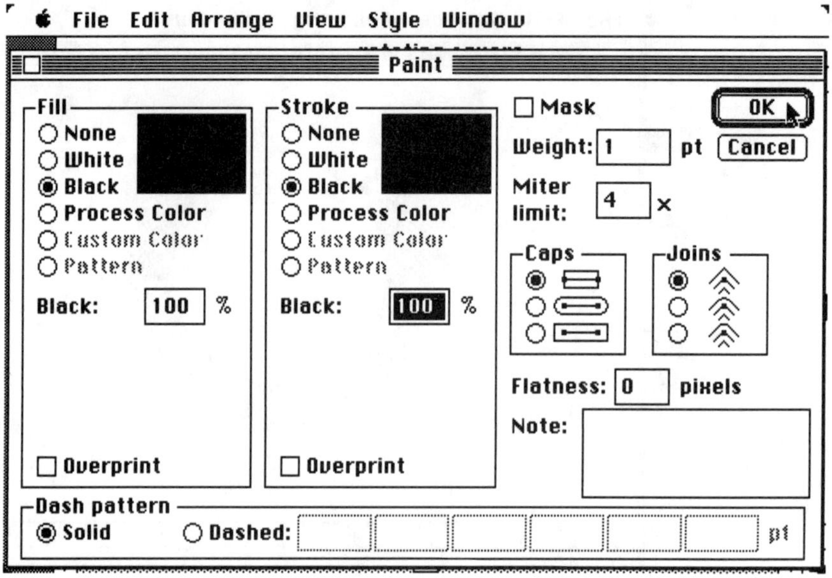

Figure 5-93.

The Paint dialog box, with black fill and black stroke set to 100 percent (you can change the black percentage to specify a shade of gray for fill and stroke). Since a stroke is specified, the dialog box also lets you specify the stroke line weight, solid or dashed lines, the pattern for dashed lines, the type of line cap and join, the miter limit for miter joins, and the flatness level for controlling the number of points in an illustration.

command brings up the Paint dialog box (Figure 5-93). You can use the Paint command to examine or change the painting attributes of a particular object by selecting the object and then choosing the Paint command, which displays the Paint settings for that object.

Adobe Illustrator 88 uses the settings of the Paint dialog box to produce the final image that is output to the printer, displayed on the screen with the Preview Illustration command, or output by the Adobe Separator program.

PostScript automatically masks objects that overlap one another, so that the painted fill and stroke of an object that is underneath another filled and stroked object does not print. It is like painting with non-transparent pieces of paper for each shape. If you ever have any doubt that two shapes overlap, choose the Preview Illustration option to see what will happen when the illustration is printed.

Adobe Illustrator 88 lets you assign custom colors to paths in an image whether or not you are using a color display. Printing presses

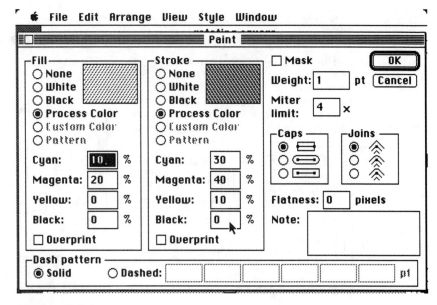

Figure 5-94.
The Paint dialog box showing percentages of process colors used for the path's fill and stroke.

use cyan, yellow, and magenta (CYM) primary subtractive colors in inks that can be applied to a white surface and combined with black ink. This color model, referred to as CYMK (for cyan, yellow, magenta, and black), is available in the Paint dialog box (Figure 5-94) for a path's fill and stroke. The program automatically displays your CYMK assignments using the proper RGB values so that you don't have to make wild guesses about how the colors will appear. Adobe Illustrator 88 also lets you adjust this conversion from time to time for your particular display, so that colors will appear the same under different lighting conditions (see Preferences: Change Progressive Colors in the Edit menu).

You can also assign more than 700 PANTONE printing inks which are also available with all printing presses. The premixed PANTONE colors are chosen by consulting the PANTONE MATCHING SYSTEM, developed by Pantone, Inc. Unlike process colors, which can be mixed by yourself to make different shades of color, PANTONE colors can't be mixed — you simply select one that looks right.

PANTONE colors are specified by clicking the Custom Color button to display a scrolling list of color names (Figure 5-95). To see

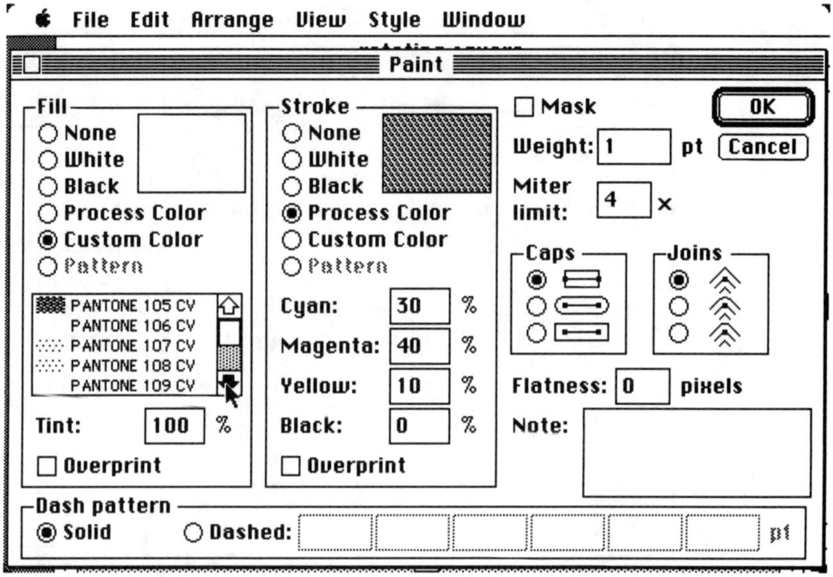

Figure 5-95.
The Paint dialog box showing PANTONE colors that can be assigned to any open document (a document containing PANTONE color assignments must be already open). PANTONE or other custom-mixed colors can be assigned to fill and stroke.

the list of PANTONE colors, you must also have open a document with PANTONE colors already specified; Adobe Systems provides two documents containing all of the PANTONE colors for both coated and uncoated paper stock. You can open one of these documents and leave it open while coloring objects in other documents. As you assign a PANTONE color to an object in a document, that particular color name is saved with the document, appearing whenever you open that document.

Colors do not usually mix when they overlap. The overprint option (available separately for fill and stroke) allows color underneath an object to mix with the color of the object, thus creating a color somewhere between the two for the overlapping area. The overprint option is useful for creating trap, because an overprinting stroke mixes its color with the color beneath it, preventing any separation between the two objects in print even if the registration is slightly off.

When a colored object is overprinted, the process colors that are common to it and the objects behind it are not affected and print

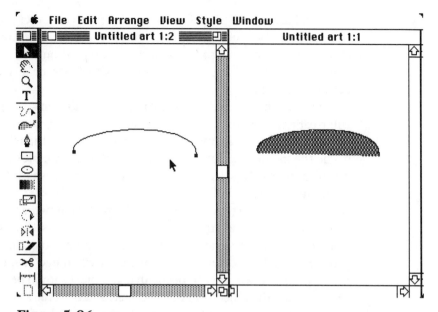

Figure 5-96.
When you paint an open path, the program draws an imaginary straight line to close the path and paints the object. The Preview Illustration window shows the result of painting the fill with 50 percent black and the stroke with 100 percent black.

normally; only the colors that are not in common are mixed. You don't need to use the overprint feature for 100 percent black because Adobe Illustrator automatically overprints black. However, tints of black must be overprinted if used for trapping.

Adobe Illustrator 88 paints objects according to how they are ordered in the document. The program starts painting the backmost object in the document and then paints objects successively until the foremost object is painted. Since the ink that Illustrator paints with is opaque (unless you turn on overprint), each layer of ink completely covers any layers under it.

If you want to change the order in which objects are painted (which is often necessary for the artwork to look right) you can use the Paste In Front and Paste In Back commands, or the Send To Back and Bring To Front commands (Edit menu). The Group command is also handy for controlling the order in which objects are painted.

When Adobe Illustrator 88 paints your document for previewing, separating, or printing, all the objects in your artwork, including the type, are treated as paths and can therefore have fills and strokes painted. Paths consisting of a single point (such as center points) are not painted. Type characters are treated as if each character were a closed path, so you can specify whether the type should be filled with black or any color or pattern, stroked with black or any color or pattern, or both.

If you fill an open path with two distinct endpoints, the program will treat the open path as if it were a closed path by connecting the two endpoints with an imaginary straight line; it will then fill the area inside the imaginary closed path (Figure 5-96). Complex paths that intersect themselves are painted according to a system called the "winding number rule" (see Chapter 6).

If you specify a stroke for a path, the path is drawn as a series of connected curve and line segments. The thickness (line weight), color (white, black, gray, process color, custom color, or custom pattern), and dash pattern of the line can be examined or specified in the Paint dialog box. If you specify that an object should be filled and stroked, then the object will be filled first, and then the stroke will be placed over the fill (the filled area will be covered by one-half the specified line weight).

When you first start the Adobe Illustrator 88 program, the Paint dialog box displays the following default settings: "Fill" is set to 100% Black (the selected areas will be filled with 100% black ink), "Stroke" is set to none (there will be no stroke delineating the paths), "Weight:" and stroke styles are grayed-out (since Stroke is set to none), "Overprint" is off, "Flatness" is set to 0 (curves will be drawn with a medium amount of flatness), and the "Note:" box is empty.

If you specify a colored (white, black, process color, custom color, or custom pattern) stroke, the default stroke "Weight" is set to 1 point, default "Miter Limit:" is set to 4, a mitered line join and butt caps are automatically selected, the "Dash pattern" is set to solid, and "Overprint" is left off.

If you select a single path, or an object consisting of a single path, then choose the Paint command (Command-I), the settings for that path or object are displayed in the dialog box. If you select more than one object and then choose the Paint command, only the settings common to all the selected objects are displayed in the dialog box, and any settings that were not the same for all the selected objects are left unspecified.

If you select an object that you don't realize is grouped with another object, and some of the settings differ, then those settings will appear blank in the Paint dialog box. Ungroup the selected objects (Command-U), select only one object at a time, and use Command-T for the Paint dialog box to see all the settings.

The first set of options in the Paint dialog box are Fill options that specify what color ink, if any, will be used to fill the selected objects. If you click the None button, the area will not be filled and will be transparent. A spot will appear inside the small circle preceding the word "None" to signify that the option is selected. The spot appears in whichever of the fill options you click.

Click the White button, and opaque (not transparent) white ink will be used to fill the selected objects. Painting areas with white ink can provide a handy way to erase things; this is analogous to using white paper tape over typing errors, only better because the edges of the "painted" tape never cause shadows on the page, which is a problem with paper tape. For example, the Nurse (Plate 2) has a wide, white tape strip along the outside of each of the four sides to create the white border around the art. The border tapes are filled with 100% white paint.

Clicking the Black button displays the number 100 in the box following the word "Black:" below the rest of the buttons, indicating that the area will be filled with 100% black ink. If you want to fill the selected objects with a shade of gray, enter the desired shade (as a percentage of black) into the box instead of the number 100. If you specify less than three percent black as a fill or stroke, it could fade away and disappear on press, or actually be printed at around five percent due to various press factors.

Click the Process Color button, and the process color percent boxes appear below the buttons set to zero. To specify colors for a four-color process (black, cyan, magenta, and yellow), click in the appropriate boxes and type in percentages between 0 and 100 that represent the amount of each of the four colors that you want the selected objects to be filled with. If your printer does not feature color printing capabilities, the program converts the specified color mix into an equivalent shade of gray while printing, and retains the specified colors. Refer to the process color charts in the back of the *Adobe Illustrator 88 Color Guide* supplied with the program.

The Custom Color button is gray unless you have already opened a document containing custom or PANTONE color assignments. The Pattern button is also gray unless you have already defined custom patterns. You can select PANTONE or custom colors with the first button, or custom patterns with the second button, rather than black or process colors.

The second set of options in the Paint dialog box are Stroke options. The color selections are exactly the same as with the Fill options.

The "Weight:" option is to the right of the Stroke options in the Paint dialog box. Weight specifies the line weight (thickness) that the selected paths will be stroked with. The Weight option is grayed-out when the stroke is set to none. To change the stroke of selected paths, click in the box after the word "Weight:" and enter a number that represents how many points of thickness (one point = 1/72 inch) you want the lines to be. Line weights can be less than 1 point, but very fine lines will appear thicker when printed on the LaserWriter than when printed on a high-resolution device such as the Linotronic 300. Line weights are not scaled unless you specify a uniform scale and click the line weight scaling option in the Scale dialog box.

The "Caps" choices affect the endpoints of open paths and dashed lines. The "Joins" choices affect the corners of paths that are stroked (it has no effect on nonstroked paths or points where paths intersect). Figures 4-5 and 4-6 (in Chapter 4) show examples.

The default setting for caps is the butt cap (at the top). If you don't change it, the butt line cap uses squared-off ends perpendicular to the path. The middle choice, round cap, creates a half-moon cap in which the diameter equals the line width. The projecting cap (bottom) offers square ends that extend half of the line width beyond the end of the line.

The default join is a miter join (at top), in which the edges of the intersecting strokes are extended until they meet in a point. The middle choice is the round join, which connects corners in a circular arc with a diameter equal to the line width. You would use both round caps and round joins because round joins do not fit well with squared-off butt caps. The bottom choice is the bevel join, which connects corners with triangular ends.

Miter joins can be modified by the "Miter limit" ratio, which is active if you select the miter join choice. When two lines intersect at a sharp angle, a miter corner extends a spike that is controlled by the miter limit ratio. The higher the ratio, the sharper the corner. You can select a ratio between 1 and 10, with 4 corresponding to a square corner and 1 corresponding to a bevel corner.

You can also specify a solid line or a dashed line pattern for the stroke. The solid pattern is usually checked (by default). If you want a dashed line, click the Dashed button, which activates six boxes for entering the length, in points, that you want the first dash to be. Then click in the next box and type the length, in points, that you want the first gap to be. Fill in the other four boxes if you want the dash and gap length pattern to vary. Whatever lengths are typed will be repeated and used for the dash pattern of the line. Remember that the type of line cap you select also affects the dash pattern, and that if you select round or projecting caps you should widen the gap width to accommodate caps that stick out an amount equal to half the current line weight setting.

In the lower right-hand side of the Paint dialog box is the Note: box that allows you to enter a text comment that is inserted into the PostScript text file when the program saves the artwork. The Note option is handy for tagging an object so that you can find it in the PostScript file. The note appears as a comment with the "%%Note" prefix in the PostScript file. For further information about Post-Script, see Chapter 6.

The Mask button lets you set an object as a masking object so that it is filled with whatever artwork lies in front of it. The masking object defines the boundaries and treats everything it touches (that is pasted in front of it) as part of a pattern for itself. To create a masking object, select an ungrouped path (usually a single object, not a blend). Then choose Paint from the Style menu, set the paint and stroke attributes, and click the Mask check box to turn on masking for this object. Finally, paste or drag artwork to be on top of the masking object, and after selecting both objects, choose the Group command. The Mask option automatically turns off when you group the masking object with the masked objects.

Setting the mask attribute for a small object (a line, single anchor point, or very small shape) can cause all the objects in front of it to be masked and not appear in the Preview Illustration view. This can happen if you set the mask attribute to the center point of an oval or rectangle. You should first ungroup an oval or rectangle and delete its center point before using it as a mask.

The last option in the Paint dialog box is the Flatness option. Flatness refers to how smoothly curves will be drawn, and it affects both previewed and printed artwork. The flatness value is measured in terms of pixels in the output device and corresponds to the distance of any point on the printed curve from any point on the theoretically ideal curve. The value used can be anywhere from 0 to 10; smaller values will produce more accurate curves but will take longer to compute. If you are willing to sacrifice image quality, you can set the value higher than the default value of zero. Printing and previewing will be faster, but the curves in the artwork will not be as smooth. Increasing the flatness value also helps when printing or previewing long paths which can be slow to draw.

If you get the PostScript limitcheck error when you try to print the file, select all or portions of the art, use Command-I to display the Paint dialog box, and increase the flatness value for the selected portions. Continue increasing the flatness until the file prints without error.

Once you have set the paint attributes the way that you want, you can click the OK button to send the dialog box away and the specified attributes in the document are changed. The double line surrounding the OK button indicates that pressing the Return key can be used as a shortcut for selecting the OK button. To cancel any attribute changes that you have just specified, click the Cancel button instead to send the Paint dialog box away and leave your document unchanged.

Type...

The Type command is used for altering type or changing the specifications for type created with the type tool. For a more detailed description of the type tool and the Type dialog box, see the section on the type tool. Since text cannot be edited directly on the drawing, if you want to change type that is already in the document, select the type block you want to edit with the selection tool or selection marquee, and then choose Type in the Style menu (or press Command-T); this will display the Type dialog box, and you can edit the plain version of the text displayed in the text window at the bottom of the box.

Text entered into the text window in the Type dialog box wraps within the window, but you must put Returns at the ends of lines. You are limited to 254 characters of text per type block. The text can be entered and edited using the standard Cut (Command-X), Copy (Command-C), Paste (Command-V), or Select All (Command-A) commands found in the Edit menu.

The text in the window appears plain (not formatted), and the Type dialog box displays settings for changing attributes of the type such as typeface, type size, spacing, and alignment. The attribute

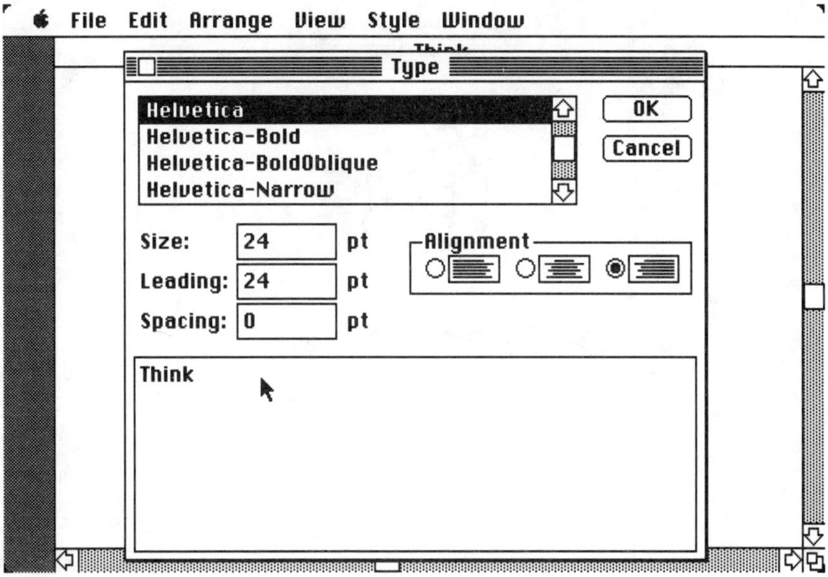

```
  ┌ ⚹  File  Edit  Arrange  View  Style  Window                    ┐
                              Think
        ┌──────────────────────── Type ────────────────────────┐
        │ ┌──────────────────────────────┐  ┌──────────┐        │
        │ │ Helvetica                  ⬆ │  │    OK    │        │
        │ │ Helvetica-Bold             ▓ │  └──────────┘        │
        │ │ Helvetica-BoldOblique      ▓ │  ┌──────────┐        │
        │ │ Helvetica-Narrow           ⬇ │  │  Cancel  │        │
        │ └──────────────────────────────┘  └──────────┘        │
        │                                                        │
        │  Size:    [24    ] pt   ┌─Alignment─────────────────┐  │
        │                         │ ○▤  ○▤  ◉▤ │               │
        │  Leading: [24    ] pt   └───────────────────────────┘  │
        │                                                        │
        │  Spacing: [0     ] pt                                  │
        │  ┌───────────────────────────────────────────────────┐│
        │  │ Think                                              ││
        │  │        ▶                                           ││
        │  │                                                    ││
        │  └───────────────────────────────────────────────────┘│
        └────────────────────────────────────────────────────────┘
```

Figure 5-97.
The Type dialog box lets you change the type specifications for a selected block of text.

settings are applied to the entire block of type when the art is printed. The default type attribute settings are Helvetica typeface, 12-point type size, 12-point leading, 0 spacing, and left alignment.

If you select only one block of type, this text is displayed in the bottom section of the Type dialog box and the attributes of the text are displayed in the upper section of the dialog box. If you select more than one block of type, only the attributes shared by all the selected blocks are displayed, and the text area at the bottom of the dialog box is blank and cannot be used. You can then change all attributes of the selected blocks that you want to be the same, such as typeface, or alignment, deselect the blocks, and then select the individual blocks of text to edit the text displayed in the window.

To set the typeface of selected text, choose a typeface from among those listed in the scroll box located in the upper left-hand region of the Type dialog box (Figure 5-97). The scroll bar located on the right side of the scroll box lets you scroll through the available typefaces if there are more than will fit into the scroll box.

To set the type size, click the small box after the word "Size:" and type the point size that you want the type to be. To set the leading,

Figure 5-98.
Type specifications can include a negative value for leading that moves the baseline of type closer to the baseline of the line above it. This type block, consisting of two lines, is set to -6 points for leading.

click the small box after the word "Leading," and then type in the leading that you want. Leading is the amount of space between the lines of type, measured from baseline to baseline. The smallest type size is 0.001 points and the largest is 1008 points. The smallest amount of leading you can have is -1008 points and the largest is 1008 points. A negative leading moves the baseline above the baseline of the line of type above (Figure 5-98).

Likewise, to set the spacing, click the small box after the word "Spacing," and type a spacing value. Spacing is the measure of space between characters; by typing a positive number you can add space between characters, or by typing a negative number you can bring characters closer together. The largest and smallest amount of spacing is 1008 and -1008 points, respectively.

To set the alignment of the type, click one of the small circles in the Alignment area of the dialog box; a small black dot will appear in the center of the small circle that you selected. Clicking in the first circle (and its accompanying image of a paragraph) selects left alignment (flush left, ragged right), clicking in the second circle selects center alignment (each line centered under the next), and clicking on the third circle selects right alignment (flush right, ragged left).

To apply the type attributes to the type block, click the OK button; this sends the dialog box away and places the specified type attributes in the document. Press the Return key as a shortcut for selecting the OK option. On the other hand, if you want to cancel any attribute changes that you have specified, click on the Cancel button instead to send the Type dialog box away and leave your document unchanged.

It's important to remember that if you have changed the x and y axes by setting the Constrain angle in the Preferences dialog box (Edit menu) to a value other than zero degrees, the placement of text blocks will be relative to the x and y axes. If you are placing type and it looks a bit slanted or askew, check the alignment of the x and y axes by looking at the Preferences dialog box. You can use this feature to type several text blocks in sequence at a certain angle.

Pattern...

Adobe Illustrator 88 lets you fill and stroke paths with a custom pattern. You can even stroke and fill type with a custom pattern. A pattern can be transformed with the shape, transformed separately, or remain the same while the shape is transformed.

A pattern is available for a document if it has been defined in that document or in another document that is open at the same time. A custom pattern is always stored with the document in which is was defined and in any document that uses the pattern as a fill or stroke. You can see the list of custom patterns stored with the documents that are currently open by choosing the Paint dialog box and clicking the Pattern button for either the fill or stroke (Figure 5-99). You can also see the pattern list by choosing the Pattern option from the Styles menu (Figure 5-100). Any pattern in the list can be used in any open document. If you intend to use a lot of patterns, it helps to define them in one document which can be left open while opening other documents and applying patterns.

To create a pattern, draw an element of the pattern in a document (see Figures 4-33 and 4-34 in Chapter 4), and paint the element as

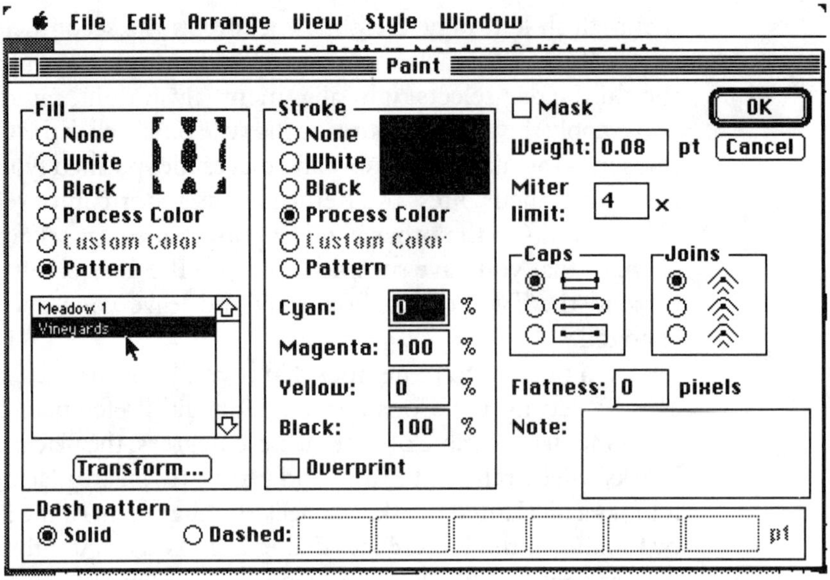

Figure 5-99.
The Paint dialog box lets you assign previously defined custom patterns to the fill and stroke of a path.

you would like it to appear in the pattern. Then clone the element several times and place the clones in appropriate places. Next, define the pattern tile with a rectangle. The pattern tile exposes the part of the pattern that will be repeated. The rectangle must have perpendicular corners (be sure that the corner radius is zero in the Preferences dialog box). You can draw the rectangle with the rectangle tool or with the pen tool as long as the constrain angle set in the Preferences dialog box is set to zero.

The pattern tile rectangle must be behind the other objects in the pattern. Whatever fill you apply to the rectangle becomes the pattern's background — if you specify no fill, the background will have no fill. You should always specify no stroke for the pattern tile rectangle unless you want the pattern tile lines to be visible in the pattern.

A placed EPS image can't be used as a pattern element, nor can a masked group be used as a pattern element. Another pattern can't act as the fill for either the pattern tile rectangle or for the pattern elements because a pattern can't be defined as containing another pattern. You can create a pattern using another pattern by using the

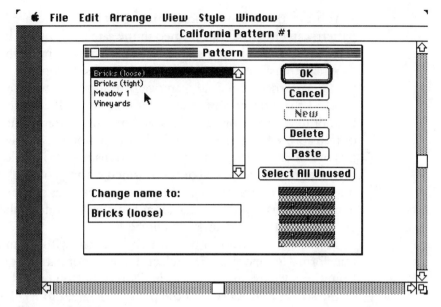

Figure 5-100.
The list of defined custom patterns also appears in the Patterns dialog box, where you can define new patterns and redefine or rename existing ones.

Paste button in the Pattern dialog box to paste the other pattern into the artwork for the new pattern. Any defined pattern can be pasted it into another document and treated as regular artwork by using this Paste button.

With both the pattern tile and the elements selected, you can define the pattern by choosing Pattern from the Style menu, and click the New button. The name New Pattern 1 appears in the pattern list and in the change name field, and you can rename it by typing over this name. A preview of the pattern appears in the Pattern dialog box.

To assign a pattern to an object's fill or stroke, click the Pattern button in the Paint dialog box (in the fill or stroke area) and click on the name of a pattern. The pattern is displayed when you choose the Preview Illustration option.

The pattern is like another layer that starts at the current ruler origin, which is usually at the lower left corner of page 5 (the center page of the drawing area). You can change the ruler origin (the point were zero appears on both rulers) by moving the ruler intersection square to the new position (see the Show Rulers command).

You can transform an object painted with a pattern fill and the pattern can either be transformed in the same fashion, or left alone. A pattern can also be transformed without transforming the object.

When transforming (including moving and cloning) an object with a pattern, if you drag to move or transform (and you haven't checked the Transform pattern tiles box in the Preferences dialog box, or in the transformation dialog box), the pattern is not moved or transformed with the object. If, however, you previously checked this option in the Preferences or in the transformation dialog boxes, the pattern tiles are moved or transformed with the object when you drag to move or transform. (Whenever you turn this option on or off in a transformation dialog box, it automatically updates the Preferences dialog box to your latest choice.)

To move or transform the pattern by itself, without moving or transforming the object, first select the object or path, choose Paint from the Style menu, and click the Pattern button for either the fill or the stroke (whichever has the pattern assigned to it). Then click the Transform button, and the program displays the Transform Pattern Style dialog box (see Figure 4-46 in Chapter 4). This dialog box lets you specify movement, scaling, rotating, reflecting, and shearing information to transform the pattern of an object without transforming the object. No matter what order you specify the information, the transformations occur in order: moving, scaling, rotating, reflecting, and shearing. When you transform a pattern, the operation doesn't change the definition of the pattern, nor does it change the pattern as it is used in other parts of the document or other documents.

You can blend two objects that have the same pattern, but not objects with different patterns unless one of the patterns is defined with artwork that is a transformation of the other pattern.

Custom Color...

You can create custom mixes of process colors that can also be listed by name along with the PANTONE colors in this scroll box of the Paint dialog box. You can also rename a PANTONE color to have a more familiar name when assigning it to documents from the Paint dialog box.

First create the custom color with the Custom Color command in the Style menu. You can simply create a custom name for a PAN-

TONE color, or mix process colors into custom color that you can use by name. The Custom Color command displays a dialog box (see Figures 3-32 and 3-33 in Chapter 3). Create a custom name for a PANTONE color in this dialog box, or mix percentages of process colors to define custom color.

To make it easy to call up custom and PANTONE colors, create a document that contains all of the regular custom and PANTONE colors that you use. As long as this document is open, you can assign those colors to objects in any other documents.

Window Menu

The Window menu contains options for showing or hiding the contents of the Clipboard, showing or hiding the Adobe Illustrator 88 toolbox, create multiple views of a document, and switch the active window to other documents. You can have several documents open at once with Adobe Illustrator 88. The Window menu can grow with the names of many documents as you open documents without closing others.

Show Clipboard

The Show Clipboard command displays the current contents of the Clipboard. The Clipboard is a temporary storage area used by Macintosh applications for objects stored by the Cut and Copy commands. Objects stored in the Clipboard can be retrieved using the Paste commands. The Clipboard is common to virtually all Macintosh applications and can be used to easily move small amounts of data between applications.

Although many types of data can be stored in the Clipboard, only three types are relevant to Adobe Illustrator 88: Illustrator artwork objects, text, and PICT data. Only Illustrator artwork objects can be pasted directly into any window. Text can be cut or copied into the Clipboard from another program, from the Note Pad, or from the Scrapbook, but it can only be pasted into the Type dialog box, and it can only be 254 characters long. (For more information about the Type dialog box, refer to the type tool section.) PICT-formatted graphic images cannot be pasted into any Illustrator window (templates cannot be altered with Illustrator), but PICT images of the artwork's Preview Illustration view can be copied into the Clipboard by holding down the Option key while you choose the Copy command.

Hide Clipboard

The Hide Clipboard command is used to hide the Clipboard after it has been displayed with the Show Clipboard command. To choose the Hide Clipboard command, either select Hide Clipboard in the Edit menu, select Close in the File menu, or click in the small close box located in the upper left-hand corner of the Clipboard window's title bar. The Clipboard can also be hidden by clicking in any other window besides the Clipboard window.

Hide Toolbox

The Hide Toolbox command removes the toolbox from view. Hiding the toolbox lets you see more of the artwork on the screen at one time. You can choose the Hide Toolbox command by selecting Hide Toolbox in the Window menu, or clicking in the small close box that is located at the top of the toolbox.

When the toolbox is hidden you can still use the tool that was selected when you hid the toolbox. You can also use the selection tool by holding down the Command key; the hand tool by holding down the space bar; and the zoom tool by either holding down the space bar and Command key to zoom in or by holding down the space bar, Command key, and Option key to zoom out. If you want to use any of the other tools, you must first bring the toolbox back onto the screen by issuing the Show Toolbox command described below.

Show Toolbox

The Show Toolbox command displays the toolbox after it has been removed from view by the Hide Toolbox command. You can choose the Show Toolbox command by selecting Show Toolbox in the

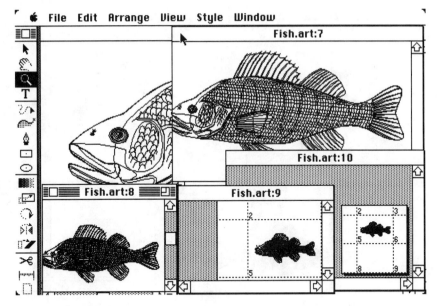

Figure 5-101.
Many documents can be open at once in Adobe Illustrator 88, but only one window is the active window at any particular time. This shows several windows for the same document created with the New Window command. Each window created for the same document is automatically numbered sequentially.

Window menu. When the toolbox is displayed, it can't be moved behind another window; if you try to place another window on top of the toolbox, the toolbox will force itself on top of the window.

New Window

The New Window command creates a new window that displays another view of the Adobe Illustrator 88 document (Figure 5-101). The command creates a new active window that is identical to the window that was active when the command was chosen. The new window and the old window are automatically numbered by the program and the numbers are placed after a colon that follows the document and template document names. Any other new views of the same document that are created are consecutively numbered in

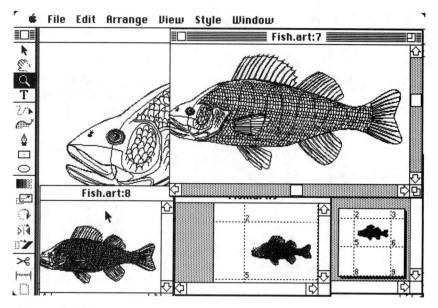

Figure 5-102.
Click inside the window to make it the active window.

the order in which they were opened. If you close one of the views of a document, the remaining view windows of that document will be automatically renumbered, removing the closed window from the sequence.

The new window can be manipulated independently of the active window. Any changes made to the document from the active window affect the document and are subsequently displayed in all views of that document.

Creating new views of a document can be helpful for such purposes as viewing a preview and a regular view of the artwork, for viewing different areas of the artwork, or for viewing the artwork at different magnifications simultaneously. You can switch the active window to any window by selecting its name in the Window menu (Figure 5-103).

Creating new views is especially useful when you are using a display larger than the standard Macintosh Plus and Macintosh SE displays. Using multiple windows with different views can slow down the system if you have limited memory.

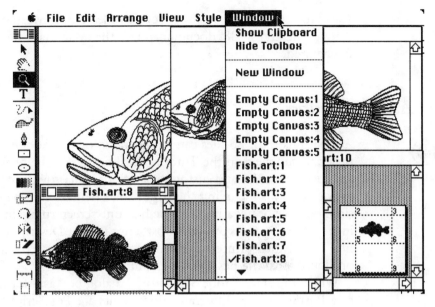

Figure 5-103.
You can switch the active window to any window by selecting its name in the Window menu.

DrawOver

DrawOver™ 1.0

The DrawOver program is supplied by Adobe Systems for converting MacDraw artwork (version 1.9 or 1.9.5) into Adobe Illustrator 88 files.

MacDraw 1.9 and 1.9.5 (Claris) creates objects that can be converted into PostScript. Straight line paths and curve paths are converted correctly, as well as geometric shapes such as rectangles and ovals. The program can also convert black, white, and shades of gray to appropriate Paint settings.

Lines drawn with the MacDraw freehand tool are converted to straight line segments. This unfortunately creates a lot of segments and anchor points.

The program displays a preview image of the artwork with an OK or Cancel button so that you can decide whether or not to convert the artwork. The program automatically appends the characters

".art" to the file name of the MacDraw file. The converted file is an Adobe Illustrator 88 document, and the MacDraw file remains unchanged.

Adobe Separator

Adobe Separator™ 2.0

Adobe Illustrator 88 files can be separated by the Adobe Separator program supplied on the Tutorial/Utilities disk. The program can produce four-color and custom separations, and provides choices for various options including the page size, orientation, type of emulsion, positive or negative, and the halftone screen ruling in lines per inch. Adobe Systems provides PostScript Printer Description (PPD) files for various printers and imagesetters so that separations are produced with the best possible control settings.

When you start Adobe Separator, a dialog box asks for the name of a PostScript file (Illustrator documents are PostScript files, and you can also select PostScript files from other applications). The program then displays the dimensions of the artwork's bounding box (see Figures 4-18 and 4-19 in Chapter 4). The bounding box, defined in PostScript units (points), defines the outside dimensions of the illustration. Trim marks, color bars, and registration symbols are printed by Adobe Separator just outside the bounding box.

After clicking OK for the bounding box dimensions, the program asks for a PostScript Printer Description file, which contains specific device information for Adobe Separator including the resolution, available page sizes, color support, and acceptable screen rulings.

Adobe Separator's dialog box (see Figure 4-21 in Chapter 4) lets you switch PPD and PostScript files, activate the Chooser to choose an output device, and change separation parameters.

Page sizes are listed by name or by dimensions, which define the printable area for the separation (including space for trim marks). The page orientation can be set to Portrait or Landscape. The emulsion type depends on your printer's requirements; film separations are usually set to have emulsion side down. You can also choose to print a positive or negative image (usually set to negative for film separations). The halftone screen ruling defines the number of halftone dots per inch, referred to as lines per inch (lpi).

Adobe Separator lets you print all of the process color separations in one operation, or separately, or as a color comp to a color printer.

The Print All button lets you print separations for all four process colors and one for each custom color. Alternatively, custom colors and PANTONE colors can be converted into percentages of process colors automatically and included in the separations for the four process colors.

To convert a custom or PANTONE color to appropriate process color percentages, select the color's name in the list of custom and PANTONE colors, and click the To Process button. The program automatically converts the custom or PANTONE color into process color percentages; to reverse the process (reverse previously converted custom or PANTONE colors), click the All Custom button.

6

PostScript and Adobe Illustrator 88

The PostScript language has emerged as the leading graphics language in use today due to its endorsement by many major computer companies including Apple and IBM. PostScript is the foundation on which Adobe built Adobe Illustrator 88. The program uses PostScript for such purposes as drawing images on the Macintosh video screen, communicating with printers and typesetting machines, and as a format for saving artwork documents. Knowing PostScript will allow advanced users to understand Adobe Illustrator 88 documents and create special PostScript effects.

What is PostScript?

PostScript is a computer language that is used for describing the appearance of graphics and text on a page. Adobe Illustrator 88 documents are PostScript programs saved as ordinary text files. PostScript is used to write programs for computers or printers, or to create special graphic effects.

PostScript describes text and graphics in a standard format that can be understood by other computers, printers, and other output devices. Printers (such as laser printers and typesetting machines) interpret PostScript page descriptions and create bit-mapped representations of the pages for printing. Video displays use PostScript to accurately interpret page descriptions, convert the result into a bit-mapped image, and display the image on the computer screen.

Since graphics and text together convey more information per page than text alone, there is a major trend in computer technology away from the text-only computer screens that have dominated computing since its inception and towards the heavy use of graphic information in both computer documents and operating systems (such as the Macintosh Finder, Microsoft Windows, and IBM's Presentation Manager). Data processing and information processing on desktop computers is rapidly becoming document processing, and the documents being processed are using much more graphics to help convey information. PostScript has emerged as the standard language for describing the text and graphics that are on the pages of computer documents.

PostScript allows pages to be described very concisely, which means that PostScript files take up less memory than many other types of page descriptions, including the typical bit-mapped descriptions. For example, a page on the Apple LaserWriter has a printable area of 8-by-10.9 inches for a total of 87.2 square inches; at the LaserWriter's resolution of 300 dots per linear inch (which equals 90,000 dots per square inch) an 87.2 square inch LaserWriter page would have 7,848,000 dots in it. To store this document as a bit-mapped document with no gray-scale (where one dot is represented by one bit of memory) would require 7,848,000 bits of memory, which is just shy of one megabyte. Considering that the standard Macintosh floppy disk only stores 800K, a full-page bit-mapped image would not fit on a floppy disk, and you'd be forced to use a hard disk. If you've ever used a scanner to digitize a page of graphics, you know that the image files are usually enormous (sometimes over two megabytes). However, a PostScript description of a page usually takes up much less memory.

Not only does PostScript offer a compact way to describe pages, but the PostScript description is also not tied to a particular device. In computer jargon this is referred to as device-independence. What device-independence means in practical terms is that PostScript files created on the Macintosh with Adobe Illustrator 88 (or any other application that works with PostScript) can be used on certain computer systems from IBM and other vendors, and these PostScript descriptions can be printed on many different PostScript printers and typesetting machines from a wide array of vendors such as Apple, IBM, DEC, Varityper, and Linotype. The advantages of PostScript, and its endorsement by both Apple and IBM, has led to its current status as the major industry standard among computer graphics languages.

PostScript was created with graphic arts in mind, and it uses a way of describing images that is modeled after graphic arts. In PostScript an image is created by putting certain types of computer-generated "ink" in specified areas. The ink can be in various forms such as lines, shapes, or spots of ink in a bit-mapped photograph. The computer-generated ink can be black, white, any shade of gray, or any shade of color. PostScript starts building a page by taking a white page and placing the ink in specified areas according to the PostScript description of the page. As ink is placed on the page, any new ink completely covers any ink it is placed on top of; in other words, every type of ink on the page is opaque and keeps its color, rather than being transparent and bleeding colors together.

Some of PostScript's capabilities include the ability to construct arbitrary shapes from straight lines and curves. Shapes may be convex, concave, contain disconnected sections and holes, and can even intersect with themselves. PostScript includes painting commands for further describing shapes; the paint commands allow PostScript to do such things as assign any thickness of line to outline a shape, fill the shape with any color, or use the shape as a clipping path to crop any other graphics or images.

PostScript features a general coordinate system that allows all types of graphics to be transformed mathematically in all the possible linear transformations such as scaling, rotating, reflecting, skewing, and translating. PostScript also has commands that allow it to be used to describe text alone, or text integrated with graphics. The language allows you to specify typefaces, type styles, and type sizes. It treats text as graphic shapes that can be manipulated and operated on by any of PostScript's graphics commands such as painting, scaling, rotating, reflecting, or slanting. PostScript also has commands for working with digitized images that are either scanned or created artificially with a computer. Digitized images of any resolution can be conveyed in PostScript and the language provides methods for assigning gray-scale and color values to the images.

The main commands used for placing images on a page are fill, stroke, image, and show. The fill command places a filled area on the page.When PostScript calculates how to fill a path, it uses the "Winding number rule." According to this system, the way in which Adobe Illustrator 88 determines whether a particular location is inside the path (for the purpose of filling the area) is to draw an imaginary ray from that location that extends to infinity (beyond the edge of the document), and then examine each place that the path of the object being filled crosses that ray. Then, starting with a value of zero, a value of one is added to the total each time the path crosses the ray from the left, and a value of one is subtracted from the total each time the path crosses the ray from the right. After the program either adds or subtracts a unit for all the places that the path crosses the ray, it can determine whether or not to fill the area by examining the total. If right-hand intersections equaled left-hand intersections, then the total would be zero — a zero total indicates that the original location was outside the object because the ray extending from that location entered and exited the object (by crossing the path) the same number of times. If a value other than zero remained as a total, then Adobe Illustrator 88 decides that the original location was inside the object and fills the area with the specified type of ink.

The stroke command draws lines on the page, the image command is used for placing a gray-scale halftone digitized image on the page, and the show command places characters on the page. Just as Adobe Illustrator 88 uses paths to create artwork, PostScript uses the concept of the "current path" as a way to draw things on the page. Commands used to describe how the path should be drawn include newpath, moveto, lineto, curveto, arc, and closepath. In addition to the current path, PostScript also features a "current clipping path" that represents an outline of the area on the page that will be displayed or printed. Usually the clipping path is the entire printable area on a page. Anything that is drawn outside that area is cut off and discarded. However, by using the PostScript clip command, you can shrink the size of the area that will be displayed or printed down to any desired size or shape. Clipping the artwork can be useful for placing it in a particular layout, or for creating special graphics effects.

In order to draw pages the same way on different types of devices, PostScript uses two different types of coordinate systems, device space and user space, for locating items on a page.

Device space is the area that can be displayed or printed on a particular output device. On the Apple LaserWriter Plus for example, the device space is an 8-by-10.9-inch area with 300 dots per linear inch for a total of about 7,848,000 dots. The characteristics of the device space such as image resolution and the shape of the dots used to create images are idiosyncratic to the particular device. PostScript's device space provides an x-axis and y-axis coordinate system that allows any dot to be located. The device space is only a consideration for the PostScript interpreter program in a printer; PostScript programs only need to concern themselves with the user space.

The user space provides a standard ideal coordinate system that is always the same for every page, regardless of the characteristics and idiosyncrasies of the output device (printer, typesetting machine, video display, etc.). The PostScript interpreter in the printer automatically converts the items in the user space into points to be printed or displayed in the device space. PostScript starts each user space out as a default user space and sets the point of origin in the lower left-hand corner of the output page, and the length of a unit of space along either the x-axis or y-axis to a default value of 1/72nd of an inch (approximately 1 point). A PostScript program can then modify the user space by using the coordinate transformation commands: translate, rotate, and scale. Translate lets you change the point of origin, rotate lets you turn the axes relative to the point of origin, and scale lets you change the length of a unit of space.

PostScript programs are usually created by other programs such as Adobe Illustrator 88. However, it is possible to use PostScript to create special graphic effects that are not feasible to draw with Adobe

Illustrator 88 program alone, such as wrapping text or graphics around models of solid objects.

PostScript and Output Devices

A PostScript page description can be rendered on a wide variety of output devices such as printers, typesetting machines, and video monitors. The PostScript page description is interpreted by a special controller known as a raster image processor (RIP) that is connected to the output device. The RIP converts the compact PostScript page description into a very large number of dots that are then printed on a specific printer or displayed on a particular video monitor.

Although the primary use of PostScript is to describe pages for printing, it should be noted that Adobe Illustrator 88 uses PostScript for drawing your artwork on the Macintosh screen. This is an example of how PostScript is used for displaying images on video monitors. Adobe System's implementation of this technology indicates that PostScript may start gaining ground as a video screen description language as well as a printed page description language. The advantage to desktop publishing of using PostScript as a screen description language as well as a printer language is that what you see on the screen will probably more closely correspond to what is printed on the page. This discrepancy can be especially bothersome when working with certain graphics and page-layout programs. The discrepancy is caused by the fact that most Macintosh applications use a graphics description language called QuickDraw to control the video display; when a document is printed on a PostScript printer, the Macintosh's native QuickDraw is translated into PostScript as part of the printing process. Inherent differences between QuickDraw and PostScript cause a certain amount of precision to be lost in the translation.

In order to solve the problem of the discrepancies between QuickDraw and PostScript, Adobe Illustrator 88 uses PostScript to draw artwork on the screen, uses PostScript as the format in which it saves the artwork, and sends a PostScript file directly to the printer. The advantage of this method is that less precision is lost between the way that the image is displayed on the screen and described to the printer. Also, since the artwork file is saved in the PostScript format, no translation is needed between QuickDraw and PostScript, which improves the speed and performance of the printing process.

Since Adobe Illustrator 88 files are saved as pure PostScript text files, you can use the standard PostScript language to understand and modify the Illustrator files.

PostScript Tutorial

If you plan on doing any special effects with Adobe Illustrator 88 documents, you will need to know the PostScript programming language. In order to help you learn PostScript we have included a tutorial that will give you some basic PostScript skills. If you want to learn more about the PostScript language, you can either take a PostScript programming class (available at some colleges and universities), or you can read the *PostScript Language Tutorial and Cookbook* and the *PostScript Language Reference Manual*, both published by Addison-Wesley and available from Adobe Systems. The *PosScript Language Tutorial and Cookbook* provides an introduction and explanation to PostScript as well as some handy tips and techniques for improving your PostScript programming skills. The *PostScript Language Reference Manual* is a more technically oriented book.

This introductory PostScript tutorial presents some of the basic principles, structures, and commands you'll need to know in order to understand the way PostScript programs operate. This tutorial assumes that you are already familiar with some other programming language or that you are a fairly experienced computer user.

PostScript is a stack-oriented language, keeping its working values, definitions, and intermediary results in a set of ordered lists, known as stacks. That makes it more like Forth than like BASIC or Pascal. In general, values and objects are either used immediately or pushed onto a stack. When the program needs data or encounters a command to retrieve a value, it pops a value back off the top of the stack again.

PostScript is also an extensible (or "threaded") language, meaning that you can define routines in terms of basic PostScript operations and then use these new terms as part of further definitions. When the LaserWriter, or other PostScript printer, interprets your PostScript program, it follows each new term back through your definitions until it reaches a description made up of primitive operations that it knows how to perform.

As a complement to the threaded-stack structure of the language, most PostScript operations are written in postfix notation — you first list the objects you want to use, and you then say what you want do with them. For example, to add 3 and 4, you write:

```
3 4 add
```

rather than the

```
3 + 4
```

infix form you would use in BASIC or ordinary math. This procedure makes it possible for PostScript to evaluate objects according to a set of simple rules, although it does make the programs harder for beginners to read and write.

In general, PostScript works its way through a program as follows. As the computer reads each set of symbols, PostScript figures out where the breaks are between the words and assigns each group to a logical unit called a *token*. As soon as a token becomes available, PostScript looks to see what type of object it represents.

If the token is a number, PostScript saves it for later use by pushing it onto the operand stack. It does the same for definitions. Likewise for specially marked command routines intended for later use.

If, on the other hand, the token is a name, PostScript checks to see if it represents an executable routine or a primitive operation. If it does, the language executes the statement, pulling as many values off the stack as the operation requests and returning any results back onto the stack.

The basic scheme is first to define any new terms and push them onto the stack. Then you supply the values you want the program to work with. Finally, you give the commands that will retrieve the values, do the required arithmetic and logic, and print out the result. In practice, it's slightly more complicated, and you usually alternate between adding values to the stack and popping them back off.

PostScript actually has four distinct stacks: operand, execution, dictionary, and graphic states. A different class of operations affects each stack.

The operand stack is much like a piece of scratch paper or the running total on a calculator. If an operation needs input values, it pops the required number of values from the operand stack. Similarly, any results produced go back on the stack for later use. This holds true for both arithmetic operations and those that handle text.

The execution stack is where PostScript stores away your program. Normally, you don't explicitly work with this stack but let PostScript do the stack management as it works its way through your program.

The dictionary stack lets you create new definitions and save libraries of procedures. PostScript searches this stack for your definitions, then for built-in operations, and flags any terms that it can't find in either.

Finally, the graphics-state stack is a holding area for sets of parameters that define how the PostScript language interfaces to a specific printer or interprets the exact graphic commands in your program. PostScript can keep track of several sets of parameters, which makes it possible to temporarily alter graphics characteristics in order to draw certain objects and then return to the original mode.

The Simplest Possible Program

You have now done enough theory to start with some practical examples, beginning with the simplest useful PostScript routine,

```
copypage
```

a one-line program that tells a PostScript printer to produce a printout of the current page. Because you haven't said to write anything on the page and the printer assumes a blank white page to begin with, this routine will simply eject an empty sheet of paper.

Suppose you want two blank pages. The routine then becomes,

```
2 {copypage} repeat
```

and the PostScript interpreter, as it reads this line, first encounters the 2. Remember, PostScript pushes values it encounters in the input stream onto the operand stack until they are needed. So the 2 is pushed onto that stack.

Then the interpreter finds {copypage}. Curly brackets (braces) tell the interpreter that it should save the enclosed commands, rather than execute them. The program treats deferred commands as a special form of text input — as operands to be saved on the operand stack until they're called for. That's what happens to the {copypage} command.

Proceeding along, the PostScript interpreter then finds the repeat command. Repeat is a word that it understands as an executable command that takes two operands. Going back to the stack, repeat treats the object on the top of the stack as a sequence of commands to execute and the next object on the stack as the number of repetitions to be made.

The object on the top of the stack is copypage, which still prints out the current page. The next object is the repeat factor, which in this case is 2. The LaserWriter responds by printing two blank pages.

To add some text to the page you'll have to gather up some more PostScript tools. To print text, you'll need to use fonts, arrays, and a positioning command.

Before the PostScript interpreter can place text within a page image, it has to know what style and size you want to use. For this example, use Times Roman.

The first token in the statement is:

```
/Times-Roman
```

which is the name of the font, preceded by a slash. The slash tells the PostScript interpreter that Times-Roman is a name that it should put on the operand stack, rather than interpreting it. Otherwise, the interpreter would look at the name Times-Roman, decide that it wasn't a built-in command or a word already defined, and flag it as an error.

With Times-Roman on the stack, you can then issue a command to select it for use. Your line then becomes:

```
/Times-Roman findfont
```

and the findfont command tells the interpreter to locate the dictionary of information about the font whose name is on top of the operand stack and push all the information about that font onto the operand stack.

Fonts are generally stored in a reference size, rather than in the actual size of letters. PostScript uses a one-point font as the reference (1/72- inch high), which it can do because it is able to smoothly scale fonts up in size without creating jagged lines.

The operator called scalefont takes the scale factor from the top of the operand stack and the font information from underneath it. You have set the font name, but you need the number. To put a number on the stack, you include it in a command as a separate token. Putting these elements together, the command is now:

```
/Times-Roman findfont 12 scalefont
```

Finally, with the font specified, you add one more command to make it the current font until further notice.

The first line now reads:

```
/Times-Roman findfont 12 scalefont setfont
```

Now that you have a font, the next step is to specify where on the page you want the typing to start. The most basic positioning command in PostScript is moveto, which tells the LaserWriter which point on the page to use as the starting point for further graphics or text commands.

Naturally enough, since a page is two-dimensional, moveto takes two numeric values as its input. In stack-language form, the two values must already be on the stack already when you execute the moveto command. The command line to start at halfway up the page, about an inch from the left margin, is:

```
72 396 moveto
```

(0,0 is at the bottom left of the page and there are 72 units to an inch).

In PostScript, the operator to place text on the page image is show, which takes a string for input, places the characters on the image, and advances the current location point as it goes. The string input, as you've probably guessed, must first be placed on the operand stack.

Strings in PostScript are made up of sequences of characters. You can create these sequences with operators, or as literal elements. First you'll learn to create arrays with literals. You set strings off by enclosing them with parentheses. Therefore your text string is:

```
(this page intentionally not left blank)
```

and the command to place the text on the page is:

```
(this page intentionally not left blank) show
```

That gets the print on the image, which, as you already know, is put on the paper with showpage.

You now have a complete Postscript program. To print your single line on the page, you run the program:

```
/Times-Roman findfont 12 scalefont setfont
72 396 moveto
(this page intentionally not left blank) show
showpage
```

You can now understand that PostScript is a stack-oriented language, and you have worked a little bit with the stacks. You have written a short program and seen the very basics of how to get an image on a page. On the way, you've encountered commands, deferred commands, arithmetic, strings, arrays, and graphics. And you've gotten the printer to actually a print a page.

Next, a closer look at the PostScript graphics commands and what you can do with them. Then, back to text in more detail.

PostScript Graphics Commands

Using a collection of saved values called "the current graphics state" for the defaults, PostScript creates on a page an image that depends on your commands. Those graphics commands, like all other PostScript commands, are written in post-fix form, with the operators following the values they work on.

In the examples that follow, lines that start with the percent sign are program comments. In these examples the comments usually appear first, followed by the command lines to which the comments refer.

The first operation in most PostScript graphics routines is to save the current graphics state. This operation allows us to change the state as you please without worrying about losing the standard values other routines might need. When we're done, you restore the original graphics state. The first and last operational lines of the program, then, are usually:

```
%save the graphics state
gsave
```

```
%restore the saved state
grestore
```

Further on, you'll change some of the graphics-state values, but right now you should consider the blank page you have to work with. The PostScript page is a two-dimensional space with the origin (0,0) point at the bottom left, and a default scale of 72 units to the inch. If you want to switch the drawing point to two inches over and four up, for example, you write:

```
144 288 moveto
```

On the LaserWriter, the page is assumed all white unless you place a mark upon it.

The most common way to make graphic designs on a PostScript page is to create a "path" of connected lines or curves, which you can then make visible, fill, replicate, or used as a template for filling with colors and shades of gray. This is, in fact, exactly what Adobe Illustrator 88 does when it creates a piece of artwork. To create a simple drawing of a house, for example, you might in turn create paths representing the walls, doors, windows, and roof. Tell the PostScript interpreter you want to start a path with the newpath command. Your sequence thus far becomes:

```
gsave
144 288 moveto
newpath
grestore
```

If you were to add a showpage command at this point, you'd still get a blank page. Moving to a position or defining a path doesn't actually draw the image. To actually draw the image, you create a path and either use the stroke command (to follow the outline of the path, much like inking in a drawing with a pen) or the fill command (to color in any area completely enclosed by the current path). You may recognize that the concept of either stroking or filling paths is identical to Adobe Illustrator 88. You now have all the elements to draw a small bar across the paper.

```
%save the state
%move to the initial position
gsave
```

```
144 288 moveto

%set up a path,
%draw a line,
%ink it in,
%output the page

newpath
288 288 lineto
stroke
showpage
grestore
```

Now, expand the program to draw a simple box and color it black. Tell it exactly where to move for the first point on the box, specify relative movements for three of the sides, and tell the interpreter to close up the path to make the fourth side. When you have completed the outline, tell the interpreter to fill in the square.

```
%set initial position
gsave
288 288 moveto

%set up a path,
%move up, over, down
%complete path,
%fill it in
newpath
0 144 rlineto
144 0 rlineto
0 -144 rlineto
closepath
fill

%print out
showpage
grestore
```

Notice that we didn't say explicitly what to fill the box with. PostScript specifies that the fill operator gets the fill color or pattern from the current graphics state, and on the LaserWriter the initial default fill pattern is black.

Can you add a round peg to your square hole? PostScript uses simple arcs and more complex Bézier curves (a class of curves connecting four points). We show arcs in this example, although Adobe Illustrator 88 relies mostly on the Bézier curves.

To make a circle, you start a new path, specify the origin point, give the radius, and finish with the starting and ending angles. A one-inch circle in the middle of a standard page becomes:

```
%save
%create a path
%specify the arc
%ink it in
gsave
newpath
288 360 72 0 360 arc
stroke

%show page, restore
showpage
grestore
```

To make this an outline, follow the arc command with stroke; to make the circle solid, follow it with fill.

You don't have to choose just a white interior or a solid black fill. By setting the color parameter in the graphics state, you can choose any gradation in between. To set a middle-darkness gray, for example, before executing a fill you write:

```
0.5 setgray
```

It may seem incongruous that leaving the image white requires a color value of 1 and filling with black needs a 0, but if you remember that PostScript is a general solution that is also designed for working with color printers, having more brightness carry the higher value makes sense.

If you want to outline your arc rather than fill it, you also have a wide variety of choices for the stroke pattern and size. In much the way you can set the brush shape and pattern in MacPaint, you can set the stroke width and the shape of the corners. Stroke width is another value saved in the graphics state, but you can change it with the setlinewidth command. For example,

```
5 setlinewidth
```

says to set the width to five units wide. The units start out as points, but you can change them and even make the vertical and horizontal units different.

Line endings and corners are set by the setlinecap and setlinejoin parameters, also part of the graphics state. Line caps (the end of lines) can be butt (squared off, ending right at the end of the stroke), rounded (semicircular arc with diameter same as line width, centered at the end of the stroke), or projecting square (squared off, projecting beyond the end of the stroke by half the line width). Similarly, line joins can be mitered (extended until they meet at an angle), rounded (circular arc with center at intersection), or beveled (flattened connections). The same choices for Caps and Joins are offered in the Adobe Illustrator 88 Paint dialog box.

Make a series of three half-boxes, each with a different stroke width, line cap, and join. Because you are going to make three identical figures, you'll use PostScript's ability to define a word by pushing a name and deferred procedure onto the stack, followed by the def operator to define the name you specified as invoking the procedure.

```
%define a procedure to start a
%path, move right 1", up 1",
%ink in the result, then move
%over 1"

/halfbox
{newpath
72 0 rlineto
0 72 rlineto
stroke
72 0 rlineto}
def

%save the state,
%move to the initial position
```

```
gsave
144 144 moveto

%set but caps and mitered joins
%set 2 unit line width
%move to an initial position,
%invoke the procedure

0 setlinecap
0 setlinejoin
2 setlinewidth
100 350 moveto
halfbox

%set rounded caps and rounded joins
%set 5 unit line
%invoke the procedure

1 setlinecap
1 setlinejoin
5 setlinewidth
halfbox

%set projecting caps and bevelled joins
%set 10 unit line
%invoke the procedure

2 setlinecap
2 setlinejoin
10 setlinewidth
halfbox

%print the result,
%reset the state

showpage
grestore
```

For the last example, draw an arrow, followed by a closing message. Write:

```
%because you are including text
%you need to set a font

gsave
/Times-Roman findfont
12 scalefont
setfont

%start off at the middle of the page
%and mark the start of the figure

newpath
288 500 moveto
%draw a vertical two-inch line
%with no change in horizontal
%position

0 -144 rlineto
currentpoint
stroke
newpath
moveto

%make the triangular head by
%moving a half inch up and right,
%an inch left, and then closing the
%path. Fill in the result.
36 36 rlineto
0 -72 rlineto
closepath
currentpoint
fill
moveto

%put our text in, make a copy
(That's all, folks) dup

% find the width, throw out
% the height, divide the result
% by two, and make it negative
```

```
stringwidth pop 2 div neg

% set -18 points for vertical,
%put the x and y in right order
%on stack, move relative

-18 exch rmoveto

% now save our string, which
% should be on top of stack

show

%finally, you print the page
%and restore the state
showpage
grestore
```

Text and PostScript

The ability to work with and manipulate text is one of the strong suits of the PostScript language. To PostScript, text is a special class of graphics shapes, and also a set of special codes. All the graphics commands that apply to other shapes in PostScript also apply to text. In addition, text has special commands and procedures.

As stated earlier, PostScript is a stack-oriented language. Operations get their inputs from this variable-length list of values, and results or other items not immediately needed are pushed back onto the stack until popped back off. PostScript actually has four stacks, but the one you should be most concerned with is the operand stack.

PostScript uses the postfix form of notation, with the input values expressed first, followed by the operation that acts on them ("3 4 add" rather than "add 3 and 4" or "3 + 4"). Programs don't need a special overall format, but lines starting with a percent sign (%) are treated as comments.

You have already seen how producing a printed line on the page entails picking a font, making it the right size, establishing a position on the page, specifying the string to be printed, and then telling the printer to output the page. The simple program was:

```
% pick a font
/Times-Roman findfont
% scale it to 12 point,
% set it as the current font
12 scalefont setfont
%move over 1 inch, up about 5
72 396 moveto
% image the text at that point
(this page intentionally) show
(not left blank) show
% print out the page
showpage
```

Now, take a look at some of the more special ways PostScript can handle text. You'll start by performing transformations on the Times Roman font included in the LaserWriter. First, make a copy of the Times Roman font, calling it Yourfont. Remember that operators and commands get their values from the stack:

```
% put a name on the stack
/Yourfont
% tell PostScript to retrieve a copy of
% Times Roman and put it on the operand stack too
/Times-Roman findfont
% define that copy as Yourfont
def
```

You're now ready to start making variations. Use the makefont command, which scales and slants a font using a six-element ordered group of numbers called a matrix. We can skip over the mechanics of matrix multiplication and follow some simple plug-in formulas for using makefont matrices.

For a start, make a version of Yourfont that's much taller than normal (much more narrow than usual for its height). To scale a font, you plug in the scale factor in the x (horizontal) direction as the first value, the scale factor in the y (vertical) direction as the fourth value, and leave the others as zero. Your code thus becomes:

```
% define Yourfont as a copy of Times-Roman
/Yourfont /Times-Roman findfont def
```

```
% put a copy on the stack, followed
% by the matrix, then create the new font
Yourfont [12 0 0 36 0 0] makefont
% make that new font the current font
setfont
% move to position on the page, write
216 432 moveto
(Tall fonts and) show
% wait to print until the next part
```

In addition to making the font larger or smaller, you can also slant the letters. Again, you use the makefont command, but this time the matrix is a bit more complex. To get a slant to the right, for example, you want the top of the letter to sit further over to the right than the bottom of the letter does, with the horizontal skew proportional to vertical distance (halfway up, the letter should be displaced half as far over as at the top, and so on).

The mathematical function gives that proportionality factor for x as a function of y and the specified angle is the tangent. To slant a letter, you put the tangent, multiplied by the horizontal-scale factor, in the matrix's third position.

There is one small additional complicating factor: PostScript doesn't have the tangent function built in, but instead expects you to find it by dividing the sine by the cosine. So, continuing on with the example, you:

```
% put a copy of the font on the stack
Yourfont
% follow it with our matrix
% with the the third position filled with the
% sine of 30 degrees divided by the cosine of 30
% degrees, multiplied by 24 points
[24 0 30 sin 30 cos div 24 mul 24 0 0]

% create the new font, set it as current
makefont setfont
% continue imaging text at our current position
(slanted fonts) show
% print the page
showpage
```

Next, see how you can get PostScript to make text fit into a specified space. You might need to do that, for example, to create justified columns in a report or to label a chart.

The basic strategy will be to measure the length of a text phrase, then subtract the length from the intended measure. Follow that by dividing the remaining distance among the spaces in the line, which you'll then add to the image. Because you want to use several values more than once (and PostScript operations take parameters from the top of the stack), you'll have to use several exchange operations to reorder the pending values on the stack.

```
% save the environment
gsave
% set up a 12-point font
/Times-Roman findfont 12 scalefont setfont
% move in 4 inches, up 8
288 572 moveto
% put two copies of the string on the stack
(All the news that fits in print) dup

% make another copy, use it to count length,
% which uses up the copy and leaves the length
dup stringwidth

% get rid of change in vertical position
% because you just want an even horizontal edge
pop
% exchange the length and the extra copy of the string
% you left on the stack with the first "dup"
exch

% now, you need to set up the stack to count
% the spaces in a line. First, you
% put a zero on the stack for a counter
0
% pull the string up above the 0 on the stack
exch
% start a procedure to do for each element
% of the string, but mark it for deferred execution;
% the procedure will count how many spaces you have in
% the string
{
```

```
% set a flag if the element is a space (code 32)
32 eq
% leave a procedure on the stack to add 1
% to top of stack, which should be our counter
% when this operation is executed
{ 1
add}
% do the add to counter procedure if
% the flag was set true
if
% end of the procedure for each member
}
% tell PostScript to execute the test and
% possibly add to counter procedure for
% each element of the string (which is on the
% stack)
forall
% now exchange so the length is
% on top of the count
exch
% now subtract the leftover space
% from a desired length of 4 inches (72 X 4)
288 exch sub
% do the division, computing length
% to add at each space
exch div
% you now have the excess space that must
% be added at each space position sitting
% on the top of the stack. You don't want
% any extra vertical increment,
% but you need a y-axis value on the stack to
% be taken off by widthshow
0
% widthshow needs the string at the top of
% the stack, and it's now 3 down,
% so pull the third element to the top and
% roll all the others down
3 -1 roll
% show the string (from the stack),
% adding the increment whenever a space
% (character code 32) is encountered
32 exch widthshow
```

```
% show the page, restore the environment
showpage grestore
```

If you were actually writing a program to justify lines of text, you might optimize the process so the stack would need less rearranging. For simple text, however, the LaserWriter's built-in computer (or any other PostScript device's RIP) is much faster than the print mechanism anyway, so optimizing isn't always worth the trouble. Instead, it's more worthwhile to write programs in logical order, with ample comments, so that they can be read and understood by others.

In this section, you saw a few ways to shape your own alphabets and how to make text fit in a defined space. Those processes are a small fraction of what PostScript can do with text, but they serve as an introduction. PostScript can literally write in circles, spirals, up and down steep angles, and even backward and forward.

Matrices in Space

PostScript keeps track of shapes and points as grid locations, but the grid may be different for the individual characters, for the page description, and for the output device. You can also set up temporary grids with new origins (0,0 position) or at an angle to the existing lines. Many of the PostScript operators are concerned with making a transformation from one grid to another.

One effective way to go between grids is by using matrix multiplication. PostScript makes extensive use of these multipliers, from mapping the character space into the user space, to mapping the user space onto the output device itself. Like many of the details of PostScript, you can start off without worrying at all about matrix mathematics and let PostScript automatically calculate the essential values. However, if you're curious or ready for more advanced operations, this is how graphic matrices work.

Starting with any point value in two dimensions, extend that (X, Y) pair to a triplet matrix of [x y 1]. You can then accomplish the three basic graphic transformations by multiplying by the appropriate three-by-three matrix. For those of you who haven't learned matrix multiplication or have forgotten it along the way, multiplying the matrix:

```
A   B   0
C   D   0   by  [X  Y    1]
E   F   1
```

yields a new three-element matrix with:

```
first term  =  (X*A)+(Y*C)+(1*E)
second term =  (X*B)+(Y*D)+(1+F)
third term  =  (1*0)+(1*0)=(1*1).
```

To translate (move position sideways), you set the matrix to:

```
1   0   0
0   1   0
dx  dy  1
```

which multiplied by [X Y 1] yields

```
[(X*1)+(Y*0)+(1*dx)   (X*0)+(Y*1)+(1*dy)
(1*0)+(1*0)+(1*1)]
```

simplifying to

```
X' = X + dx, Y' = Y + dy, 1 = 1
```

To scale (move up or down in size), the matrix becomes:

```
Sx  0   0
0   Sy  0
0   0   1
```

which multiplied by [X Y 1] yields

```
[(X*Sx)+(Y*0)+(1*0)   (X*0)+(Y*Sy)+(1*0)
(1*0)+(1*0)+(1*1)]
```

simplifying to

```
X' = X * Sx, Y' = Y + Sy, 1 = 1
```

Finally, to rotate the axes at an angle, the matrix is:

```
cos(a) -sin(a) 0
sin(a) cos(a)     0
0      0          1
```

which multiplied by [X Y 1] yields

```
[(X*cos(a))+(Y*sin(a))+(1*0)
(X*-sin(a))+(Y*cos(a))+(1*0)  (1*0)+(1*0)+(1*1)]
```

simplifying to

```
X' = X * cos(a) + y * sin(a)
Y' = X * -sin(a) + Y * cos(a)
1 = 1
```

Although these matrix operations seem tedious by hand, they're reasonably easy for a computer. More complex transformations can be constructed using combinations of displacement, scale, and rotation in the proper sequence.

If you'd like to try your hand at PostScript programming, you'll need access to a LaserWriter or another PostScript printer connected to an AppleTalk or serial connection. You can write the PostScript programs on just about any word processing program. To send the program to the printer that is connected to your computer via AppleTalk, use the SendPS program included on the Adobe Illustrator Gallery Disk.

If you want to send your program to a printer connected via the serial port, you can use a communications package such as MacTerminal or MicroPhone. Set your communications parameters to 8 data bits, 1 stop bit, no parity, and the X-ON/X-OFF protocol. You can use 1200 bps (set the Mode control on the LaserWriter to 1), 9600 bps (Mode 2), or AppleTalk (Mode 3). Send the LaserWriter a Control-D to stop any current job, a Control-T to have it report the job's status, and the Executive command to tell it to echo back your input. Then, enter your PostScript programs.

The Artwork Document

An Adobe Illustrator 88 artwork document is a PostScript program that describes the appearance of a piece of artwork that you create with the Adobe Illustrator 88 program. An artwork document is saved as a text file that can be opened and edited using a standard word processing program such as Word, MacWrite, or WriteNow. The document communicates a description of the artwork to Post-Script output devices such as the Macintosh screen, printers, and typesetting machines; and to graphics software such as Illustrator program itself.

Adobe Illustrator 88 artwork document files consist of a prologue and data. The prologue defines the procedures that are used by Adobe Illustrator 88 to describe the artwork. The data part of the artwork document consists of calls to the procedures defined in the prologue and the associated target groups of data about the compo-nents of the artwork such as coordinates and positions of all the lines and curves, their associated line weights, gray-scale or color values, paint and type specifications, and page breaks.

The procedures in the prologue relate to many of the functions that are available within the Adobe Illustrator 88 program with the notable exception that transformations such as scaling, rotating, reflecting, and skewing are performed within the Adobe Illustrator 88 program itself and only the information about the resultant transformation is contained in the artwork document. Although commands for performing the transformations are available within PostScript, saving the transformed objects saves time during printing since the PostScript interpreter in the printer (the RIP) doesn't have to be burdened with the task of the transformation, which can be a relatively slow process.

Adobe Illustrator 88 can also save a document in the Macintosh Encapsulated PostScript format or the IBM PC Encapsulated Post-Script format (EPS). These formats contain a reduced resolution image of the artwork in addition to its PostScript description, and therefore, cannot be opened with a standard word processing program. This image provides a 72 dot-per-inch representation of the artwork in either the QuickDraw PICT format (in Macintosh

Encapsulated PostScript) and Aldus/Microsoft TIFF format (in IBM PC Encapsulated PostScript). The representation of the artwork can be used by another program such as a page layout program for placement of the artwork in a layout, or for scaling or cropping the image. The page layout program can use the bit-mapped representation of the image to provide a displayed preview without requiring the program to understand PostScript.

The PostScript portion of Encapsulated PostScript documents created by Adobe Illustrator 88 follows the bit-mapped representation of the artwork and conforms to the Adobe PostScript Document Structuring Conventions, version 2.0, the Adobe Encapsulated PostScript File Format For Apple Macintosh and IBM PC Application, version 1.2, the Aldus Encapsulated PostScript File Format for PageMaker Import for PC Windows and Macintosh Applications, version 1.2, and the Altsys Encapsulated PostScript File Format for Apple Macintosh and PC-Windows Applications, version 1.2.

Another convention used by all the Adobe Illustrator 88 artwork document formats is not to include the PostScript command showpage (or copypage) at the end of the document as is often the case in other PostScript documents. The showpage command causes the PostScript output device to print (or display) the page and clear the page from the printer's memory after the page is printed. The copypage command is similar to the showpage command except that the image of the page is left unchanged in the printer's memory after the page has been printed.

Since artwork document files are usually created for the purpose of becoming a component in another document (such as a page layout), printing the page at the end of the artwork is not usually desirable because it would interfere with the normal printing process of that page by causing it to be printed prematurely. Adobe Illustrator 88 temporarily appends a showpage command to the end of the document as part of the program's normal printing process that is invoked by either selecting Print in the File menu or by typing Command-P as a shortcut. If you want to print an artwork document from outside of Adobe Illustrator 88, you can add the showpage command to the end of the document while you are editing it, or you can use the SendPS program, which has an option for temporarily appending the showpage command to a PostScript file for the purpose of printing.

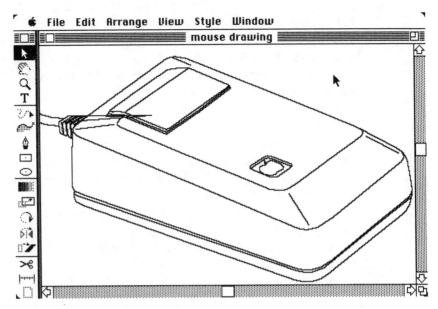

Figure 6-1.
The mouse drawing, a result of executing the PostScript code in the artwork document.

The Artwork Document Structure

Adobe Illustrator 88 uses a standard text file format to store its documents. One of the advantages of using the text format is that people can easily read and modify an artwork document with just about any word processing program.

To understand the document structure, refer to the following listing of the contents of the artwork document, which is in Post-Script, and to the mouse drawing (Figure 6-1) that results from executing the PostScript code. Following the artwork document listing is an explanation of what the various elements in the document mean.

```
%!PS-Adobe-2.0 EPSF-1.2
%%Creator:Adobe Illustrator(TM) 1.0
%%For:Fred Davis
```

```
%%Title:Mouse art
%%CreationDate:4/25/87 1:39 PM
%%DocumentProcSets:Adobe_Illustrator_1.0 0 0
%%DocumentSuppliedProcSets:Adobe_Illustrator_1.0 0 0
%%DocumentFonts:Courier
%%BoundingBox:27 -366 526 -55
%%TemplateBox:0 -720 576 0
%%EndComments
%%BeginProcSet:Adobe_Illustrator_1.0 0 0
% Copyright (C) 1987 Adobe Systems Incorporated.
% All Rights Reserved.
% Adobe Illustrator is a trademark of Adobe Systems
Incorporated.
/Adobe_Illustrator_1.0 dup 100 dict def load begin
/Version 0 def
/Revision 0 def
% definition operators
/bdef {bind def} bind def
/ldef {load def} bdef
/xdef {exch def} bdef
% graphic state operators
/_K {3 index add neg dup 0 lt {pop 0} if 3 1 roll}
bdef
/_k /setcmybcolor where
{/setcmybcolor get}{{1 sub 4 1 roll _K _K _K
setrgbcolor pop} bind} ifelse def
/g {/_b xdef /p {_b setgray} def} bdef
/G {/_B xdef /P {_B setgray} def} bdef
/k {/_b xdef /_y xdef /_m xdef /_c xdef /p {_c _m _y
_b _k} def} bdef
/K {/_B xdef /_Y xdef /_M xdef /_C xdef /P {_C _M _Y
_B _k} def} bdef
/d /setdash ldef
/_i currentflat def
/i {dup 0 eq {pop _i} if setflat} bdef
/j /setlinejoin ldef
/J /setlinecap ldef
/M /setmiterlimit ldef
/w /setlinewidth ldef
% path construction operators
/_R {.25 sub round .25 add} bdef
/_r {transform _R exch _R exch itransform} bdef
```

```
/c {_r curveto} bdef
/C /c ldef
/v {currentpoint 6 2 roll _r curveto} bdef
/V /v ldef
/y {_r 2 copy curveto} bdef
/Y /y ldef
/l {_r lineto} bdef
/L /l ldef
/m {_r moveto} bdef
% error operators
/_e [] def
/_E {_e length 0 ne {gsave 0 g 0 G 0 i 0 J 0 j 1 w
10 M [] 0 d
/Courier 20 0 0 1 z [0.966 0.259 -0.259 0.966
_e 0 get _e 2 get add 2 div _e 1 get _e 3 get add 2
div] e _f t T grestore} if} bdef
/_fill {{fill} stopped
{/_e [pathbbox] def /_f (ERROR: can't fill, increase
flatness)
def n _E} if}
bdef
/_stroke {{stroke} stopped
{/_e [pathbbox] def /_f (ERROR: can't stroke, in-
crease flatness) def n _E} if} bdef
% path painting operators
/n /newpath ldef
/N /n ldef
/F {p _fill} bdef
/f {closepath F} bdef
/S {P _stroke} bdef
/s {closepath S} bdef
/B {gsave F grestore S} bdef
/b {closepath B} bdef
% text block construction and painting operators
/_s /ashow ldef
/_S {(?) exch {2 copy 0 exch put pop dup false
charpath currentpoint _g setmatrix
_stroke _G setmatrix moveto 3 copy pop rmoveto}
forall pop pop pop n} bdef
/_A {_a moveto _t exch 0 exch} bdef
/_L {0 _l neg translate _G currentmatrix pop} bdef
/_w {dup stringwidth exch 3 -1 roll length 1 sub _t
```

```
mul add exch} bdef
/_z [{0 0} {dup _w exch neg 2 div exch neg 2 div}
{dup _w exch neg exch neg}] bdef
/z {_z exch get /_a xdef /_t xdef /_l xdef exch
findfont exch scalefont setfont} bdef
/_g matrix def
/_G matrix def
/_D {_g currentmatrix pop gsave concat _G currentma-
trix pop} bdef
/e {_D p /t {_A _s _L} def} bdef
/r {_D P /t {_A _S _L} def} bdef
/a {_D /t {dup p _A _s P _A _S _L} def} bdef
/o {_D /t {pop _L} def} bdef
/T {grestore} bdef
% group construction operators
/u {} bdef
/U {} bdef
% font construction operators
/Z {findfont begin currentdict dup length dict begin
{1 index /FID ne {def} {pop pop} ifelse} forall /
FontName exch def dup length 0 ne
{/Encoding Encoding 256 array copy def 0 exch {dup
type /nametype eq
{Encoding 2 index 2 index put pop 1 add} {exch pop}
ifelse} forall} if pop
currentdict dup end end /FontName get exch defin-
efont pop} bdef
end
%%EndProcSet
%%EndProlog
%%BeginSetup
Adobe_Illustrator_1.0 begin
n
%%EndSetup
0 g
0 G
1 i
0 J
0 j
0.2 w
10 M
[]0 d
```

```
%%Note:
163.75 -161.25 m
156.75 -165.75 152.75 -171.25 160.75 -174.25 C
344.25 -249.75 l
360.25 -251.75 361.75 -254.25 377.75 -242.75 c
393.75 -231.25 459.75 -185.75 y
464.811 -180.343 457.938 -177.323 452.25 -174.75 c
447.156 -172.445 243.25 -91.75 y
232.625 -88.125 224.25 -88.25 216.25 -93.25 c
208.25 -98.25 104.569 -169.953 102.25 -173.25 c
99.875 -176.625 97.75 -182.75 118.25 -189.25 c
138.75 -195.75 365.25 -291.25 371.75 -294.25 c
378.25 -297.25 393.75 -307.25 421.75 -284.75 c
449.75 -262.25 507.75 -217.75 y
513.25 -212.75 513.75 -206.75 502.75 -200.75 c
491.75 -194.75 457.625 -177.25 y
S
101 -176.625 m
98.5 -209.625 99.25 -239.25 99.25 -242.25 C
99.75 -251.5 102.625 -251.25 113.75 -255.25 c
130.714 -261.349 376.25 -345.25 y
384.75 -347.25 399.75 -351.5 420.75 -335.75 c
444.19 -318.169 516.75 -260.25 y
523.625 -253.312 521.25 -247.75 520.25 -242.25 c
519.25 -236.75 515.75 -216.25 y
514.75 -210.875 509.875 -206.375 y
S
103 -251.25 m
98.5 -253.75 102.25 -254.75 107.25 -256.75 c
112.25 -258.75 377.75 -348.25 y
389.75 -352 401 -350 410.75 -344.75 c
419.421 -340.08 519.75 -260.25 y
521.875 -258.187 520.937 -253.937 y
S
521.187 -256.937 m
518.25 -275.312 510.255 -279.244 507.25 -282.25 c
503.75 -285.75 416.75 -351.5 y
404 -362 388.75 -363.75 374.75 -359.25 c
360.75 -354.75 116.25 -269.25 y
106.375 -265.25 101.5 -264.625 101 -253.125 c
S
85 -181 m
```

```
83 -167.5 l
96 -159.75 l
199.75 -160 l
86.5 -167.75 l
88.5 -182.5 l
85 -181 l
s
89.899 -182.811 m
88.014 -168.234 l
101.639 -160.26 l
105.642 -160.525 l
91.75 -168.5 l
93.634 -184.403 l
89.899 -182.811 l
s
95.076 -185.032 m
93.036 -169.254 l
107.784 -160.622 l
112.117 -160.909 l
97.079 -169.541 l
99.119 -186.755 l
95.076 -185.032 l
s
100.392 -187.333 m
98.309 -170.254 l
114.274 -160.91 l
118.464 -161.221 l
102.686 -170.565 l
103.02 -172.323 l
S
90.25 -163 m
71.5 -161 48 -168 42.25 -115.5 c
36.5 -63 35.75 -57 y
S
83.5 -172 m
70 -170.75 41 -174 35.5 -124.5 c
29.668 -72.009 29 -66 y
S
147.125 -154.25 m
145.125 -155.875 145.125 -156.25 144.25 -158.5 C
```

```
158.25 -157.5 162.25 -157.75 163.75 -158.75 c
165.25 -159.75 216.492 -180.796 217.75 -180.25 C
220.562 -182.187 296.375 -127.562 296.375 -126.062 c
S
144.25 -158.625 m
144.5 -160.375 144.875 -161 y
S
104.25 -176.25 m
152.75 -170.75 l
S
226.75 -90.75 m
248.75 -99.75 l
S
218.312 -177.125 m
217.875 -179.75 l
S
294.19 -126.316 m
283.092 -134.798 234.443 -168.174 221.228 -175.821 C
218.228 -177.446 217.009 -176.519 214.384 -176.144 C
202.719 -171.863 166.924 -157.366 165.25 -156.25 c
163.991 -155.41 159.772 -155.025 150.615 -155.595 C
145.365 -156.22 145.838 -155.079 148.588 -152.829 C
166.414 -141.471 215.09 -106.17 220 -105 c
223.715 -104.114 243.875 -101.625 246 -103 C
294.299 -123.469 L
295.486 -124.219 295.253 -125.441 294.19 -126.316 C
s
294.687 -123.75 m
295.564 -124.353 296.125 -124.812 296.375 -126.062 C
S
296.375 -126.125 m
296.5 -127 296.625 -128.437 y
S
144.125 -159.375 m
142.375 -160.375 141.187 -160.812 142.312 -161.062 C
156.312 -160.062 162.25 -160.25 163.75 -161.25 c
165.25 -162.25 214.75 -182.25 217.75 -182.75 c
220.75 -183.25 298.149 -128.899 297.812 -127.437 c
297.625 -126.625 296.875 -126.687 296.5 -126.5 c
S
```

```
368.25 -255.25 m
392.25 -293.25 l
S
465.25 -186.25 m
505.25 -207.25 l
S
322.5 -220.75 m
338.5 -210.75 l
340.25 -209.5 343.5 -209 346.25 -210 c
351.45 -211.891 371 -219.5 y
373 -221 372.25 -222.25 370.25 -224 c
365.984 -227.732 353.75 -235.25 y
352 -236.25 349.5 -236.5 346.75 -235.5 c
341.844 -233.716 322.5 -226 y
319.5 -225 318.75 -223.25 322.5 -220.75 C
s
321.25 -224.75 m
338.75 -213.5 l
340.5 -212.25 343.75 -211.75 346.5 -212.75 c
351.7 -214.641 371.25 -222.25 y
S
339.687 -220.375 m
335.687 -220.75 332.125 -222.125 331.875 -224.5 c
331.625 -226.875 332.375 -230 338.25 -231.875 c
344.125 -233.75 347.936 -233.396 351.375 -232.25 c
354 -231.375 353.462 -229.617 354.5 -228.75 c
356.463 -227.107 359.564 -227.437 361.5 -225.625 c
365.411 -221.963 354.219 -216.578 348.5 -215.625 c
347 -215.375 346.319 -215.056 344 -215.875 c
342.024 -216.572 341.375 -217.125 341 -218.125 c
340.625 -219.125 341.125 -221.5 340.25 -219.25 c
339.375 -217 339.125 -215.25 338.25 -215.25 C
337.875 -216.75 337.937 -219.75 339.687 -220.375 C
338.812 -220.375 339.687 -220.375 y
s
167.25 -155.25 m
245.125 -103.875 l
S
217.812 -180.375 m
217.125 -181.812 217.875 -182.562 y
S
%%Trailer
_E end
```

The Document Structure Explained

As stated earlier, the document consists of two major sections, a prologue followed by a script. The prologue contains a set of specific definitions that are used by the script. These definitions describe Adobe Illustrator 88 output functions in PostScript language primitives.

The script describes the component graphic elements that are used to create the artwork. The description consists of references to the definitions made in the prologue, interspersed with operands and the data required by those operations. Below is an overview of the artwork document's component sections and subsections, and the order in which they appear in the document. Following the overview is a more detailed description of the prologue definitions and the component descriptions within script.

The following section, which describes an Adobe Illustrator artwork document, focuses primarily on the document's overall structure as defined by a set of PostScript comments. Comments can be recognized by the percentage sign (%) that precedes them. Comments are totally ignored by a PostScript interpreter. However, they convey structural information about the document to other programs that operate on the document. Some comments serve primarily to mark the boundaries between the various parts of the document (the prologue and the script). Others provide information such as a bounding box that encloses all the marks painted as a result of executing the document and the set of fonts that may need to be downloaded to a PostScript printer before the document can be printed.

The Prologue of an Artwork Document

The document's prologue section is subdivided into header and definition subsections.

Prologue Header Subsection

```
%!PS-Adobe-2.0 EPSF-1.2
```

is the first line in the document and indicates that the document conforms to version 2.0 of the Adobe PostScript Document Structuring

Conventions and version 1.2 of the Encapsulated PostScript Document Format.

```
%%Creator:Adobe Illustrator(TM) version serial
```

indicates that the document was created by the specified version of Adobe Illustrator optionally serialized with the specified serial value. The version value and the optional serial value consist of arbitrary text delimited by white space.

```
%%For:name organization
```

indicates that the document was created by a version of Adobe Illustrator personalized for the specified name and organization. The name and organization values consist of arbitrary text, including white space. Organization is terminated by a newline.

```
%%Title:name
```

indicates the title of the document. The name value consists of arbitrary text (such as the filename) terminated by a newline.

```
%%Creation Date:date time
```

indicates the date and time at which the document was created. The date and time values consist of arbitrary text, including white space. Time is terminated by a newline.

```
%%DocumentProcSets:Adobe_Illustrator_version
level revision
```

indicates that the document requires the specified prologue procedure set. The version, level, and revision values consist of arbitrary text delimited by white space.

```
%%DocumentSuppliedProcSets:Adobe_Illustrator_version
level revision
```

indicates that the document supplies the specified prologue procedure set. The version, level, and revision values consist of arbitrary text delimited by white space.

```
%%DocumentFonts:font...
```

indicates that the document uses the specified fonts. These fonts may need to be downloaded to the PostScript printer before the document is sent. The font values consist of PostScript font names delimited by white space.

```
%%+font...
```

when following the %%DocumentFonts comment, this comment indicates that the document uses the specified fonts, in addition to those given by the %%DocumentFonts comment. The font values consist of PostScript font names delimited by white space.

```
%%BoundingBox:llx lly urx ury
```

indicates the bounding box (the smallest rectangle that encloses all the marks painted as a result of executing (for example, printing) the document). All four values are integers: lower left x, lower left y, upper right x, and upper right y. The coordinates (llx, lly) and (urx, ury) are the lower left and upper right corners of the bounding box, respectively. The coordinates are specified in the default user coordinate system in which the unit length along both of the axes is 1/72 of an inch, the positive x axis extends horizontally to the right, and the positive y axis extends vertically upwards (and negative x extends left, negative y extends down) The value urx - llx, which must be an integer, provides an upper bound on the width of the illustration. The value ury - lly, which must be an integer, provides an upper bound on the height of the illustration.

```
%%TemplateBox:llx lly urx ury
```

indicates the bounding box that encloses all the samples in the document's template. All four values are integers: lower left x, lower left y, upper right x, and upper right y. The coordinates (llx, lly) and (urx, ury) are the coordinates of the lower left and upper right corners of the bounding box, respectively. The coordinates are specified in the default user coordinate system in which the unit length along both axes is 1/72 of an inch: Adobe Illustrator assumes that the size of each sample is 1/72-by-1/72- inch. The value urx - llx, which must be an integer, equals the number of rows of samples. If the document has no template, llx equals urx and lly equals ury.

When Adobe Illustrator opens the document, the illustration is placed on the drawing area in such a way that the coordinate ((llx +urx)/2), ((lly +ury)/2) is centered in the drawing area. (Use these coordinates; lower left, center and upper right, to determine adjustments to make to the bounding box when using the Adobe Separator program, to adjust the page size to print trim marks, etc. outside a larger sized bounding box.)

```
%%EndComments
```

explicitly ends the prologue header subsection and marks the beginning of the prologue definition subsection.

Prolog Definition Subsection

```
%%BeginProcSet:Adobe_Illustrator_version level
revision prologue definitions
%%EndProcSet
```

The %%BeginProcSet and %%EndProcSet comments explicitly delimit the prologue definitions of the document. These definitions are used by the script section to match the Adobe Illustrator 88 output functions to the capabilities and primitives that PostScript supports. The entire prologue is packaged as a single procedure set identified by the version, level, and revision values, each of which is delimited by white space.

```
%%EndProlog
```

The %%EndProlog remark explicitly ends the prologue section and marks the beginning of the script section.

The Script Section

The document's script section is subdivided into setup, body, and trailer subsections.

Script Setup Subsection

```
%%BeginSetup
script setup
%%End Setup
```

The %%BeginSetup and %%EndSetup comments explicitly delimit the script setup, which performs various graphics state and error recovery initialization and font reencoding operations required by the document's prologue and script.

Script Body Subsection

```
script body
```

The script body describes the set of component graphic elements that define the illustration. The script consists of references to definitions made in the prologue, interspersed with operands and data required by those operations.

```
%%Trailer
```

The %%Trailer remark explicitly ends the script body subsection of the document and marks the beginning of the script trailer subsection.

Script Trailer Subsection

```
script trailer
```

The script trailer performs various cleanup and error recovery operations required by the document's prologue and script.

Illustrator Document Prologue Definitions

This section specifies and defines the operations provided by the prologue of an Adobe Illustrator document. These operations are used within the script to match Adobe Illustrator's output functions to the capabilities and primitives provided by PostScript.

Graphic State Operations

The prologue maintains a graphics state that establishes a context in which its graphic operations execute. The graphics state inherits most of its functionality from the underlying graphics state supplied by the PostScript interpreter. Many of the prologue's graphics state operations have a one-for-one mapping into a single PostScript primitive, and hence, they simply provide a set of abbreviated primitive names or aliases.

The primary difference between the prologue's graphics state and that of PostScript is in the handling of color state and font metric information. The prologue maintains two separate current color parameters: a filling color and a stroking color. These two parameters determine the color of subsequently filled and stroked shapes, respectively (see g, G, k, and K). They are provided to match Adobe Illustrator's capability of filling and stroking a single path with different colors.

The font metric information included in the graphics state, in addition to the current font, consists of the spacing (also called kerning) adjustment to the x width of each character, the leading distance between each successive line of text, and a specification of the alignment method that aligns each line of text. These parameters are provided to support the Adobe Illustrator 88 operators.

Several of PostScript's graphic state parameters are not directly accessible through prologue operators. These parameters include the current transformation matrix, the clipping path, the halftone screen, the transfer function, and the output device. Values for these parameters are inherited by the prologue when the prologue is executed by a specific physical device (such as an Apple LaserWriter laser printer or a Linotype L300 imagesetter) and remain unchanged throughout the execution of the rest of the document. (This statement may not be strictly true if the document's script contains embedded documents. However, the graphics state may be restored and all printer virtual memory recovered by embedding the document itself within a save/restore context.)

```
d array offset d -
```

sets the dash pattern parameter in the graphics state which determines the dash pattern of subsequently stroked paths (see s and S). The array and offset parameter values have meaning identical to those of the PostScript setdash operator. That is, if array is empty, normal unbroken stroked lines are produced. If array is not empty, dashed lines, whose pattern (in user space) is given by the elements of array, which must all be non-negative, but not all zero, are produced. The offset parameter, which must be non-negative, is interpreted as a distance (in user space) into the dash pattern at which the pattern should be started.

```
g gray g -
```

sets the current filling color parameter in the graphics state which determines the color of subsequently filled paths (see f and F). The gray parameter value has a meaning identical to that of the PostScript setgray operator. That is, the filling color is set to a gray shade corresponding to gray, which must be a number between 0 and 1, where 0 corresponds to black, 1 corresponds to white, and intermediate values correspond to intermediate shades of gray. If no shade is specified, the default fill shade of black is used. The specified gray shade remains in effect for all fills until another setgray operator changes it.

```
G gray G -
```

sets the current stroking color parameter in the graphics state which determines the color of subsequently stroked paths (see s and S). The gray parameter value has a meaning identical to that of the PostScript setgray operator. That is, the stroking color is set to a gray shade corresponding to gray, which must be a number between 0 and 1, where 0 corresponds to black, 1 corresponds to white, and intermediate values correspond to intermediate shades of gray. If no shade is specified, the default stroke shade of black is used. The specified gray shade remains in effect for all strokes until another setgray operator changes it.

```
i flat i -
```

sets the current flatness parameter in the graphics state which determines the accuracy with which curved path segments are to be rendered on the output device. A positive flat parameter value has a meaning identical to that of the PostScript setflat operator. That is, its value gives the maximum error tolerance (measured in output device pixels) of a straight line segment approximation of any portion of a curve. If flat is 0, the flatness is set to the flatness value in effect when the document's prologue section is executed, which normally equals the device's default, built-in flatness.

```
j join j -
```

sets the current line join parameter in the graphics state which determines the shape to be placed at the corners of stroked paths (see s and S). The join parameter value has a meaning identical to that of the PostScript setlinejoin operator. That is, the value 0 establishes miter joins, 1 establishes round joins, and 2 establishes bevel joins.

```
J cap J -
```

sets the current line cap parameter in the graphics state which determines the shape to be placed at the ends of open stroked paths and at the ends of dashed line segments (see s and S). The cap parameter value has a meaning identical to that of the PostScript setlinecap operator. That is, the value 0 establishes butt caps, 1 establishes round caps, and 2 establishes projecting caps.

```
k cyan magenta yellow black k -
```

sets the current filling color parameter in the graphics state which determines the color of subsequently filled paths (see f and F). The cyan, magenta, yellow, and black parameter values have meaning identical to those of the PostScript setcmybcolor operator (contact Adobe Systems Technical Support for a definition of this operator). That is, each value must be a number between 0 and 1, where 0 corresponds to no contribution at all of that color, 1 corresponds to maximum intensity of that color, and intermediate values correspond to intermediate intensities.

If the setcmybcolor operator is not known in any of the dictionaries on the current dictionary stack when the document's prologue section is executed, then the current filling or stroking color parameter is set to the color obtained by the following operation

```
red green blue setrgbcolor
```

where
red = 1 - min(1, cyan + black)
green = 1 - min(1, magenta + black)
blue = 1 - min(1, yellow + black)

That is, the black component is added to each of the other three components, and the resulting values are converted to a color specified by the red-green-blue color model.

On most existing black-and-white PostScript printers, the setrgbcolor operator is implemented as if the following operation were performed

```
gray setgray
```

where gray is an NTSC (video standard) weighed average of the three color components given by

```
gray = .3* red + .59* green+.11* blue
```

Of course, page composition systems and other printing managers may produce color separations on black-and-white printers by redefining the setcmybcolor and setgray operators and establishing the appropriate halftone screens and transfer functions before sending the document.

```
K cyan magenta yellow black K -
```

sets the current stroking color parameter in the graphics state which determines the color of subsequently stroked paths (see s and S). The cyan, magenta, yellow, and black parameter values have meaning identical to those of the PostScript setcmybcolor operator. That is, each value must be a number between 0 and 1, where 0 corresponds to no contribution at all of that color, 1 corresponds to maximum intensity of that color, and intermediate values correspond to intermediate intensities of that color.

See the k operator for a discussion of the setcmybcolor operator.

```
M miter M -
```

sets the current miter limit parameter which determines when the objectionably long spikes produced at the corners of sharply angled stroked paths by mitered joins should be cut off with bevels (see j). The miter parameter value has a meaning identical to that of the PostScript setmiterlimit operator. That is, miter specifies the maximum desired ratio between the miter length at the corner and the line width.

```
w width w -
```

sets the current line width parameter in the graphics state which determines the thickness of stroked lines (see s and S). The width parameter value has a meaning identical to that of the PostScript setlinewidth operator. That is, all points whose perpendicular distance from the current path (in user space) is less than or equal to one-half of width are painted. As usual, a value of 0 is permitted: it is interpreted as the thinnest line that can be rendered on the output device.

```
z font scale leading kerning alignment z -
```

sets the current font parameter in the graphics state which establishes the font dictionary to be used by subsequent text-block painting operators (see a, e, o, and r). The positive scale factor (z) is applied to the font dictionary given by the literal name font, producing a new font whose characters are scaled by the positive number scale (in both x and y). The resulting font is established as the current font.

This operator also sets the current leading, spacing, and alignment method parameters in the graphics state. The spacing parameter, given by the number kerning, specifies a spacing value (in user space) that is added to the x width of each character in the scaled font, thus modifying the horizontal spacing between the characters. The leading parameter, given by the non-negative leading, specifies the vertical spacing (in user space) between successive lines of text composing the text block. The alignment method parameter, given by the integer alignment, specifies how the lines of text are aligned with one another. That is, an alignment value of 0 specifies align left (flush left, ragged right), 1 specifies align center (ragged left and right), and 2 specifies align right (ragged left, flush right).

```
Z array newfont font Z -
```

creates a new reencoded font, whose name is given by the literal name newfont, that is a copy of an existing font, whose name is given by font, except that portions of the new font's encoding vector have been modified as specified by the array parameter value. Array is an array of encoding numbers and literal character names organized as follows:

```
[code1 name11 name12...name1m1
code2 name21 name22....name2m2
....
coden namen1 namen2...namenmn]
```

where codei for $1 <= i <= n$ are encoding numbers between 0 and 255, and nameij for $1 <= i <= n$, $1 <= mi$ are literal character names. The encoding vector of the new font is identical to that of the existing font except that the element at index codei + j equals nameij for $1 <= i <= n$, $1 <= j <= mi$. It is assumed that all of the encoding numbers codei + j are distinct. In addition, n may be equal to 0, in which case array is an empty array, and the encoding vector of the new font is identical to that of the existing font.

Path Construction Operations

A path is built up by executing one or more path construction operations that append a sequence of connected straight or curved line segments onto the path. Once a path is completely built up, it is painted with one of the path painting operations.

Only one path may be built up at a time. This path is called the current path. The current path is initially empty and is reset to empty by all of the path painting operations.

The trailing endpoint of the most recently appended segment is referred to as the current point. All of the path construction operations that append a segment start at the current point. Each segment is specified by a set of coordinates specified in user space. A new path is begun by executing a special operation that establishes a current point on an otherwise empty path.

As the path is built up, each point that joins two segments is marked a smooth point or a corner point. If the point is marked smooth, then the point and the two associated Bézier direction points of the segments that the point connects are assumed to be colinear. If the point is marked corner, then no constraint is assumed. (A straight line segment can be thought of as a degenerate Bézier curve whose direction points are coincident with its endpoints).

```
c x1 y1 x2 y2 x3 y3 c -
```

adds a Bézier curve segment to the current path between the current point and the point (x3, y3), using (x1, y1) and then (x2, y2) as the Bézier direction points; (x3, y3) then becomes the current point. The new current point is marked a smooth point.

```
C x1 y1 x2 y2 x3 y3 C -
```

adds a Bézier curve segment to the current path between the current point and the point (x3, y3), using (x1, y1) and then (x2, y2) as the Bézier direction points; (x3, y3) then becomes the current point. The new current point is marked a corner point.

```
l x y l -
```

appends a straight line segment to the current path. The line extends from the current point to the point (x, y); (x, y) then becomes the current point. The new current point is marked a smooth point.

```
L x y L -
```

appends a straight line segment to the current path. The line extends from the current point to the point (x, y); (x, y) then becomes the current point. The new current point is marked a corner point.

```
m x y m -
```

starts a new current path by setting the current point to (x, y) without adding any segment to the path. Initially, the path must be empty and have no current point.

```
v x2 y2 x3 y3 v -
```

adds a Bézier curve segment to the current path between the current point and the point (x3, y3), using the current point and then (x2, y2) as the Bézier direction points; (x3, y3) then becomes the current point. The new current point is marked a smooth point.

```
V x2 y2 x3 y3 V -
```

adds a Bézier curve segment to the current path between the current point and the point (x3, y3), using the current point and then (x2, y2) as the Bézier direction points; (x3, y3) then becomes the current point. The new current point is marked a corner point.

```
y x1 y1 x3 y3 y -
```

adds a Bézier curve segment to the current path between the current point and the point (x3, y3), using (x1, y1) and then (x3, y3) as the Bézier direction points; (x3, y3) then becomes the current point. The new current point is marked a smooth point.

```
Y x1 y1 x3 y3 Y-
```

adds a Bézier curve segment to the current path between the current point and the point (x3, y3), using (x1, y1) and then (x3, y3) as the Bézier direction points; (x3, y3) then becomes the current point. The new current point is marked a corner point.

Path Painting Operations

The prologue provides a set of painting operations that can convert the current path to represent marks on the current page. All of these operations are based on combinations of the underlying PostScript primitives closepath, fill, and stroke.

The results of these painting operations are controlled by the prologue's current graphics state (see the earlier section, "Graphic State Operations").

All of the painting operations assume that the current path has been previously built-up by a sequence of path construction operations. After the painting operation is completed, the current path is initialized to be empty.

b - b-

indicates that the current path should be closed and then first filled (see f and F) with the current filling color and then stroked (see s and S) with the current stroking color. The stroke line width (see w) is set by the current line width parameter.

B - B -

indicates that the current path should be first filled (see f and F) with the current filling color and then stroked (see s and S) with the current stroking color. The stroke line width (see w) is set by the current line width parameter.

f - f -

closes the current path and then paints (fills) the area enclosed by the current path with the current filling color. The inside of the current path is determined by the normal PostScript non-zero winding number rule. Any previous contents of that area on the current page are obscured.

F - F -

paints (fills) the area enclosed by the current path with the current filling color. The inside of the current path is determined by the normal PostScript non-zero winding number rule. Any previous contents of that area on the current page are obscured.

n - n -

closes the current path and then neither fills (see f and F) nor strokes (see s and S) the path.

```
N  -  N  -
```

neither fills (see f and F) nor strokes (see s and S) the current path.

```
s  -  s  -
```

closes the current path and then paints (strokes) a line following the path with the current stroking color. This line is centered on the path, has sides parallel to the path segments, and has a width given by the current line width parameter (see w).

The joints between connected path segments are painted with the current line join (see j). The ends of the line's dash segments, if any, are painted with the current line cap (see J). The line is either solid or broken according to the current dash pattern (see d).

```
S  -  S  -
```

paints (strokes) a line following the path with the current stroking color. This line is centered on the path, has sides parallel to the path segments, and has a width given by the current line width parameter (see w).

The joints between connected path segments are painted with the current line join (see j). The ends of the path and the ends of the line's dash segments, if any, are painted with the current line cap (see J). The line is either solid or broken according to the current dash pattern (see d).

Text Block Painting Operations

The prologue provides a set of text block painting operations that paint the successive lines of text composing the text block, using the current font, spacing (also called kerning), leading, and alignment method parameters in the graphics state.

```
a matrix a  -
```

indicates the start of a text block whose character outlines should be neither filled (see e) nor stroked (see r). Matrix specifies a matrix that is concatenated with the current transformation matrix to define a new user space whose coordinates are transformed into the former user space according to matrix. This new space establishes an origin for the first line of text.

```
e matrix e -
```

indicates the start of a text block whose character outlines should be filled with the current filling color. Matrix specifies a matrix that is concatenated with the current transformation matrix to define a new user space whose coordinates are transformed into the former user space according to matrix. This new space establishes an origin for the first line of text.

```
o matrix o -
```

indicates the start of a text block whose character outlines should be first filled (see e) with the current filling color and then stroked (see r) with the current stroking color. Matrix specifies a matrix that is concatenated with the current transformation matrix to define a new user space whose coordinates are transformed into the former user space according to matrix. This new space establishes an origin for the first line of text.

```
r matrix r -
```

indicates the start of a text block whose character outlines should be stroked with the current stroking color. The stroked line is centered on the character's outline, has sides parallel to the outline's segments, and has a width given by the current line width parameter (see w). The joints between connected outline segments are painted with the current line join (see j). The ends of the line's dash segments, if any, are painted with the current line cap (see J). The outline is either solid or broken according to the current dash pattern (see d). The width and dash parameters' lengths are interpreted in terms of the user space in effect prior to the start of the text block. Matrix specifies a matrix that is concatenated with the current transformation matrix to define a new user space whose coordinates are transformed into the former user space according to matrix. This new space establishes an origin for the first line of text.

```
t string t -
```

prints the characters of string starting at the point (Sx, Sy) in the user space established by either the a, e, o, or r operator at the start of the text block or by the prior t operator. The characters are printed using a combination of the outline filling and stroking methods as specified by the a, e, o, or r operator. The characters are painted using the current font. While painting, the width of each character is adjusted by adding the current spacing to its x width.

The starting point (Sx, Sy) is defined as follows:

alignment method	(Sx, Sy)
align left	(0, 0)
align center	(-wx/2, -wy/2)
align right	(-wx, wy)

where wx and wy are the sum of the x and y widths of all the characters printed, respectively (where the x widths have been adjusted by the spacing parameter value).

After painting, the origin of user space is translated by the current leading in the negative y direction to establish an origin for the next line of text.

```
T - T -
```

indicates the end of a text block and restores the user space in effect prior to the start of the text block.

Group Construction Operations

The prologue provides two group construction operators that support Illustrator's ability to combine several objects into groups that are then treated as one composite object. These operators have no affect on the graphics state, nor do they place marks on the page. They provide structural information only.

```
u - u -
```

indicates that the subsequent objects (paths, text blocks, and groups), up to the next matching U operator, are to be grouped together as a single object.

```
U - U -
```

when matched with a previous u operator, indicates the end of a group of objects.

Prologue Implementaton

The following is a complete listing of the version 1.1 PostScript implementation of the prologue's definitions. Indented descriptions are included throughout the listing to provide additional documentation.

```
%%BeginProcSet:Adobe_Illustrator_1.1 0 0
% Copyright (C) 1987 Adobe Systems Incorporated.
% All Rights Reserved.
% Adobe Illustrator is a trademark of Adobe Systems
Incorporated.
```

The entire prologue is packaged as a single procedure set identified by the %%BeginProcSet comment. Copyright and trademark information are also included.

```
/Adobe_Illustrator_1.1 dup 100 dict def load begin
/Version 0 def
/Revision 0 def
```

All of the prologue's definitions are placed within a dictionary created just for this purpose. This definition dictionary is associated with the key Adobe_Illustrator_1.1 in the current dictionary. The new dictionary is then placed on the top of the dictionary stack so that all of the following definitions will be defined within it.

The Version and Revision keys specify that the dictionary contains the version 0, revision 0 procedure set definitions. The version and revision fields are both 0 since version information is included in the dictionary's name.

In some environments, the entire prologue may be permanently downloaded. The following program tests for its presence. The program writes true to the standard output file if the proper version and revision of the prologue are present and writes false otherwise.

```
Adobe_Illustrator_1.1 where
{begin Version 0 eq Revision 0 eq and end}
{false} ifelse = flush
% definition operators
/bdef {bind def} bind def
/ldef {load def} bdef
/xdef {exch def} bdef
```

These three definition operators all associate a key with a value in the current dictionary. They are provided to conserve virtual memory within the printer and to reduce the execution time required by the operators.

```
% graphic state operators
/_K {3 index add neg dub 0 it {pop 0} if 3 1 roll} bdef
/_k /setcmybcolor where
{/setcmybcolor get} {{1 sub 4 1 roll _K _K _K setrgbcolor
pop} bind} ifelse def
/g {/_b xdef /p {_b setgray} def} bdef
/G {/_B xdef /P {_B setgray} def} bdef
/k {/_b xdef /_y xdef /_m xdef /_c xdef /p {_c _m _y _b
_k} def} bdef
/K {/_B xdef /_Y xdef /_M xdef /_C xdef /P {_C _M _Y _B
_k} def} bdef
```

The four variables _c, _m, _y, and _b maintain the component cyan, magenta, yellow, and black color values, respectively, that represent the current filling color, and the execution of p establishes the current filling color as the current color in the PostScript graphics state. The variables perform a similar function with respect to the current stroking color. When executed, the four operators g, G, k, and K update the values of the appropriate subset of these eight variables.

The operators _k and _K provide an interface to the setcmybcolor operator. See the k operator for a discussion of their behavior.

```
/d /setdash ldef
/_l currentflat def
/l {dup 0 eq {pop _l} if setflat} bdef
/j /setlinejoin ldef
/J /setlinecap ldef
/M /setmiterlimit ldef
/w /setlinewidth ldef
```

The above are implementations of several of the simpler graphics state operators.

```
% path construction operators
/_/R {.25 sub round .25 add} bdef
/_r {transform _/r exch _R exch itransform} bdef
/c {_r curveto} bdef
/C /c ldef
/v {currentpoint 6 2 roll _r curveto} bdef
/V /v ldef
/y {_r 2 copy curveto} bdef
/Y /y ldef
/l {_r lineto} bdef
/L /l ldef
/m {_r moveto} bdef
```

Although path coordinates are specified in a device-independent user space, this independence leads to slight variations in stroke weight due to differences in the device subpixel location of the coordinates. For example, if a vertical line is drawn with a width of 2.5 device pixels, then the line will overlap 3 pixel columns if its center is at a .5 subpixel location, while it will overlap 4 columns if its center is at a .0 location. To eliminate this plus or minus one variation in stroke weight, the endpoints of each path segment are moved to a uniform subpixel location of .25. This operation is called path phase locking.

The choice of .25 as opposed to other possible subpixel locations for phase locking is based on a desire that the location should not produce more even stroke weights than odd ones, and vice versa. For example, a choice of .0 would never produce an odd stroke width, while .5 would never produce an even width. The choice of .25

provides an unbiased balance of these two extreme behaviors.

All the path construction operations are based on the PostScript primitives: moveto, lineto, and curveto. Before executing these primitives, however, the segment's endpoints are phase-locked by executing the _r operator. The Bézier direction points are not phase-locked, unless they are coincident with the segment's endpoints.

```
% error operators
/_e [] def
/_/E {_e length 0 ne {gsave 0 g 0 G 0 1 0 J 0 j 1 w 10
M [] 0 d
/Courier 20 0 0 1 z [0.966 0.259 -0.259 0.966
_e 0 get _e 2 get add 2 div _e 1 get _e 3 get add 2 div]
e _f t T grestore} if} bdef
/_fill {{fill} stopped
{/_e [pathbbox] def /_f (ERROR: can't fill, increase
flatness) def n _E} if}
bdef
/_stroke {{stoke} stopped
{/_e [pathbbox] def /_f (ERROR: can't stroke, increase
flatness) def n
_E} if} bdef
```

The _fill and _stroke operators provide an error recovery method for the PostScript fill and stroke primitives, respectively. If the filling or stroking of the current path would cause some limit to be exceeded within the PostScript interpreter, these operators will catch the error, display an appropriate error message, and then allow the execution of the document to continue.

When an error is caught by the stopped primitive, _e is set equal to a four-element array containing the bounding box of the current path, and _f is set equal to the string containing the error message. The operator _E is then invoked to display the message. Since the error message may be obscured by the painting of subsequent elements, _E is defined so that it may be called in the document's trailer subsection. If any errors occurred, the message associated with the last occurring error is redisplayed.

```
% path painting operators
/n /newpath ldef
/N /n ldef
/F {p _fill} bdef
```

```
/f {closepath F} bdef
/S {P _stroke} bdef
/s {closepath S} bdef
/B {gsave F grestore S} bdef
/b {closepath B} bdef
```

The path painting operators are easily implemented by calling the appropriate PostScript fill and stroke primitives. When the current path must be filled as well as stroked, it is preserved across the fill via the PostScript gsave and grestore primitives. Before the primitives are called, however, the current color in the PostScript graphics state is established by executing either p or P, which are defined by the implementations of g, G, k, and K.

```
% text block construction and painting operators
/_s /ashow ldef
/_S {(?) exch {2 copy 0 exch put pop dup false charpath
currentpoint _g
setmatrix
_stroke _G setmatrix moveto 3 copy pop rmoveto} forall
pop pop pop    n} bdef
```

The _s and _S operators are used to fill and stroke the outlines of the characters in an argument string, respectively. Both of these operators expect three arguments on the stack like the PostScript primitive ashow: the x and y width displacement values and the string.

Filling the outlines is especially easy: ashow is simply executed. Stroking the outlines involves a loop that enumerates each character of the string. The primitive charpath is executed to obtain the character's outline, which is stroked by the primitive stroke, in the set line width.

Before the outline is stroked, however, the user space that was in effect prior to the start of the text block is restored. This must be done so that the width and dash parameter lengths are interpreted properly. The matrix _g contains the transformation matrix that defines this space. After the outline is stroked, the matrix _G is used to reestablish the prior user space. It is the responsibility of the a, e, o, r, and t operators to define and maintain proper values for these matrices.

A special property of the charpath primitive is used to establish the proper spacing between each character in the string and the next: charpath leaves the current point displaced from its initial position by the width of the character. Before the outline is stroked, this displaced current point is placed on the stack. Afterwards, a current point is reestablished by executing moveto, which takes its arguments from the stack. The rmoveto primitive is then used to emulate the width adjustment performed by ashow.

```
/_A {_a moveto _t exch 0 exch} bdef
/_L {0 _l neg translate _G currentmatrix pop} bdef
```

The _A and _L operators are used just prior and just after a single line of text is painted. _A takes the line of text as a string argument and returns x and y width displacement values and the string, in preparation for the ashow operator. In addition, it sets the current point equal to the line's starting point. This is accomplished by executing the alignment method associated with the operator _a, which expects a string argument and leaves the string along with the starting point on the stack. Then a moveto is executed. The x width displacement value is defined by the current spacing value, associated with _t. The y width displacement value is 0. It is the responsibility of the z operator to define _a and _t properly.

After the line is painted, the origin of user space is translated by the current leading in the negative y direction to establish an origin for the next line of text. The current leading is associated with _l. After the translation, the matrix _G is updated to reflect the new translated user space.

```
/_w {dup stringwidth exch 3 -1 roll length 1 sub _t mul
add exch} bdef
/_z [{0 0} bind {dup _w exch neg 2 div exch neg 2 div}
bind {dup _w exch neg exch neg} bind] def
/z {_z exch get /_a xdef /_t xdef /_l xdef exch findfont
exch scalefont setfont} bdef
```

The three variables _l, _t, and _a maintain the current leading, spacing, and alignment method parameters, respectively. The alignment method is implemented as an operator "t" takes the line of text as a string argument and returns the string along with the x and y coordinates of the line's starting point in the current user space. The computation of the starting point is based on the PostScript primitive stringwidth, along with the current spacing value.

The three different alignment methods are implemented as elements of the array associated with _z. When z is executed, the appropriate element is selected from the array and bound to _a.

```
/_g matrix def
/_G matrix def
/_D {_g currentmatrix pop gsave concat _G currentmatrix
pop} bdef
/e {_D p /t {_A _s _L} def} bdef
/r {_D P /t {_A _S _L} def} bdef
/a {_D /t {dup p _A _s P _A _S _L} def} bdef
/o {_D /t {pop _L} def} bdef
/T {grestore} bdef
```

The a, e, o, and r operators all begin by executing the operator _D to establish the user space associated with the text block. _D saves the transformation matrix associated with the current user space in the matrix _g, concatenates its argument matrix with the current transformation matrix to define the new user space, and then saves the transformation matrix associated with the new space in the matrix _G. These two matrices are used by the character stroking operations as described above.

Then the t operator is bound to the appropriate character filling and stroking method. In general, t first establishes the current filling or stroking color by executing the p or P operator, respectively. Then the _A operator is executed to establish the line's starting point. Next, the _s or _S operator is invoked to fill or stroke the line, respectively. Finally, the _L operator is executed to translate the user space for the next line of text.

At the end of the text block, the T operator executes the primitive grestore to restore the user space prior to the start of the text block. This grestore matches the gsave executed by the _D operator.

```
% group construction operators
/u {} bdef
/U {} bdef
```

These operators provide structural information within the script, hence their implementations do nothing.

```
% font construction operators
/Z {findfont begin currentdict dup length dict begin
{1 index /FID ne {def} {pop pop} ifelse} forall
/FontName exch def dup
length 0 n e
{/Encoding Encoding 256 array copy def 0 exch {dup type
/nametype
eq
{Encoding 2 index 2 index put pop 1 add} {exch pop}
ifelse} forall} if pop currentdict dup end
end /FontName get exch definefont pop} bdef
```

The Z operator builds the reencoded font by first copying all the entries in the base font dictionary to the new dictionary, except for the FID field. Then, the new font name is installed. Next, the elements of the argument array are enumerated to update the new font's character encoding vector. Finally, the definefont primitive is executed to create the new font.

```
e n d
%%EndProcSet
```

The %%EndProcSet comment defines the end of the prologue's definitions. The definition dictionary is removed from the dictionary stack.

The Illustrator Document Script Subsection

The Adobe Illustrator 88 script section was designed to meet two goals. First, it must be executable by a PostScript interpreter, and second, it must be easily parsable so that a complete description of the illustration's graphic elements may be obtained without having to directly interpret the PostScript program. These goals result in a script consisting of a sequence of tokens that conforms to a strict syntactic form.

Syntax Notation

In the syntax notation used to describe the script, syntactic categories are indicated by italic type, and literal names by bold type. Alternative categories are listed on separate lines. Occurrences of the newline character are explicitly included as instances of the category newline. The category text specifies an arbitrary sequence of characters excluding a newline character.

The category arbitrary_text specifies an arbitrary PostScript program consisting of a sequence of characters possibly including newline characters. Prologue operator argument categories, such as pattern, offset, gray, and so forth, are left unspecified. Consult the section on Adobe Illustrator Document Prologue Definitions beginning on page 362.

Script Syntax

```
script:
  script_setup script_body script_trailer

script_setup:
  script_setup_begin script_setup_init
script_setup_encode

script_setup_begin:
  %%BeginSetup newline

script_setup_init:
  arbitrary_text newline

script_setup_encode:
  font_encode
  font_encode script_setup_encode

script_setup_end:
  %%EndSetup newline
```

```
font_encode:
  font_encode_begin font_encode_body font_encode_end

font_encode:begin
  %%Begin Encoding:newfont font newline

font_encode_body:
  array newfont font Z newline

font_encode_end
  %%EndEncoding newline

script_body:
  script_element
  script_element script_body

script_element:
  state_element
  object_element

state_element:
  pattern offset d newline
  gray g neline
  gray G newline
  flat i newline
  join j newline
  cap J newline
  cyan magenta yellow black k newline
  cyan magenta yellow black K newline
  miter M newline
  width w newline
  font scale leading kerning alignment z newline
  %%Note: text newline

object_element:
  path
  text
```

```
    embed
    group

 path:
    path_begin path_body path_end

 path_begin:
    x y m newline

 path_body:
    path_segment
    path_segment path_body

 path_segment:
    x1 y1 x2 y2 x3 y3 c newline
    x1 y1 x2 y2 x3 y3 C newline
    sx y l newline
    x y L newline
    x2 y2 x3 y3 v newline
    x2 y2 x3 y3 V newline
    x1 y1 x3 y3 y newline
    x1 y1 x3 y3 Y newline

 path_end:
    b newline
    B newline
    f newline
    F newline
    n newline
    N newline
    s newline
    S newline

 text:
    text_begin text_body text_end

 text_begin:
```

```
     matrix a newline
     matrix e newline
     matrix o newline
     matrix r newline

text_body:
  text_line
  text_line text_body

text_line:
  string t newline

text_end:
  T newline

group:
  group_begin script_body group_end

group_begin:
  u newline

group_end:
  U newline

embed:
  embed_begin embed_body embed_end

embed_begin:
  %%BeginDocument: text newline

embed_body
  arbitrary_text newline

embed_end
  %%EndDocument newline
script_trailer:
  script_trailer_begin script_trailer_body
```

```
script_trailer_begin:
  %%Trailer

script_trailer_body:
Marbitrary_text newline
```

Other Illustrator Document Resources

On the Macintosh, the resource fork of an Adobe Illustrator document contains several ancillary resources that are described here.

```
PICT ID = 256
```

An Adobe Illustrator 88 document may have a graphical screen representation provided so that a preview of the illustration may be manipulated on the screen by other applications, such as a page composition system. On the Macintosh, this representation is saved as a QuickDraw PICT picture resource within the resource fork of the document. The resource is assigned a resource type of PICT and a resource number of 256.

The picture's picFrame bounding box matches the bounding box of the illustration, as specified by the %%BoundingBox comment. That is, the width and height of picFrame equals the width and height of the bounding box, respectively.

The picture resource is composed of two bitmap images: the image itself and its mask. If a particular bit is set in the mask, then the illustration has actually painted the corresponding bit in the image; otherwise, the corresponding bit has not been painted and hence should be transparent.

The mask is placed in the picture first in the QuickDraw srcBic mode. It punches a white hole in just those areas that are painted. Then the image is placed in the QuickDraw srcOr mode, which fills in the punched areas but leaves the other areas unaffected.

```
PAGE ID = 256
```

This resource contains the x and y coordinates of the document's page origin, as specified by the page tool, in the default user coordinate system in which the unit length along both axes is 1/72 of an inch. The resource consists of two 32-bit fixed point numbers; the first specifies the y (vertical) coordinate, the second the x (horizontal) coordinate. The resource is given a resource type of PAGE and a resource number of 256.

```
PREC ID = 256
```

This resource contains the standard 120-byte Macintosh Printing Manager print record. It describes the document's user-specified printing preferences selected from the Page Setup and Print dialog boxes. The resource is given a resource type of PREC and a resource number of 256.

```
TEMP ID = 256
```

This resource identifies the name of the document's template file, if it has one. It consists of a 32-bit integer containing the directory identifier of the folder containing the template file, followed by a Pascal string containing the name of the volume on which the template file resides, followed by a Pascal string containing the name of the template file itself.

If the document has no template, then the directory identifier integer is zero, and both strings are empty. The resource is given a resource type of TEMP and a resource number of 256.

Index